Robert Gordon Latham

A Hand-book of the English Language

For the use of Students of the Universities and Higher Classes of Schools

Robert Gordon Latham

A Hand-book of the English Language

For the use of Students of the Universities and Higher Classes of Schools

ISBN/EAN: 9783744778046

Printed in Europe, USA, Canada, Australia, Japan

Cover: Foto ©Paul-Georg Meister /pixelio.de

More available books at **www.hansebooks.com**

A HAND-BOOK

OF

THE ENGLISH LANGUAGE,

FOR THE USE OF

STUDENTS OF THE UNIVERSITIES AND
HIGHER CLASSES OF SCHOOLS.

BY

R. G. LATHAM, M. D., F. R. S.,

LATE PROFESSOR OF THE ENGLISH LANGUAGE AND LITERATURE, UNIVERSITY
COLLEGE, LONDON.

NEW YORK:
D. APPLETON AND COMPANY,
90, 92 & 94 GRAND STREET.
1870.

CONTENTS.

PART I.

GENERAL ETHNOLOGICAL RELATIONS OF THE ENGLISH LANGUAGE.

CHAPTER I.

GERMANIC ORIGIN OF THE ENGLISH LANGUAGE.—DATE.

SECTION	PAGE
1. English language not British	1
2. Real origin German	1
3. Accredited immigrations and settlements . . .	2
4, 5. Criticism	4, 5

CHAPTER II.

GERMANIC ORIGIN OF THE ENGLISH LANGUAGE.—THE GERMANIC AREA OF THE PARTICULAR GERMANS WHO INTRODUCED IT.—EXTRACT FROM BEDA.

6, 7. Jutes, Angles, and Saxons . .	6
8, 9. Extract from Beda	6, 7
10—13. Criticism	8—11
14, 15. Angles	11, 12
16. Saxons of Beda	12, 13
17. Anglo-Saxon area . .	13
18, 19. The Frisians . . .	13, 14
20. Anglo-Saxon area	14

CHAPTER III.

OF THE DIALECTS OF THE SAXON AREA, AND OF THE SO-CALLED OLD SAXON.

SECTION   PAGE
21—29. Old Saxon and Anglo-Saxon   . . 16, 17

CHAPTER IV.

AFFINITIES OF THE ENGLISH WITH THE LANGUAGES OF GERMANY AND SCANDINAVIA.

30, 31. Gothic languages   . . . 18
32—34. Divisions of the Gothic stock   . . 18
35. Mœso-Gothic   19
36. Old High German   19
37. Low German   19
38. Frisian and Dutch   19
39. Platt-Deutsch   20
40, 41. Comparison   . . . . 21—23

CHAPTER V.

ANALYSIS OF THE ENGLISH LANGUAGE.—GERMANIC ELEMENTS.— THE ANGLES.

42. Analysis   24
43—54. Angles—their relations   . . . 24—28
55, 56. The Frisians 29, 30

CHAPTER VI.

THE CELTIC STOCK OF LANGUAGES AND THEIR RELATIONS TO THE ENGLISH.

57. Branches of the Celtic stock   . . 31
58—60. Structure of Celtic tongues   . . 31—33
61—63. The Picts   . . . . 33—35

CHAPTER VII.

THE ANGLO-NORMAN, AND THE LANGUAGES OF THE CLASSICAL STOCK.

SECTION	PAGE
64. The classical languages	36
65—67. Latin branch	36—40
68, 69. Norman French	40, 41

PART II.

HISTORY AND ANALYSIS OF THE ENGLISH LANGUAGE.

CHAPTER I.

HISTORICAL AND LOGICAL ELEMENTS OF THE ENGLISH LANGUAGE.

70. Celtic elements	45
71. Latin of first period	46
72. Anglo-Saxon	47
73. Danish or Norse	47
74. Roman of second period	49
75. Anglo-Norman element	49
76. Indirect Scandinavian elements	50
77. Latin of third period	51
78. Latin of fourth period	51
79. Greek	52
80—82. Tables	53—55
83—90. Miscellaneous elements	55—60
91—94. Hybridism and new words	60—62
95. Historical and logical analysis	63

CHAPTER II.

THE RELATION OF THE ENGLISH TO THE ANGLO-SAXON, AND THE STAGES OF THE ENGLISH LANGUAGE.

96. Ancient and modern tongues	64
97. Details	65—68
98. Stages of the English language	68

SECTION	PAGE
99. Semi-Saxon	69
100—103. *Old* English, &c.	70—72
104. Present tendencies	73

PART III.

SOUNDS, LETTERS, PRONUNCIATION, SPELLING.

CHAPTER I.

GENERAL NATURE AND CERTAIN PROPERTIES OF ARTICULATE SOUNDS.

105. Spelling and speaking	77
106. Sounds and syllables	79
107. Vowels	79
108. Divisions	80
109. Sharp and flat sounds	80
110. Continuous and explosive	80
111. General statements	81
112. The sound of *h*	81

CHAPTER II.

SYSTEM OF ARTICULATE SOUNDS.

113. Certain foreign sounds	82
114. System of mutes	82
115. Lenes and aspirates	83
116. Fourfold character of mutes	84
117. Y and *w*	84
118, 119. Diphthongs	84
120. Compound sounds	85
121. *Ng*	85
122, 123. Broad, slender; long, short; dependent, independent vowels	86, 86
124—126. System of sounds	86, 87

CHAPTER III.

OF CERTAIN COMBINATIONS OF ARTICULATE SOUNDS.

SECTION	PAGE
127. Sharp and flat mutes	88
128. Unstable combinations	89
129. Effect of *y*	89
130, 131. Double consonants rare	89
132. True aspirates rare	90

CHAPTER IV.

EUPHONY AND THE PERMUTATION OF LETTERS.

133. Euphony	92
134. Permutation	93

CHAPTER V.

ON THE FORMATION OF SYLLABLES.

135. Syllabification	95—97

CHAPTER VI.

ON QUANTITY.

136. Long and short sounds	98
137. Quantity of vowels—of syllables	98
138. Classical and English measurements	99

CHAPTER VII.

ON ACCENT.

139. Place of accents	101
140. Distinctive accents	101
141. Emphasis	102

CHAPTER VIII.

ORTHOGRAPHY.

142. Orthoepy	103
143—146. Principle of an alphabet	103—105

1*

SECTION		PAGE
147. Violations of it		105
148. Rules		107
149—151. Details of English		107—109
152. Insufficiency		109
153. Inconsistency		109
154. Erroneousness		110
155. Redundancy		110
156. Unsteadiness		110
157. Other defects		111
158. Historical propriety		113
159. Conventional spelling		113

CHAPTER IX.

HISTORICAL SKETCH OF THE ENGLISH ALPHABET.

160—166. Phœnician, Greek, Roman stages	116—124
166—172. Anglo-Saxon alphabet	124—126
173. Anglo-Norman alphabet	126
174. Extract from *Ormulum*	127
175. Order of alphabet	128

PART IV.

ETYMOLOGY.

CHAPTER I.

ON THE PROVINCE OF ETYMOLOGY.

176—179. Meaning of term	131—133

CHAPTER II.

ON GENDER.

180. *Boy* and *girl*	134
181. *Man*-servant and *maid*-servant	134
182, 183. Forms like *genitrix*	135

CONTENTS.

SECTION	PAGE
184. Forms like *domina*	136
185—189. Genders in English	136, 137
190—192. *The sun in his glory; the moon in her wane*	138
193. Miscellaneous forms	139—142

CHAPTER III.

THE NUMBERS.

194—197. Numbers in English	143, 144
198. Rule	145
199. Remarks	145
200. Addition of *-es*	146
Pence, alms, &c.	147
Mathematics	147
201. *Children*	149
202. Form in *-en*	150
203. *Men, feet*, &c.	150
204. *Brethren*, &c.	150
205. *Houses*	152
206. *Wives*, &c.	152

CHAPTER IV

ON THE CASES.

207—211. Nature of cases	151—156
212. Accusatives	156
213. Datives	157
214. Genitives	157
215. Instrumental	158
All the better	158, 159
216. Determination of cases	159
217. Analysis of cases	160
218. Form in *-s*	160

CHAPTER V.

THE PERSONAL PRONOUNS.

219, 220. *I, we, us*, &c.	162
221. *You*	162

SECTION	PAGE
222. *Me*	163
223—225. Cautions	163, 164

CHAPTER VI.

ON THE TRUE REFLECTIVE PRONOUN IN THE GOTHIC LANGUAGES, AND ON ITS ABSENCE IN ENGLISH.

226. How far found in English	165

CHAPTER VII.

THE DEMONSTRATIVE PRONOUNS, ETC.

227. *He, she, it*	166
228. *She*	166
229. *Her, him, his, its,* &c.	167
230. *Theirs*	167
231. Table	168
232. *These*	169
233. *Those*	171

CHAPTER VIII.

THE RELATIVE, INTERROGATIVE, AND CERTAIN OTHER PRONOUNS.

234. *Who, what,* &c.	173
235. *Same,* &c.	173
236. *Other, whether*	177

CHAPTER IX.

ON CERTAIN FORMS IN -ER.

237—239. Idea expressed by *-er*	179—181

CHAPTER X.

THE COMPARATIVE DEGREE.

240. Form in *-s*	182
241. *Elder,* &c.	183
242. *Rather*	183

CONTENTS.

SECTION	PAGE
243, 244. Excess of expression	183
245—247. Better	183—185
248. Worse	185
249. More	185
250. Less	185
251—253. Near, &c.	186
254. Origin of superlative	186

CHAPTER XI.

THE SUPERLATIVE DEGREE.

255, 256. Former	188
257. Nearest	188
258. Next	188
259, 260. Upmost, &c.	189, 190

CHAPTER XII.

THE CARDINAL NUMBERS.

261. How far undeclined	191

CHAPTER XIII.

THE ORDINAL NUMBERS.

262—264. Seven, nine, ten	192
265, 266. Thirteen, thirty	193

CHAPTER XIV.

THE ARTICLES.

267. A, an, the	194

CHAPTER XV.

DIMINUTIVES, AUGMENTATIVES, AND PATRONYMICS.

268—270. Diminutives	197—199
271. Augmentatives	200
272. Patronymics	200, 201

CHAPTER XVI.

GENTILE FORMS.

SECTION	PAGE
273. *Wales*	202

CHAPTER XVII.

ON THE CONNEXION BETWEEN THE NOUN AND VERB, AND ON THE INFLECTION OF THE INFINITIVE MOOD.

274—281. The verb, how far a noun	203—206

CHAPTER XVIII.

ON DERIVED VERBS.

282. Divisions of verbs	207
282. Derivation	208, 209

CHAPTER XIX.

ON THE PERSONS.

283. Persons in English	210
284, 285. Historical view	211
286. Form in *-t*	212
287. *Thou spakest*, &c.	212
288. *We loves*	213

CHAPTER XX.

ON THE NUMBERS OF VERBS.

289. Numbers in English	214
290. *Ran, run*, &c.	215

CHAPTER XXI.

ON MOODS.

291—292. Moods in English	216

CHAPTER XXII.

ON TENSES IN GENERAL.

SECTION	PAGE
293. *Strike, struck*	217
294—296. Ἔτυπτον, &c.	217, 218
297. Reduplication	219
298. *Weak* or *strong*	220

CHAPTER XXIII.

THE STRONG TENSES.

299. *Sing, sang, sung*	221
300—303. Tables	222—225

CHAPTER XXIV.

THE WEAK TENSES.

304. *Stabbed*, &c.	226
305—307. Divisions	227, 228
308. *Bought, sought*	228
309. Forms in *-te* and *-ode*	229
310—312. *Bred, beat,* &c.	230
313. *Leave, left*	231
314. *Made, had*	231
314. *Would, should, could*	231
315. *Aught*	231
316. *Durst, must,* &c.	232
317. *This will do*	233
318. *Mind*	234
319. *Yode*	234
320. *Did*	234

CHAPTER XXV.

ON CONJUGATION.

321, 322. Weak and strong conjugations natural	235—237

CHAPTER XXVI.

DEFECTIVENESS AND IRREGULARITY

SECTION	PAGE
323—325. Irregularity	238
326. Vital and obsolete processes	240
327. Processes of necessity, &c.	241
328. Ordinary processes	241
329. Positive	242
330. Normal	242
331. *Could*	243
332. *Quoth*	244
333. Real irregular verbs few	244

CHAPTER XXVII.

THE IMPERSONAL VERBS.

334, 335. *Me-seems, me-listeth*	246

CHAPTER XXVIII.

THE VERB SUBSTANTIVE.

336. Not irregular	247
337. *Was*	247
338—341. *Be*	248, 249
342. *An*	249
343. *Worth*	250

CHAPTER XXIX.

THE PRESENT PARTICIPLE.

344. Forms in *-ing*	251
345. Forms in *-ung*	252

CHAPTER XXX.

THE PAST PARTICIPLE.

346. Forms in *-en*	254
347, 348. *Drunken*	254

CONTENTS.

SECTION		PAGE
349. *Forlorn*	. . . .	255
350. Forms in *-ed*	. . . . .	255
351. The prefix *Y*	. . . .	256

CHAPTER XXXI.

COMPOSITION.

352—357. Nature of compounds	. . .	258—261
358—361. Accent	. . . .	261—266
362. Obscure compounds	. . . .	266
363—365. Exceptions .	. . . .	266, 267, 268
366. *Peacock, peahen*	. . . .	269
367. *Nightingale*	. . . .	269
368. Improper compounds	. . . .	270
369. Decomposites	. . . . .	270
370. Combinations	. . . .	270, 271

CHAPTER XXXII.

ON DERIVATION AND INFLECTION.

371—373. Their nature	. . .	272—275

CHAPTER XXXIII.

ADVERBS.

374, 375. Their division	. . . .	276
376—379. Adverbs of deflection	. . .	277
380. *Darkling*	. . . .	278

CHAPTER XXXIV.

ON CERTAIN ADVERBS OF PLACE.

381—384. *Hither, thither,* &c.	. . .	279
385. *Hence,* &c.	. . . .	280
386. *Yonder*	. . . .	280
387. *Anon* .	. . . .	281

CHAPTER XXXV.

ON WHEN, THEN, AND THAN.

388, 389. Their origin	. . .	282

CHAPTER XXXVI.

PREPOSITIONS AND CONJUNCTIONS.

SECTION	PAGE
390. Prepositions	283
391. Conjunctions	283
392. *Yes, No*	283
393. Particles	283

CHAPTER XXXVII.

ON THE GRAMMATICAL POSITION OF THE WORDS *mine* AND *thine*.

394—407. Equivalent to *meus* and *tuus*, rather than possessive cases . . . . . 284—290

CHAPTER XXXVIII.

ON THE CONSTITUTION OF THE WEAK PRETERITE.

408. Grimm's view	291
409, 410. Remarks of Dr. Trithen	291—293

PART V.

SYNTAX.

CHAPTER I.

ON SYNTAX IN GENERAL.

	PAGE
411, 412. Syntax	294
413. Personification	294
414. Ellipsis	295
415. Pleonasm	295
416. Leugma	295
417. *Pros to semainomenon*	296
418. Apposition	296
419. Collectiveness	297

CONTENTS. xix

SECTION	PAGE
420. Reduction	297
421. Determination of part of speech	298
422—424. Convertibility	298, 299
425. *The Blacks of Africa*	299
426. *None of your ifs*	300
427. Convertible words numerous in English	300

CHAPTER II.

SYNTAX OF SUBSTANTIVES.

428. *Rundell and Bridge's*	301
429. *Right and left*	301

CHAPTER III.

SYNTAX OF ADJECTIVES.

430. Pleonasm	302
431. Collocation	302
432. Government	302
433. *More wise, wiser*	303
434. *The better of the two*	304
435. Syntax of adjectives simple	304

CHAPTER IV.

SYNTAX OF PRONOUNS.

436. Pleonasm	305
437. *Father's*, not *father his*	305
438. Pleonasm and ellipses allied	306

CHAPTER V.

THE TRUE PERSONAL PRONOUNS.

439. *Pronomen reverentiæ*	307
440. *Dativus ethicus*	307
441. Reflected pronoun	307
442. Reflected neuters	308
443. Equivocal reflective	308

CHAPTER VI.

ON THE SYNTAX OF THE DEMONSTRATIVE PRONOUNS, AND THE PRONOUNS OF THE THIRD PERSON.

SECTION	PAGE
414, 415. *His* and *its*	310, 311

CHAPTER VII.

ON THE CONSTRUCTION OF THE WORD *self*.

446, 447. *Myself, himself,* &c. . . .	312, 313

CHAPTER VIII.

ON THE POSSESSIVE PRONOUNS.

448—451. *My* and *mine*	314—316

CHAPTER IX.

THE RELATIVE PRONOUNS.

452—456. Their concord	317, 318
457. Ellipsis	318
458. Equivocal antecedent	319

CHAPTER X.

ON THE INTERROGATIVE PRONOUN.

459, 460. Direct and oblique questions . . .	320

CHAPTER XI.

THE RECIPROCAL PRONOUNS.

461, 462. Their construction . . .	322, 323

CHAPTER XII.

THE INDETERMINATE PRONOUNS.

463—466. Use of *it*	324, 325
467, 468. Use of *them*	325

CHAPTER XIII.

THE ARTICLES.

SECTION	PAGE
469. *A* and *the*	326

CHAPTER XIV.

THE NUMERALS.

470. Their numbers	327
471. *First two*, and *two first*	327

CHAPTER XV.

ON VERBS IN GENERAL.

472—474. Their division	328, 329

CHAPTER XVI.

THE CONCORD OF VERBS.

475, 476. Rules	330—332
477. *It is I your master who command (commands) you*	332—334
478. Concord of number	334, 335
479. Subject and predicate of different numbers	335, 336

CHAPTER XVII.

ON THE GOVERNMENT OF VERBS.

480. Of two kinds	336, 337

CHAPTER XVIII.

ON THE PARTICIPLES.

481. *Dying-day*	338
482. *I am beaten*	338

CHAPTER XIX.

ON THE MOODS.

483, 484. The infinitive	340
485. The imperative	341

CHAPTER XX.

ON THE TENSES.

SECTION		PAGE
485. Present		342
486, 487. Preterite		342

CHAPTER XXI.

SYNTAX OF THE PERSONS OF VERBS.

488, 489. Their concord		344

CHAPTER XXII.

ON THE VOICES OF VERBS.

490. *Hight*		345

CHAPTER XXIII.

ON THE AUXILIARY VERBS.

491. Their classification		346—348
492. *I have ridden*		348
493. *I am to speak*		351
494. *I am to blame*		351
495. *I am beaten*		351

CHAPTER XXIV.

OF ADVERBS.

496, 497. Their syntax simple		352
498. Termination *-ly*		354
499. *To walk and ride*		354
500. *From whence*, &c.		354, 355

CHAPTER XXV.

ON PREPOSITIONS.

501. *Climb up a tree*		356
502. *Part of the body*		356

CHAPTER XXVI.

ON CONJUNCTIONS.

SECTION	PAGE
503, 504. Their nature	357—359
505. Their government	359
506—511. The subjunctive mood	359—364
512. Use of *that*	364
513. Succession of tenses	364
514. Disjunctives	365

CHAPTER XXVII.

THE SYNTAX OF THE NEGATIVE.

515. Its place	366
516. Its distribution	366
517. Two negatives	367
518. Questions of appeal	367

CHAPTER XXVIII.

ON THE CASE ABSOLUTE.

519. Its participial character	369

PART VI.

PROSODY.

520. Derivation of the word	371
521, 522. Importance of accent	371
523—526. Measures	372, 373
527. Metrical notation	374
528—535. Rhyme	374—377
536. Blank verse	377
537, 538. Last syllable indifferent	378
539, 540. Names of common English metres	379—384

PART VII.

DIALECTS OF THE ENGLISH LANGUAGE.

SECTION	PAGE
541. Saxons and Angles	385
542—544. Dialects not coincident	385, 386
545, 546. Traces of the Danes	386, 387
547 Mercian origin of the written English	387
Notes	393

AN INTRODUCTION

TO THE STUDY OF

THE ENGLISH LANGUAGE.

PART I.

GENERAL ETHNOLOGICAL RELATIONS OF THE ENGLISH LANGUAGE.

CHAPTER I.

GERMANIC ORIGIN OF THE ENGLISH LANGUAGE.—DATE.

§ 1. THE first point to be remembered in the history of the English language, is that it was not the primitive and original tongue of any of the British Islands, nor yet of any portion of them. Indeed, of the *whole* of Great Britain it is not the language at the present moment. Welsh is spoken in Wales, Manks in the Isle of Man, and Scotch Gaelic in the Highlands of Scotland; besides which there is the Irish Gaelic in Ireland.

§ 2. The next point to be considered is the real origin and the real affinities of the English language.

Its *real* origin is on the continent of Europe, and its *real* affinities are with certain languages there spoken. To speak more specifically, the native country of the

English language is *Germany;* and the *Germanic* languages are those that are the most closely connected with our own. In Germany, languages and dialects allied to each other and allied to the mother-tongue of the English have been spoken from times anterior to history; and these, for most purposes of philology, may be considered as the aboriginal languages and dialects of that country.

§ 3. *Accredited details of the different immigrations from Germany into Britain.*—Until lately the details of the different Germanic invasions of England, both in respect to the particular tribes by which they were made, and the order in which they succeeded each other, were received with but little doubt, and as little criticism.

Respecting the tribes by which they were made, the current opinion was, that they were chiefly, if not exclusively, those of the Jutes, the Saxons, and the Angles.

The particular chieftains that headed each descent were also supposed to be known, as well as the different localities upon which they descended.[1] These were as follows:—

First settlement of invaders from Germany.—The account of this gives us A. D. 449 for the first permanent Germanic tribes settled in Britain. Ebbsfleet, in the Isle of Thanet, was the spot where they landed; and the particular name that these tribes gave themselves was that of *Jutes.* Their leaders were Hengist and Horsa. Six years after their landing they had established the kingdom of Kent; so that the county of Kent was the first district where the original British was superseded by the mother-tongue of the present English, introduced from Germany.

Second settlement of invaders from Germany.—A. D. 477 invaders from Northern Germany made the second permanent settlement in Britain. The coast of Sussex was the spot whereon they landed. The particular name that these tribes gave themselves was that of *Saxons*. Their leader was Ella. They established the kingdom of the South Saxons (Sussex or Suð-Seaxe); so that the county of Sussex was the second district where the original British was superseded by the mother-tongue of the present English, introduced from Germany.

Third settlement of invaders from Germany.—A. D. 495 invaders from Northen Germany made the third permanent settlement in Britain. The coast of Hampshire was the spot whereon they landed. Like the invaders last mentioned, these tribes were Saxons. Their leader was Cerdic. They established the kingdom of the West Saxons (Wessex or West-Seaxe); so that the county of Hants was the third district where the original British was superseded by the mother-tongue of the present English, introduced from Germany.

Fourth settlement of invaders from Germany.—A. D. 530, certain Saxons landed in Essex, so that the county of Essex [East-Seaxe] was the fourth district where the original British was superseded by the mother-tongue of the present English, introduced from Northern Germany.

Fifth settlement of invaders from Germany.—These were *Angles* in Norfolk and Suffolk. The precise date of this settlement is not known. The fifth district where the original British was superseded by the mother-tongue of the present English was the counties of Norfolk and Suffolk; the particular dialect introduced being that of the *Angles*.

Sixth settlement of invaders from Germany.—A. D. 547 invaders from Northern Germany made the sixth permanent settlement in Britain. The southeastern counties of Scotland, between the rivers Tweed and Forth, were the districts where they landed. They were of the tribe of the Angles, and their leader was Ida. The south-eastern parts of Scotland constituted the sixth district where the original British was superseded by the mother-tongue of the present English, introduced from Northern Germany.

§ 4. It would be satisfactory if these details rested upon contemporary evidence. This, however, is far from being the case.

1. *The evidence to the details just given, is not historical, but traditional.*—*a.* Beda,[2] from whom it is chiefly taken, wrote nearly 300 years after the supposed event, *i. e.*, the landing of Hengist and Horsa, in A. D. 449.

b. The nearest approach to a contemporary author is Gildas,[3] and *he* wrote full 100 years after it.

2. *The account of Hengist's and Horsa's landing, has elements which are fictional rather than historical*— *a.* Thus "when we find Hengist and Horsa approaching the coasts of Kent in three keels, and Ælli effecting a landing in Sussex with the same number, we are reminded of the Gothic tradition which carries a migration of Ostrogoths,[4] Visigoths, and Gepidæ, also in three vessels, to the mouth of the Vistula."—Kemble, " Saxons in England."

b. The murder of the British chieftains by Hengist is told *totidem verbis*, by Widukind[5] and others, of the Old Saxons in Thuringia.

c. Geoffry of Monmouth[6] relates also, how "Hengist obtained from the Britons as much land as could be enclosed by an ox-hide; then, cutting the hide into thongs, enclosed a much larger space than the granters intended, on which he erected Thong Castle—a tale too familiar to need illustration, and which runs throughout the mythus of many nations. Among the Old Saxons, the tradition is in reality the same, though recorded with a slight variety of detail. In their story, a lapfull of earth is purchased at a dear rate from a Thuringian; the companions of the Saxon jeer him for his imprudent bargain; but he sows the purchased earth upon a large space of ground, which he claims, and, by the aid of his comrades, ultimately wrests it from the Thuringians."—Kemble, "Saxons in England."

3. *There is direct evidence in favour of their having been German tribes in England anterior to* A. D. 447.—*a*. At the close of the Marcomannic war,[7] Marcus Antoninus transplanted a number of Germans into Britain.

b. Alemannic auxiliaries served along with Roman legions under Valentinian.[8]

c. The *Notitia utriusque Imperii*,[9] of which the latest date is half a century earlier than the epoch of Hengist, mentions, as an officer of state, the *Comes littoris Saxonici per Britannias;* his government extending along the coast from Portsmouth to the Wash.

§ 5. *Inference.*—As it is nearly certain, that 449 A. D. is *not* the date of the first introduction of German tribes into Britain, we must consider that the displacement of the original British began at an *earlier* period than the one usually admitted, and, consequently, that it was more *gradual* than is usually supposed.

Perhaps, if we substitute the middle of the *fourth*, instead of the middle of the *fifth* century, as the epoch of the Germanic immigrations into Britain, we shall not be far from the truth.

CHAPTER II.

GERMANIC ORIGIN OF THE ENGLISH LANGUAGE.—THE GERMANIC AREA OF THE PARTICULAR GERMANS WHO INTRODUCED IT.—EXTRACT FROM BEDA.

§ 6. OUT of the numerous tribes and nations of Germany, *three* have been more especially mentioned as the chief, if not the exclusive, sources of the present English population of Great Britain. These are the *Jutes*, the *Saxons*, and the *Angles*.

§ 7. Now, it is by no means certain that this was the case. On the contrary, good reasons can be given for believing that the Angles and Saxons were the same people, and that no such nation as the *Jutes* ever left Germany to settle in Great Britain.

§ 8. The chief authority for the division of the German invaders into the three nations just mentioned is Beda; and the chief text is the following extract from his "Ecclesiastical History." It requires particular attention, and will form the basis of much criticism, and frequently be referred to.

" Advenerunt autem de tribus Germaniæ populis fortioribus, id est Saxonibus, Anglis, Jutis. De Jutarum origine sunt Cantuarii, et Victuarii, hoc est ea gens quæ Vectam tenet insulam et ea quæ usque hodie in provincia Occidentalium Saxonum Jutarum natio nominatur, posita contra ipsam insulam Vectam. De

Saxonibus, id est, ea regione quæ nunc Antiquorum Saxonum cognominatur, venere Orientales Saxones, Meridiani Saxones, Occidui Saxones. Porro de Anglis hoc est de illa patria quæ Angulus dicitur, et ab illo tempore usque hodie manere desertus inter provincias Jutarum et Saxonum perhibetur, Orientales Angli, Mediterranei Angli, Merci, tota Northanhymbrorum progenies, id est illarum gentium quæ ad Boream Humbri fluminis inhabitant, cæterique Anglorum populi sunt orti."—" Historia Ecclesiastica," i. 15.

§ 9. This was written about A.D. 731, 131 years after the introduction of Christianity, and nearly 300 after the supposed landing of Hengist and Horsa in A.D. 449.

It is the first passage which contains the names of either the *Angles* or the *Jutes*. Gildas, who wrote more than 150 years earlier, mentions only the *Saxons*—" ferocissimi illi nefandi nominis *Saxones*."

It is, also, the passage which all subsequent writers have either translated or adopted. Thus it re-appears in Alfred, and again in the Saxon Chronicle.[10]

" Of Jotum comon Cantware " and Wihtware, þæt is seo " mæiað þe nú eardaþ on Wiht, " and þæt cynn on West-Sexum " ðe man gyt hæt Iútnacynn. " Of Eald-Seaxum comon East- " Seaxan, and Suð-Seaxan and " West-Seaxan. Of Angle co- " mon (se á siððan stód westig " betwix Iútum and Seaxum) " East - Engle, Middel - Angle, " Mearce, and calle Norðym- " bra.'	From the Jutes came the inhabitants of Kent and of Wight, that is, the race that now dwells in Wight, and that tribe amongst the West-Saxons which is yet called the Jute tribe. From the Old-Saxons came the East-Saxons, and South-Saxons, and West-Saxons. From the Angles, land (which has since always stood waste betwixt the Jutes and Saxons) came the East-Angles, Middle-Angles, Mercians, and all the Northumbrians.

§ 10. A portion of these extracts will now be submitted to criticism; that portion being the statement concerning the *Jutes*.

The words *usque hodie—Jutarum natio nominatur* constitute contemporary and unexceptionable evidence to the existence of a people with a name like that of the *Jutes* in the time of Beda—or A.D. 731.

The exact name is not so certain. The term *Jutnacyn* from the Anglo-Saxon Chronicle is in favour of the notion that it began with the sounds of *j* and *u*, in other words that it was *Jut*.

But the term *Geatum*, which we find in Alfred, favours the form in *g* followed by *ea*.

Thirdly, the forms *Wihtware*, and *Wihttan*, suggest the likelihood of the name being *Wiht*.

Lastly, there is a passage in Asserius [11] which gives us the form *Gwith*—" Mater" (of Alfred the Great) " quoque ejusdem Osburgh nominabatur, religiosa nimium fœmina, nobilis ingenio, nobilis et genere; quæ erat filia Oslac famosi pincernæ Æthelwulf regis; qui Oslac Gothus erat natione, ortus enim erat de Gothis et Jutis; de semine scilicet Stuf et Wihtgur, duorum fratrum et etiam comitum, qui acceptâ potestate Vectis insulæ ab avunculo suo Cerdic rege et Cynric filio suo, consobrino eorum, paucos Britones ejusdem insulæ accolas, quos in câ invenire potuerant, in loco qui dicitur, *Gwithgaraburgh* occiderunt, cæteri enim accolæ ejusdem insulæ ante sunt occisi aut exules aufugerant."—Asserius, " De Gestis Alfredi Regis."

Now, *Gwith-gara-burgh* means the *burg* or *town of* the *With-ware*; [12] these being, undoubtedly, no Germans at all, but the native Britons of the Isle of Wight (Vectis), whose designation in Latin would be *Vecticolæ* or *Vectienses*.

This being the case, how can they be descended from German or Danish *Jutes*? and how can we reconcile the statement of Beda with that of Asser?

§ 11. The answer to this will be given after another fact has been considered.

Precisely the same confusion between the sounds of *w*, *j*, *g*, *io*, *eœ*, *u*, and *i*, which occurs with the so-called *Jutes* of the Isle of Wight, occurs with the Jutlanders of the peninsula of Jutland. The common forms are *Jutland*, *Jute*, *Jutones*, and *Jutenses*, but they are not the only ones. In A. D. 952, we find "Dania cismarina quam *Vitland* incolæ appellant."—" Annales Saxonici."[13]

§ 12. Putting these facts together I adopt the evidence of Asser as to the *Gwithware* being British, and consider them as simple *Vecti-colæ*, or inhabitants of the Isle of *Wight*. They are also the *Vectuarii* of Beda, the *Wihtware* of the Saxon Chronicle, and the *Wihtsætan* of Alfred.

The Jutes of Hampshire—*i. e.*, the " Jutarum natio— posita contra ipsam insulam Vectam," and the *Jutnacyn*, I consider to have been the same; except that they had left the Isle of Wight to settle on the opposite coast; probably flying before their German conquerors, in which case they would be the *exules* of Asser.

The statement of Beda, so opposed to that of Asser, I explain by supposing that it arose out of an inaccurate inference drawn from the similarity of the names of the Isle of Wight and the peninsula of Jutland, since we have seen that in both cases, there was a similar confusion between the syllables *Jut-* and *Vit-*. This is an error into which even a careful writer might fall. That Beda had no authentic historical accounts of the conquest of Britain, we know from his own statements in the Preface to his Ecclesiastical History,[14] and that he par tially tried to make up for the want of them by inference is exceedingly likely. If so, what would be more natural than for him to conclude that Jutes as well as Angles helped to subdue the country. The fact itself was probable; besides which he saw at one and the same time, in England *Vitæ* (called also *Jutæ*), in immediate contact with *Saxons*,* and on the continent *Jutæ* (called also *Vitæ*) in the neighborhood of Angles† and Saxons. Is it surprising that he should connect them?

§ 13. If the inhabitants of the Isle of Wight were really *Jutes* from *Jutland*, it is strange that there should be no traces of the difference which existed, then as now, between them and the proper Anglo-Saxons—a difference which was neither inconsiderable nor of a fleeting nature.

The present Jutlanders are not Germans but Danes, and the Jutes of the time of Beda were most probably the same. Those of the 11th century were *certainly* so, " Primi ad ostium Baltici Sinus in australi ripa versus nos *Dani, quos Juthas appellant*, usque ad Sliam lacum habitant." Adamus Bremensis,[15] " De Situ Daniæ " c. 221. Also, " Et prima pars Daniæ, quæ Jutland dicitur, ad Egdoram‡ in Boream longitudine pretenditur. . . . . .in cum angulum qui Windila dicitur, ubi Jutland finem habet," c. 208.

At the time of Beda they must, according to the received traditions, have been nearly 300 years in possession of the Isle of Wight, a locality as favourable for the preservation of their peculiar manners and customs as any in Great Britain, and a locality wherein we have no evidence of their ever having been disturbed. Nevertheless, neither trace nor shadow of a trace, either

---

* In Hampshire. † In Northern Germany.
‡ The Eyder.

in early or modern times, has ever been discovered of their separate nationality and language; a fact which stands in remarkable contrast with the very numerous traces which the Danes of the 9th and 10th century left behind them as evidence of their occupancy.

§ 14. The words *England* and *English* are derived from the *Angles* of Beda. The words *Sussex*, *Essex*, *Middlesex* and *Wessex*, from his *Saxons*. No objection lies against this; indeed to deny that populations called *Angle* and *Saxon* occupied *England* and spoke the *Anglo-Saxon* language would display an unnecessary and unhealthy scepticism. The real question concerning these two words consists in the relation which the populations to which they were applied bore to each other. And this question is a difficult one. Did the Angles speak one language, whilst the Saxons spoke another? or did they both speak dialects of the same tongue? Were these dialects slightly or widely different? Can we find traces of the difference in any of the present provincial dialects? Are the idioms of one country of Angle, whilst those of another are of Saxon origin? Was the Angle more like the Danish language, whilst the Saxon approached the Dutch? None of these questions can be answered at present. They have, however, been asked for the sake of exhibiting the nature of the subject.

§ 15. The extract from Beda requires further remarks.

The Angles of Beda.—The statement of Beda respecting the Angles, like his statement concerning the Jutes, reappears in the Anglo-Saxon Chronicle, and in Alfred.

Ethelweard [16] also adopts it:—" *Anglia vetus* sita est inter Saxones et Giotos, habens oppidum capitale quod sermone Saxonico *Sleswic* nuncupatur, secundum vere Danos *Hathaby.*"

Nevertheless, it is exceptionable and unsatisfactory; and like the previous one, in all probability, an incorrect inference founded upon the misinterpretation of a name.

In the eighth century there *was*, and at the present moment there *is*, a portion of the duchy of Sleswick called *Anglen* or *the corner*. It is really what its name denotes, a triangle of irregular shape, formed by the Slie, the firth of Flensborg, and a line drawn from Flensborg to Sleswick. It is just as Danish as the rest of the peninsula, and cannot be shown to have been occupied by a Germanic population at all. Its area is less than that of the county of Rutland, and by no means likely to have supplied such a population as that of the Angles of England. The fact of its being a desert at the time of Beda is credible; since it formed a sort of *March* or *Debatable Ground* between the Saxons and Slavonians of Holstein, and the Danes of Jutland.

Now if we suppose that the real Angles of Germany were either so reduced in numbers as to have become an obscure tribe, or so incorporated with other populations as to have lost their independent existence, we can easily see how the similarity of name, combined with the geographical contiguity of Anglen to the Saxon frontier, might mislead even so good a writer as Beda, into the notion that he had found the country of the *Angles* in the *Angulus* (Anglen) of Sleswick.

The true *Angles* were the descendants of the *Angli* of Tacitus. Who these were will be investigated in §§ 47—54.

§ 16. *The Saxons of Beda.*—The Saxons of Beda reached from the country of the Old Saxons* on the

* See §§ 21—29.

Lippe, in Westphalia, to that of the Nordalbingian*
Saxons between the Elbe and Eyder; and nearly,
but not quite, coincided with the present countries of
Hanover, Oldenburg, Westphalia, and part of Holstein.
This we may call the *Saxon*, or (as reasons will be given
for considering that it nearly coincided with the country
of the Angles) the *Anglo-Saxon* area.

§ 17. *River-system and sea-board of the Anglo-Saxon
area.*—As the invasion of England took place by sea,
we must expect to find in the invaders a maritime population. This leads to the consideration of the physical
character of that part of Germany which they occupied.
And here comes a remarkable and unexpected fact.
The line of coast between the Rhine and Elbe, the line
which in reasoning *a priori*, we should fix upon as the
most likely tract for the bold seamen who wrested so
large an island as Great Britain from its original occupants (changing it from *Britain* to *England*), to
have proceeded from, is *not* the country of the Anglo-
Saxons. On the contrary, it is the country of a similar
but different section of the Germanic population, a section
which has not received the attention from the English
historian which it deserves. The country in question is
the area of—

§ 18. *The Frisians.*—At the present moment the
language of the Dutch province of Friesland is materially
different from that of the other parts of the kingdom
of Holland. In other words it is not Dutch. Neither
is it German — although, of course, it resembles
both languages. On the other hand, it is more like
the English than any other language or dialect in Germany is.

It is a language of considerable antiquity, and al-

* Saxons *North of the Elbe* (*Albis*).

though at present it is spoken by the country-people only, it possesses a considerable literature. There is the *Middle* Frisian of Gysbert Japicx,[17] and the *Old* Frisian of the Frisian Laws.[18] The older the specimen of the Frisian language the more closely does it show its affinity to the English; hence the earliest Frisian and the Anglo-Saxon are exceedingly alike. Nevertheless they differ.

§ 19. The Frisian was once spoken over a far greater area than at present. It was the original language of almost all Holland. It was the language of East Friesland to a late period. It was, probably, the language of the ancient Chauci. At the present time (besides Friesland) it survives in Heligoland, in the islands between the Ems and Weser, in part of Sleswick, and in a few localities in Oldenburg and Westphalia.

Hence it is probable that the original Frisian, extending to an uncertain and irregular distance inland, lay between the Saxons and the sea, and stretched from the Zuyder Zee to the Elbe; a fact which would leave to the latter nation the lower Elbe and the Weser as their water-system: the extent to which they were in direct contact with the ocean being less than we are prepared to expect from their subsequent history.

On the other hand the *a priori* probabilities of there being Frisians as well as Anglo-Saxons amongst the conquerors of Great Britain are considerable.—See §§ 55, 56.

§ 20. The Anglo-Saxon area coincided—

1. *Politically.*—With the kingdom of Hanover, the duchy of Oldenburg, and parts of Westphalia and Holstein.

2. *Physically.*—With the basin of the Weser.

It was *certainly* from the Anglo-Saxon, and *probably*

from a part of the Frisian area that Great Britain was first invaded.

This is as much as it is safe to say at present. The preceding chapter investigated the *date* of the Germanic migration into Britain; the present has determined the *area* from which it went forth.

CHAPTER III.

OF THE DIALECTS OF THE SAXON AREA, AND OF THE SO-CALLED OLD SAXON.

§ 21. The area occupied by the Saxons of Germany has been investigated; and it now remains to ask, how far the language of the occupants was absolutely identical throughout, or how far it fell into dialects or subdialects.

There were at least *two* divisions of the Saxon; (1st) the Saxon of which the extant specimens are of English origin, and (2nd), the Saxon of which the extant specimens are of Continental origin. We will call these at present the Saxon of England, and the Saxon of the Continent.

§ 22. Respecting the Saxon of England and the Saxon of the Continent, there is good reason for believing that the *first* was spoken in the *northern*, the *second* in the *southern* portion of the Saxon area, *i.e.*, the one in Hanover and the other in Westphalia, the probable boundaries between them being the line of highlands between Osnaburg and Paderborn.

§ 23. Respecting the Saxon of England and the Saxon of the Continent, there is good reason for believing that, whilst the *former* was the mother-tongue of the Angles and the conquerors of England, the *latter* was that of the Cherusci of Arminius, the conquerors and the annihilators of the legions of Varus.[19]

§ 24. Respecting the Saxon of England and the

Saxon of the Continent, it is a fact that, whilst we have a full literature in the former, we have but fragmentary specimens of the latter—these being chiefly the following: (1) the Heliand,[20] (2) Hildubrand and Hathubrant,[21] (3) the Carolinian Psalms.[22]

§ 25. The preceding points have been predicated respecting the difference between the two ascertained Saxon dialects, for the sake of preparing the reader for the names by which they are known.

THE SAXON OF THE CONTINENT MAY BE CALLED	THE SAXON OF ENGLAND MAY BE CALLED
1. Continental Saxon.	Insular Saxon.
2. German Saxon.	English Saxon.
3. Westphalian Saxon.	Hanoverian Saxon.
4. South Saxon.	North Saxon.
5. Cheruscan Saxon.	Angle Saxon.
6. Saxon of the Heliand.	Saxon of Beowulf.[23]

§ 26. The Saxon of England *is* called Anglo-Saxon; a term against which no exception can be raised.

§ 27. The Saxon of the Continent *used* to be called *Dano*-Saxon, and *is* called *Old* Saxon.

§ 28. *Why called* Dano-*Saxon*.—When the poem called *Heliand* was first discovered in an English library, the difference in language between it and the common Anglo-Saxon composition was accounted for by the assumption of a *Danish* intermixture.

§ 29. *Why called* Old *Saxon*.—When the Continental origin of the *Heliand* was recognised, the language was called *Old* Saxon, because it represented the Saxon of the mother-country, the natives of which were called *Old* Saxons by the *Anglo*-Saxons themselves. Still the term is exceptionable; as the Saxon of the Heliand is probably a *sister*-dialect of the *Anglo*-Saxon, rather the *Anglo*-Saxon itself in a Continental locality. Exceptionable, however, as it is, it will be employed.

CHAPTER IV.

AFFINITIES OF THE ENGLISH WITH THE LANGUAGES OF GERMANY AND SCANDINAVIA.

§ 30. Over and above those languages of Germany and Holland which were akin to the dialects of the Anglo-Saxons, cognate languages were spoken in Denmark, Sweden, Norway, Iceland, and the Feroe isles, *i.e.*, in Scandinavia.

§ 31. The general collective designation for the Germanic tongues of Germany and Holland, and for the Scandinavian languages of Denmark, Sweden, Norway, Iceland, and the Feroe Isles, is taken from the name of those German tribes who, during the decline of the Roman Empire, were best known to the Romans as the *Goths;* the term *Gothic* for the Scandinavian and Germanic languages, collectively, being both current and convenient.

§ 32. Of this great *stock* of languages the Scandinavian is one *branch;* the Germanic, called also Teutonic, another.

§ 33. The Scandinavian branch of the Gothic stock comprehends, 1. The dialects of Scandinavia Proper, *i.e.*, of Norway and Sweden; 2. of the Danish isles and Jutland; 3. of Iceland; 4. of the Feroe Isles.

§ 34. The Teutonic branch falls into three divisions:—
1. The Mœso-Gothic.
2. The High Germanic.

3. The Low Germanic.

§ 35. It is in the Mœso-Gothic that the most ancient specimen of any Gothic tongue has been preserved. It is also the Mœso-Gothic that was spoken by the conquerors of ancient Rome; by the subjects of Hermanric, Alaric, Theodoric, Euric, Athanaric, and Totila.

In the reign of Valens, when pressed by intestine wars, and by the movements of the Huns, the Goths were assisted by that emperor, and settled in the Roman province of Mœsia.

Furthermore, they were converted to Christianity; and the Bible was translated into their language by their Bishop Ulphilas.

Fragments of this translation, chiefly from the Gospels, have come down to the present time; and the Bible translation of the Arian Bishop Ulphilas, in the language of the Goths of Mœsia, during the reign of Valens, exhibits the earliest sample of any Gothic tongue.

§ 36. The Old High German, called also Francic[24] and Alemannic,[25] was spoken in the ninth, tenth, and eleventh centuries, in Suabia, Bavaria, and Franconia.

The Middle High German ranges from the thirteenth century to the Reformation.

§ 37. The low Germanic division, to which the Anglo-Saxon belongs, is currently said to comprise six languages, or rather four languages in different stages.

I. II.—The Anglo-Saxon and Modern English.
III. The Old Saxon.
IV. V.—The Old Frisian and Modern Dutch.
VI.—The Platt-Deutsch, or Low German.

§ 38. *The Frisian and Dutch.*—It is a current statement that the Old Frisian bears the same relation to the Modern Dutch of Holland that the Anglo-Saxon does to the English.

The truer view of the question is as follows:—

1. That a single language, spoken in two dialects, was originally common to both Holland and Friesland.

2. That from the northern of these dialects we have the Modern Frisian of Friesland.

3. From the southern, the Modern Dutch of Holland.

The reason of this refinement is as follows:—

The Modern Dutch has certain grammatical forms *older* than those of the old Frisian; *e.g.*, the Dutch infinitives and the Dutch weak substantives, in their oblique cases, end in *-en;* those of the Old Frisian in *-a:* the form in *-en* being the older.

The true Frisian is spoken in few and isolated localities. There is—

1. The Frisian of the Dutch state called Friesland.

2. The Frisian of the parish of Saterland, in Westphalia.

3. The Frisian of Heligoland.

4. The North Frisian, spoken in a few villages of Sleswick. One of the characters of the North Frisian is the possession of a dual number.

In respect to its stages, we have the Old Frisian of the Asega-bog, the Middle Frisian of Gysbert Japicx,* and the Modern Frisian of the present Frieslanders, Westphalians, and Heligolanders.

39. *The Low German and Platt-Deutsch.*—The words *Low-German* are not only lax in their application, but they are *equivocal;* since the term has two meanings, a *general* meaning when it signifies a division of the Germanic languages, comprising English, Dutch, Anglo-Saxon, Old Saxon, and Frisian, and a limited one when it means the particular dialects of the Ems, the Weser, and the Elbe. To avoid this the dialects in question

* See Notes 17 and 18.

are conveniently called by their continental name of *Platt-Deutsch*, just as in England we say *Broad* Scotch.

§ 40. The most characteristic difference between the Saxon and Icelandic (indeed between the Teutonic and Scandinavian tongues) lies in the peculiar position of the definite article in the latter. In Saxon, the article corresponding with the modern word *the*, is þæt, se, seó, for the neuter, masculine, and feminine genders respectively; and these words, regularly declined, are *prefixed* to the words with which they agree, just as is the case with the English and with the majority of languages. In Icelandic, however, the article instead of preceding, *follows* its noun, *with which it coalesces*, having previously suffered a change in form. The Icelandic article corresponding to þæt, se, seó, is *hitt, hinn, hin* : from this the *h* is ejected, so that, instead of the regular inflection (*a*), we have the forms (*b*).

a.

	Neut.	Masc.	Fem.
Sing. Nom.	Hitt	Hinn	Hin.
Acc.	Hitt	Hinn	Hina.
Dat.	Hinu	Hinum	Hinni.
Gen.	Hins	Hins	Hinnar.
Plur. Nom.	Hin	Hinir	Hinar.
Acc.	Hin	Hina	Hinar.
Dat.	Hinum	Hinum	Hinum.
Gen.	Hinna	Hinna	Hinna.

b.

	Neut.	Masc.	Fem.
Sing. Nom.	-it	-inn	-in
Acc.	-it	-inn	-ina (-na).
Dat.	-nu	-num	-inni (-nui).
Gen.	-ins	-ins	-innar (-nnar).
Plur. Nom.	-in	-nir	-nar.
Acc.	-in	-na	-nar.
Dat.	-num	num	-num.
Gen.	-nna	nna	-nna.

Whence, as an affix, in composition,

	Neut.	Masc.	Fem.
Sing. Nom.	Augat	Boginn	Túngan
Acc.	Augat	Boginn	Túngum
Dat.	Auganu	Boganum	Túngunni
Gen.	Augans	Bogans	Túngunnor
Plur. Nom.	Augun	Bogarnir	Túngurnar.
Acc.	Augun	Bogana	Túngurnar.
Dat.	Augunum	Bogunum	Túngunum.
Gen.	Augnanna	Boganna	Túngnanna.

In the Swedish, Norwegian, and Danish this peculiarity in the position of the definite article is preserved. Its origin, however, is concealed; and an accidental identity with the indefinite article has led to false notions respecting its nature. In the languages in point the *i* is changed into *e*, so that what in Icelandic is *it* and *in*, is in Danish *et* and *en*. *En*, however, as a separate word, is the numeral *one*, and also the indefinite article *a*; whilst in the neuter gender it is *et*—en sol, *a sun*; et bord, *a table*: solon, *the sun*; bordet, *the table*. From modern forms like those just quoted, it has been imagined that the definite is merely the indefinite article transposed. This it is not.

To apply an expression of Mr. Cobbet's, *en* = *a*, and -*en* = *the*, are *the same combination of letters, but not the same word*.

§ 41. Another characteristic of the Scandinavian language is the possession of a *passive* form, or a *passive* voice, ending in -*st*:—ek, þu, hann brennist = *I am, thou art, he is burnt*; ver brennumst = *we are burnt*; þér brennizt = *ye are burnt*; þeir brennast = *they are burnt*. Past tense, ek, þu, hann brendist; ver brendumst, þér brenduzt, þeir brendust. Imperat.: brenstu = *be thou burnt*. Infinit.: brennast = *to be burnt*.

In the modern Danish and Swedish, the passive is still preserved, but without the final *t*. In the *older* stages of Icelandic, on the other hand, the termination was not -*st* but -*sc;* which -*sc* grew out of the reflective pronoun *sik*. With these phenomena the Scandinavian languages give us the evolution and development of a passive voice; wherein we have the following series of changes:—1. the reflective pronoun coalesces with the verb, whilst the sense changes from that of a reflective to that of a middle verb; 2. the *c* changes to *t*, whilst the middle sense passes into a passive one; 3. *t* is dropped from the end of the word, and the expression that was once reflective then becomes strictly passive.

Now the Saxons have no passive voice at all. That they should have one *originating* like that of the Scandinavians was impossible, inasmuch as they had no reflective pronoun, and, consequently, nothing to evolve it from.

CHAPTER V.

ANALYSIS OF THE ENGLISH LANGUAGE.—GERMANIC ELEMENTS.
—THE ANGLES.

§ 42. The language of England has been formed out of three elements.

a. Elements referable to the original British population, and derived from times anterior to the Anglo-Saxon invasion.

b. Anglo-Saxon, Germanic, or imported elements.

c. Elements introduced since the Anglo-Saxon conquest.

§ 43. Each of these requires a special analysis, but that of the second will be taken first, and form the contents of the present chapter.

All that we have at present learned concerning the Germanic invaders of England, is the geographical area which they originally occupied. How far, however, it was simple Saxons who conquered England single-handed, or how far the particular Saxon Germans were portions of a complex population, requires further investigation. Were the Saxons one division of the German population, whilst the Angles were another? or were the Angles a section of the Saxons, so that the latter was a generic term including the former? Again, although the Saxon invasion may be the one which has had the greatest influence, and drawn the most attention, why may there not have been separate and independent migrations, the effects and record of which have, in the lapse of time, become fused with those of the more important divisions?

§ 44. *The Angles; who were they? and what was their relation to the Saxons?*—The first answer to this question embodies a great fact in the way of internal evidence, *viz.*, that they were the people from whom *England* derives the name it bears = Angle land, i. e., *land of the Angles*. Our language too is *English*, i. e., *Angle*. Whatever, then, they may have been on the Continent, they were a leading section of the invaders here. Why then has their position in our inquiries been hitherto so subordinate to that of the Saxons? It is because their importance and preponderance are not so manifest in Germany as we infer them to have been in Britain. Nay more, their historical place amongst the nations of Germany, is both insignificant and uncertain; indeed, it will be seen from the sequel, that *in and of themselves* we know next to nothing about them, knowing them only in their *relations, i. e.,* to ourselves and to the Saxons.

§ 45. Although they are the section of the immigration which gave the name to England, and, as such, the preponderating element in the eyes of the present *English,* they were not so in the eyes of the original British; who neither knew at the time of the Conquest, nor know now, of any other name for their German enemies but *Saxon*. And *Saxon* is the name by which the present English are known to the Welsh, Armorican, and Gaelic Celts.

Welsh	*Saxon*.
Armorican	*Soson*.
Gaelic	*Sassenach*.

§ 46. Although they are the section of the immigration which gave the name to *England*, &c., they were quite as little Angles as Saxons in the eyes of foreign cotemporary writers; since the expression *Saxoniæ trans-marinæ*, occurs as applied to England.

§ 47. *Who were the Angles?*—Although they are the section of the immigration which gave the name to *England*, &c., the notices of them as Germans in Germany, are extremely limited.

Extract from Tacitus.—This merely connects them with certain other tribes, and affirms the existence of certain religious ordinances common to them:—

"Contra Langobardos paucitas nobilitat: plurimis ac valentissimis nationibus cincti, non per obsequium sed prœliis et periclitando tuti sunt. Reudigni deinde, et Aviones, et *Angli*, et Varini, et Eudoses, et Suardones, et Nuithones, fluminibus aut silvis muniuntur: nec quidquam notabile in singulis, nisi quod in commune Herthum, id est, Terram matrem colunt, eamque intervenire rebus hominum, invehi populis, arbitrantur. Est in insula Oceani Castum nemus, dicatumque in eo vehiculum, veste contectum, attingere uni sacerdoti concessum. Is adesse penetrali deam intelligit, vectamque bobus feminis multâ cum veneratione prosequitur. Læti tunc dies, festa loca, quæcumque adventu hospitioque dignatur. Non bella ineunt, non arma sumunt, clausum omne ferrum; pax et quies tunc tantùm nota, tunc tantùm amata, donec idem sacerdos satiatam conversatione mortalium deam templo reddat; mox vehiculum et vestes, et, si credere velis, numen ipsum secreto lacu abluitur. Servi ministrant, quos statim idem lacus haurit. Arcanus hinc terror, sanctaque ignorantia, quid sit id, quod tantùm perituri vident."[*]

Extract from Ptolemy.—This connects the Angles with the *Suevi*, and *Langobardi*, and places them on the Middle Elbe.—Ἐντὸς καὶ μεσογείων ἐθνῶν μέγιστα μέν

[*] De Mor. Germ. 40.

ἐστὶ τό τε τῶν Σουήβων τῶν Ἀγγειλῶν, οἵ εἰσιν ἀνατολικώτεροι τῶν Λαγγοβάρδων, ἀνατείνοντες πρὸς τὰς ἄρκτους μέχρι τῶν μέσων τοῦ Ἄλβιος ποταμοῦ.

Extract from Procopius.—For this see § 55.

Heading of a law referred to the age of Charlemagne.—This connects them with the Werini (Varni) and the Thuringians—"Incipit lex *Angliorum* et *Werinorum* hoc est *Thuringorum.*"

§ 48. These notices agree in giving the Angles a *German* locality, and in connecting them ethnologically, and philologically with the *Germans* of Germany. And such was, undoubtedly, the case. Nevertheless, it may be seen from § 15 that a *Danish* origin has been assigned to them.

The exact Germanic affinities of the Angles are, however, difficult to ascertain, since the tribes with which they are classed are differently classed. This we shall see by asking the following questions:—

§ 49. What were the *Langobardi*, with whom the Angles were connected by Tacitus? The most important fact to be known concerning them is, that the general opinion is in favour of their having belonged to either the *High*-German, or Mœso-Gothic division, rather than to the *Low*.

§ 50. What were the *Suevi*, with whom the Angles were connected by Tacitus? The most important fact to be known concerning them is, that the general opinion is in favour of their having belonged to either the *High*-German or Mœso-Gothic division rather than to the *Low*.

§ 51. What were the *Werini*, with whom the Angles were connected in the *Leges Anglorum et Werinorum?* Without having any particular *data* for connecting the Werini (Varni, Οὐάρνοι) with either the High-German, or the Mœso-Gothic divisions, there are certain facts in favour of their being *Slavonic*.

§ 52. What were the *Thuringians*, with whom the Angles are connected in the *Leges Anglorum?* Germanic in locality, and most probably allied to the Goths of Mœsia in language. If not, High-Germans.

§ 53. Of the Reudigni, Eudoses, Nuithones, Suardones, and Aviones, too little is known in detail to make the details an inquiry of importance.

§ 54. The reader has now got a general view of the extent to which the position of the Angles, as a German tribe, is complicated by conflicting statements; statements which connect them with (probably) *High*-German Thuringians, Suevi, and Langobardi, and with (probably) *Slavonic* Werini, or Varni; whereas in England, they are scarcely distinguishable from the *Low*-German Saxons. In the present state of our knowledge, the only safe fact seems to be, that of the common relation of both *Angles* and Saxons to the present *English* of England.

This brings the two sections within a very close degree of affinity, and makes it probable, that, just as at present, descendants of the Saxons are English (*Angle*) in Britain, so, in the third and fourth centuries, ancestors of the Angles were Saxons in Germany. Why, however, the one name preponderated on the Continent, and the other in England is difficult to ascertain.

§ 55. The Frisians have been mentioned as a Germanic population *likely* to have joined in the invasion of Britain; the *presumption* in favor of their having done so arising from their geographical position.

There is, however, something more than mere presumption upon this point.

Archbishop Usher, amongst the earlier historians, and

Mr. Kemble amongst those of the present day, as well as other intermediate investigators, have drawn attention to certain important notices of them.

The main facts bearing upon this question are the following:—

1. Hengist, according to some traditions, was a Frisian hero.

2. Procopius[2] wrote as follows:—Βριττίαν δὲ τὴν νῆσον ἔθνη τρία πολυανθρωπότατα ἔχουσι, βασιλεύς τε εἷς αὐτῶν ἑκάστῳ ἐφέστηκεν, ὀνόματα δὲ κεῖται τοῖς ἔθνεσι τούτοις Ἀγγίλοι τε καὶ Φρίσσονες καὶ οἱ τῇ νήσῳ ὁμώνυμοι Βρίττωνες. Τοσαύτη δὲ ἡ τῶνδε τῶν ἐθνῶν πολυανθρωπία φαίνεται οὖσα ὥστε ἀνὰ πᾶν ἔτος κατὰ πολλοὺς ἐνθένδε μετανιστάμενοι ξὺν γυναιξὶ καὶ παισὶν ἐς Φράγγους χωροῦσιν.—Procop. B. G. iv. 20.

3. In the Saxon Chronicle we find the following passage:—"That same year, the armies from among the East-Anglians, and from among the North-Humbrians, harassed the land of the West-Saxons chiefly, most of all by their 'æses,' which they had built many years before. Then king Alfred commanded long ships to be built to oppose the æses; they were full-nigh twice as long as the others; some had sixty oars, and some had more; they were both swifter and steadier, and also higher than the others. They were shapen neither like the *Frisian* nor the Danish, but so as it seemed to him that they would be most efficient. Then some time in the same year, there came six ships to Wight, and there did much harm, as well as in Devon, and elsewhere along the sea coast. Then the king commanded nine of the new ships to go thither, and they obstructed their passage from the port towards the outer sea. Then went they with three of their ships out against them; and three lay in the upper part of the port in the dry; the men were gone

from them ashore. Then took they two of the three ships at the outer part of the port, and killed the men, and the other ship escaped; in that also the men were killed except five; they got away because the other ships were aground. They also were aground very disadvantageously, three lay aground on that side of the deep on which the Danish ships were aground, and all the rest upon the other side, so that no one of them could get to the others. But when the water had ebbed many furlongs from the ships, then the Danish men went from their three ships to the other three which were left by the tide on their side, and then they there fought against them. There was slain Lucumon the king's reeve, and Wulfheard the *Frisian*, and Æbbe the *Frisian*, and Æthelhere the *Frisian*, and Æthelferth the king's 'geneat,' and of all the men, *Frisians* and English, seventy-two; and of the Danish men one hundred and twenty."

§ 56. I believe then, that, so far from the current accounts being absolutely correct, in respect to the Germanic elements of the English population, the *Jutes*, as mentioned by Beda, formed *no* part of it, whilst the *Frisians*, *not* so mentioned, *were a real constituent therein;* besides which, there may, very easily, have been other Germanic tribes, though in smaller proportions.

CHAPTER VI.

THE CELTIC STOCK OF LANGUAGES, AND THEIR RELATIONS TO THE ENGLISH.

§ 57. THE languages of Great Britain at the invasion of Julius Cæsar were of the Celtic stock.

Of the Celtic stock there are two branches.

1. The British or Cambrian branch, represented by the present Welsh, and containing, besides, the Cornish of Cornwall (lately extinct), and the Armorican of the French province of Brittany. It is almost certain that the old British, the ancient language of Gaul, and the Pictish were of this branch.

2. The Gaelic or Erse branch, represented by the present Irish Gaelic, and containing, besides, the Gaelic of the Highlands of Scotland and the Manks of the Isle of Man.

§ 58. Taken altogether the Celtic tongues form a very remarkable class. As compared with those of the Gothic stock they are marked by the following characteristics:—

The scantiness of the declension of Celtic nouns.—In Irish there is a peculiar form for the dative plural, as *cos = foot, cos-aibh = to feet* (ped-*ibus*); and beyond this there is nothing else whatever in the way of *case*, as found in the German, Latin, Greek, and other tongues. Even the isolated form in question is not found in the

Welsh and Breton. Hence the Celtic tongues are pre eminently uninflected in the way of *declension*.

§ 59. *The agglutinate character of their verbal inflections.*—In Welsh the pronouns for *we*, *ye*, and *they*, are *ni*, *chwyi*, and *hwynt respectively*. In Welsh also the root = *love* is *car*. As conjugated in the plural number this is—

<p align="center">car-wn = am-amus.
car-<i>ych</i> = am-<i>atis</i>.
car-<i>ant</i> = am-<i>ant</i>.</p>

Now the *-wn*, *-ych*, and *-ant*, of the persons of the verbs are the personal pronouns, so that the inflection is really a verb and a pronoun in a state of *agglutination*; *i.e.*, in a state where the original separate existence of the two sorts of words is still manifest. This is probably the case with languages in general. The Celtic, however, has the peculiarity of exhibiting it in an unmistakable manner; showing, as it were, an inflection in the process of formation, and (as such) exhibiting an early stage of language.

§ 60. *The system of initial mutations.*—The Celtic, as has been seen, is deficient in the ordinary means of expressing case. How does it make up for this? Even thus. The noun changes its initial letter according to its relation to the other words of the sentence. Of course this is subject to rule. As, however, I am only writing for the sake of illustrating in a general way the peculiarities of the Celtic tongues, the following table, from Prichard's "Eastern Origin of the Celtic Nations," is sufficient.

Câr, *a kinsman.*
  1. *form*, Câr agos, *a near kinsman.*
  2.   Ei gâr, *his kinsman.*
  3. *form*, Ei châr, *her kinsman.*
  4.   Vy nghâr, *my kinsman.*

Tâd, *a father.*
1. *form,* Tâd y plentyn, *the child's father.*
2. Ei dâd, *his father.*
3. Ei thâd, *her father.*
4. Vy nhâd, *my father.*

Pen, *a head.*
1. *form,* Pen gwr, *the head of a man.*
2. Ei ben, *his head.*
3. Ei phen, *her head.*
4. Vy nhen, *my head.*

Gwas, *a servant.*
1. *form,* Gwâs fydhlon, *a faithful servant.*
2. Ei wâs, *his servant.*
3. Vy ngwas, *my servant.*

Duw, *a god.*
1. *form,* Duw trugarog, *a merciful god.*
2. Ei dhuw, *his god.*
3. Vy nuw, *my god.*

Bara, *bread.*
1. *form,* Bara cann, *white bread.*
2. Ei vara, *his bread.*
3. Vy mara, *my bread.*

Lhaw, *a hand.*
1. *form,* Lhaw wenn, *a white hand.*
2. Ei law, *his hand.*

Mam, *a mother.*
1. *form,* Mam dirion, *a tender mother.*
2. Eivam, *his mother.*

Rhwyd, *a net.*
1. *form,* Rhwyd lawn, *a full net.*
2. Ei rwyd, *his net.*
From the Erse.

Súil, *an eye.*
1. *form,* Súil.
2. A húil, *his eye.*

Sláinte, *health.*
2. *form,* Do hláinte, *your health.*

§ 61. The Celtic tongues have lately received especial illustration from the researches of Mr. Garnett. Amongst others, the two following points are particularly investigated by him:—

1. The affinities of the ancient language of Gaul.
2. The affinities of the Pictish language or dialect.

§ 62. *The ancient language of Gaul Cambrian.*— The evidence in favour of the ancient language of Gaul being Cambrian rather than Gaelic, lies in the following facts:—

The old Gallic glosses are more Welsh than Gaelic.

a. Petorritum = a four-wheeled carriage, from the Welsh, *peder = four,* and *rhod = a wheel.* The Gaelic for *four* is *ceathair*, and the Gaelic compound would have been different.

b. Pempedula, the *cinque-foil*, from the Welsh *pump* =*five*, and *dalen* = *a leaf*. The Gaelic for *five* is *cuig*, and the Gaelic compound would have been different.

c. Candetum = a measure of 100 feet, from the Welsh *cant* = 100. The Gaelic for *a hundred* is *cead*, and the Gaelic compound would have been different.

d. Epona = *the goddess of horses*. In the old Armorican the root *ep* = *horse*. The Gaelic for a horse is *each*.

e. The evidence from the names of geographical localities in Gaul, both ancient and modern, goes the same way: *Nantuates, Nantouin, Nanteuil*, are derived from the Welsh *nant* = *a valley*, a word unknown in Gaelic.

f. The evidence of certain French provincial words, which are Welsh and Armorican rather than Erse or Gaelic.

§ 63. *The Pictish most probably Cambrian.*—The evidence in favour of the Pictish being Cambrian rather than Gaelic lies in the following facts:

a. When St. Columbanus preached, whose mother-tongue was Irish Gaelic, he used an interpreter. This shows the *difference* between the Pict and Gaelic. What follows shows the affinity between the Pict and Welsh.

b. A manuscript in the Colbertine library contains a list of Pictish kings from the fifth century downwards. These names are more Welsh than Gaelic. *Taran* = *thunder* in Welsh. *Uven* is the Welsh *Owen*. The first syllable in *Talorg* (=*forehead*) is the *tal* in *Talhaiarn* = *iron forehead*, *Taliessin* = *splendid forehead*, Welsh names. *Wrgust* is nearer to the Welsh *Gwrgust* than to the Irish *Fergus*. Finally, *Drust, Drostan, Wrad, Necton*, closely resemble the Welsh *Trwst, Trwst-*

an, Gwriad, Nwython. Cincod and *Domhnall* (*Kenneth* and *Donnell*) are the only true Erse forms in the list.

c. The only Pictish common name extant is the well-known compound *pen val*, which is, in the oldest MS. of Beda, *peann fahel.* This means *caput valli*, and is the name for the eastern termination of the Vallum of Antoninus. Herein *pen* is unequivocally Welsh, meaning *head.* It is an impossible form in Gaelic. *Fal*, on the other hand, is apparently Gaelic, the Welsh for a *rampart* being *gwall. Fal*, however, occurs in Welsh also, and means *inclosure.*

The evidence just indicated is rendered nearly conclusive by an interpolation, apparently of the twelfth century, of the Durham MS. of Nennius, whereby it is stated that the spot in question was called in Gaelic *Cenail.* Now Cenail is the modern name *Kinneil*, and it is also a Gaelic translation of the Pict *pen val*, since *cean* is the Gaelic for *head*, and *fhail* for *rampart* or *wall.* If the older form were Gaelic, the substitution, or translation, would have been superfluous.

d. The name of the *Ochil Hills* in Perthshire is better explained from the Pict *uchel* = *high*, than from the Gaelic *uasal.*

e. Bryneich, the British form of the province Bernicia, is better explained by the Welsh *bryn* = *ridge* (*hilly country*), than by any word in Gaelic.—Garnett, in Transactions of Philological Society."

CHAPTER VII.

THE ANGLO-NORMAN, AND THE LANGUAGES OF THE CLASSICAL STOCK.

§ 64. THE languages of Greece and Rome belong to one and the same stock.

The Greek and its dialects, both ancient and modern, constitute the Greek of the Classical stock.

The Latin in all its dialects, the old Italian languages allied to it, and the modern tongues derived from the Roman, constitute the Latin branch of the Classical stock.

Now, although the Greek dialects are of only secondary importance in the illustration of the history of the English language, the Latin elements require a special consideration.

This is because the Norman French, introduced into England by the battle of Hastings, is a language derived from the Roman, and consequently a language of the Latin branch of the Classical stock.

§ 65. The Latin language overspread the greater part of the Roman empire. It supplanted a multiplicity of aboriginal languages; just as the English of North America *has* supplanted the aboriginal tongues of the native Indians, and just as the Russian *is* supplanting those of Siberia and Kamskatka.

Sometimes the war that the Romans carried on against the old inhabitants was a war of extermination. In this case the original language was superseded *at once*. In other cases their influence was introduced gradually. In this case the influence of the original language was greater and more permanent.

Just as in the United States the English came in contact with an American, whilst in New Holland it comes in contact with an Australian language, so was the Latin language of Rome engrafted, sometimes on a Celtic, sometimes on a Gothic, and sometimes on some other stock. The nature of the original language must always be borne in mind.

From Italy, its original seat, the Latin was extended in the following chronological order:—

1. To the Spanish Peninsula; where it overlaid or was engrafted on languages allied to the present Biscayan.

2. To Gaul, or France, where it overlaid or was engrafted on languages of the Celtic stock.

3. To Dacia and Pannonia where it overlaid or was engrafted on a language the stock whereof is undetermined, but which was, probably, Sarmatian. The introduction of the Latin into Dacia and Pannonia took place in the time of Trajan.

§ 66. From these different introductions of the Latin into different countries we have the following modern languages—1st Italian, 2nd Spanish and Portuguese, 3rd French, 4th Wallachian; to which must be added a 5th, the Romanese of part of Switzerland.

Specimen of the Romanese.

Luke xv. 11.

11. Ün Hum veva dus Filgs:
12. Ad ilg juven da quels schet alg Bab, "Bab mi dai la Part de la Rauba c' aud' à mi: ad el parchè or ad els la Rauba.
13. A bucca bears Gis suenter, cur ilg Filg juven vet tut mess an-

semel, scha tilà 'l navent en üuna Terra dalunsch: a lou sûget el tut sia Rauba cun viver senza spargn.

14. A cur el vet tut sfaig, scha vangit ei en quella Terra üu grond Fumaz: ad el antschavet a ver basengs.

15. Ad el mà, à: sa plidò enn ün Burgeis da quella Terra; a quel ilg tarmatet or sin sés Beius a parchirar ils Porcs.

16. Ad el grigiava dad amplanir sieu Venter cun las Criscas ch' ils Porcs malgiavan; mo nagin lgi deva.

17. Mo el mà en sasez a schet: "Quonts Fumelgs da mieu Bab han budonza da l'ann, a jou miei d' fom!"

18. "Jou vi lavar si, ad ir tier mieu Bab, e vi gir a lgi: 'Bab, jou hai faig puccau ancunter ilg Tschiel ad avout tei;

19. "' A sunt bucca pli vaugonts da vangir numnaus tieu Filg; fai mei esser sco ün da tes Fumelgs.'"

Specimen of the Wallachian.

Luke xv. 11.

11. Un om evea doi fee ori.

12. Shi a zis c'el mai tinr din ci tatlui su: tat, dmi partea c'e mi se kade de avucie: shi de a impreit lor avuciea.

13. Shi nu dup multe zile, adunint toate fee orul e el mai tinr, s'a dus intr 'o car departe, shi akolo a rsipit toat avucica ea, vieeuind intr dezmierdri.

14. Shi keltuind el toate, c'a fkut foamete mare intr' ac'ea car: shi el a inc'eput a se lipsi.

15. Shi mergina c'a lipit de unul din lkuitorii crii ac'eia: si 'l a trimis pre el la carinide sale e pask porc'ii.

16. Shi doria e 'shi sature pinctec'ele sii de roshkobele c'e minka porc'ii! shi nimini nu i da lui.

17. Iar viind intru siue, a zis; kici argaci ai tatlui mieu sint indestulaci de piine, iar cu piciu de foame.

18. Skula-m-viou, shi m' voiu duc'e la tata mieu, shi viou zic'e lui:

19. Tat, greshit-am la c'er shi iuaintea ta, shi nu mai sint vrednik a ni kema fiul tu; fm ka pre unul din argacii ti.

§ 67. Such is the *general* view of the languages derived from the Latin, *i. e.*, of the languages of the Latin branch of the Classical stock.

The French requires to be more minutely exhibited.

Between the provincial French of the north and the provincial French of the south, there is a difference, at the present day, at least of dialect, and perhaps of language. This is shown by the following specimens: the first from the canton of Arras, on the confines of Flanders; the second from the department of Var, in Provence. The date of each is A.D. 1807.

I.

Luke xv. 11.

11. Ain homme avoüait deeux garchéons.

12. L'pus jone dit a saiu père, "Maiu père, baillé m'cheu qui doüo me 'r'v'nir ed vous bien," et lue père lou partit saiu bien.

13. Ain n'sais yur, tro, quate, chéon jours après l'pus tiò d'cués déeux éféans oyant r'cuéllé tout s'u' héritt'main, s'ot' ainvoye dains nâiu pahis gramain loüon, dú qu'il échilla tout s'u' argint ain fageant l'braingand dains chés cabarets.

14. Abord qu'il o eu tout bu, tout mié et tout drôlé, il o v'nu adone dains ch' pahis lo ainu' famaine cruüelle, et i c'mainchouait d'avoir fou-ye d' pon-ye (*i. e.* faim de pain).

II.

THE SAME.

11. Un homé avié dous enfaus.

12. Lou plus pichoun diguét a son püiré, "Moun püiré, dounas mi ce què mi reven de vouastré ben;" lou pairé faguet lou partagé de tout ce que poussédavo.

13. Paou de jours après, lou pichoun vendét tout se què soun püiré li avié desamparat, et s'eu anét dius un püis fourco luench, ounté dissipét tout soun ben en debaucho.

14. Quand aguét tou arcaba, uno grosso famino arribet dins aqueou päis et, leou, si veguét reducch à la derniero misèro.

Practically speaking, although in the central parts of France the northern and southern dialects melt into each other, the Loire may be considered as a line of demarcation between two languages; the term language being employed because, in the Middle Ages, whatever may be their real difference, their northern tongue and the southern tongue were dealt with not as separate dialects, but as distinct languages—the southern being called Provençal, the northern Norman-French.

Of these two languages (for so they will in the following pages be called, for the sake of convenience) the southern, or Provençal, approaches the dialects of Spain; the Valencian of Spain and the Catalonian of Spain being Provençal rather than standard Spanish or Castilian.

The southern French is sometimes called the Langue d'Oc, and sometimes the Limousin.

§ 68. The Norman-French, spoken from the Loire to the confines of Flanders, and called also the Langue d'Oyl, differed from the Provençal in (amongst others) the following circumstances.

1. It was of later origin; the southern parts of Gaul having been colonized at an early period by the Romans.

2. It was in geographical contact, not with the allied languages of Spain, but with the Gothic tongues of Germany and Holland.

§ 69. It is the Norman-French that most especially bears upon the history of the English language.

Specimen from the Anglo-Norman poem of Charlemagne.

 Un jur fu Karléun al Seint-Denis muster,
 Reout prise sa corune, en croiz seignat suu chef,
 E ad ceinte sa espée : li pons fud d'or mer.
 Dux i out e demeines e baruns e chevalers.
 Li emperéres reguardet la reine sa muillers.

Ele fut ben corunée al plus bel e as meuz.
Il la prist par le poin desuz un oliver,
De sa pleine parole la prist à reisuner:
"Dame, véistes unkes hume nul de desuz ceil
Tant beu séist espée ne la corone el chef?
Uncore cuuquerrei-jo citez ot mun espeez."
Cele ne fud pas sage, folement respondeit:
"Empercre," dist-ele, trop vus poez preiser.
"Uncore en sa-jo un ki plus se fait léger,
Quant il porte corune entre ses chevalers;
Kaunt il met sur sa teste, plus belement lui set."

In the northern French we must recognise not only a Celtic and a Classical, but also a Gothic element: since Clovis and Charlemagne were no Frenchmen, but Germans. The Germanic element in French has still to be determined.

In the northern French of *Normandy* there is a second Gothic element, *viz.*, a Scandinavian element. See § 76.

QUESTIONS

1. WHAT are the *present* languages of Wales, the Isle of Man, the Scotch Highlands, and Ireland?

2. What are the *present* languages of Germany and Holland? How are they related to the *present* language of England? How to the original language of England?

3. Enumerate the chief *supposed* migrations from Germany to England, giving (when possible) the *date* of each, the particular German tribe by which each was undertaken, and the parts of Great Britain where the different landings were made. Why do I say *supposed* migrations? Criticise, in detail, the evidence by which they are supported, and state the extent to which it is exceptionable. Who was Beda? What were the sources of his information?

4. Give reasons for believing the existence of Germans in England anterior to A. D. 447.

5. Who are the present Jutlanders of Jutland? Who the inhabitants of the district called Anglen in Sleswick? What are the reasons for connecting these with the Jutes and Angles of Beda? What those for denying such a connection?

6. What is the meaning of the termination *-uarii* in *Cant-uarii* and *Veet-uarii?* What was the Anglo-Saxon translation of *Antiqui Saxones, Occidentales Saxones, Orientales Saxones, Meridionales Saxones?* What are the known variations in the form of the word *Vectis*, meaning the Isle of Wight? What those of the root *Jut-* as the name of the inhabitants of the peninsula of Jutland?

7. Translate *Cantware, Wihtware,* into Latin. How does Alfred translate *Jutæ?* How does the Anglo-Saxon Chronicle? What is the derivation of the name *Carisbrook,* a town in the Isle of Wight?

8. Take exception to the opinions that *Jutes*, from *Jutland*, formed part of the Germanic invasion of England; or, rather, take exceptions to the evidence upon which that opinion is based.

9. From what part of Germany were the *Angles* derived? What

is Beda's? what Ethelweard's statement concerning them? Who were the *Angli* of Tacitus?

10. What is the derivation of the word Mercia?

11. Give the localities of the Old Saxons, and the Northalbingians. Investigate the area occupied by the Anglo-Saxons.

12. What is the present population of the Dutch province of Friesland? What its language? What the dialects and stages of that language?

13. What was the language of the Asega-bog, the Heliand, Beowulf, Hildubrand and Hathubrant, the Carolinian Psalms, the Gospels of Ulphilas, and the poems of Gysbert Japicx?

14. Make a map of Ancient Germany and Scandinavia according to languages and dialects of those two areas. Exhibit, in a tabular form, the languages of the *Gothic* stock. Explain the meaning of the words *Gothic*, and *Mœso-Gothic*, and *Platt-Deutsch*.

15. Analyze the Scandinavian forms *Solen*, *Bordet*, and *brennast*.

16. Exhibit the difference between the *logical* and the *historical* analysis of a language.

17. What are the Celtic names for the *English language?*

18. Enumerate the chief Germanic populations connected by ancient writers with the *Angles*, stating the Ethnological relations of each, and noticing the extent to which they coincide with those of the Angles.

19. What are the reasons for believing that there is a *Frisian* element in the population of England?

20. Exhibit, in a tabular form, the languages and dialects of the Celtic stock. To which division did the Gallic of ancient Gaul, and the Pict belong? Support the answer by reasons. What were the relations of the Picts to the Gaelic inhabitants of Scotland? What to the Lowland Scotch? What to the Belgæ?

21. Explain the following words—*petorritum, pempedula, candetum, Epona, Nantuates, peann fahel* and *Bernicia*. What inferences do you draw from the derivation of them?

22. Exhibit, in a tabular form, the languages and dialects of the Classical stock.

23. What is the bearing of the statements of Tacitus and other ancient writers respecting the following Germanic populations upon the ethnological relations of the Angles,—Aviones, Reudigni, Suevi, Langobardi, Frisii, Varini?

24. What is meant by the following terms, Provençal, Langue d'Oc, Langue d'Oyl, Limousin, and Norman-French?

25. What languages, besides the Celtic and Latin, enter into the composition of the French?

PART II.

HISTORY AND ANALYSIS OF THE ENGLISH LANGUAGE.

CHAPTER I.

HISTORICAL AND LOGICAL ELEMENTS OF THE ENGLISH LANGUAGE.

§ 70. THE Celtic elements of the present English fall into five classes.

1. Those that are of late introduction, and cannot be called original and constituent parts of the language. Some of such are the words *flannel, crowd* (a fiddle), from the Cambrian; and *kerne* (an Irish foot-soldier), *galore* (enough), *tartan, plaid,* &c., from the Gaelic branch.

2. Those that are originally common to both the Celtic and Gothic stocks. Some of such are *brother, mother,* in Celtic *brathair, mathair;* the numerals, &c.

3. Those that have come to us from the Celtic, but have come to us through the medium of another language. Some of such are *druid* and *bard,* whose *immediate* source is, not the Celtic but the Latin.

4. Celtic elements of the Anglo-Norman, introduced into England after the Conquest, and occurring in that language as remains of the original Celtic of Gaul.

5. Those that have been retained from the original Celtic of the island, and which form genuine constituents of our language. These fall into three subdivisions.

a. Proper names—generally of geographical localities; as *the Thames, Kent,* &c.

b. Common names retained in the provincial dialects of England, but not retained in the current language; as *gwethall* = *household stuff*, and *gwlanen* = *flannel* in Herefordshire.

c. Common names retained in the current language.— The following list is Mr. Garnett's:—

Welsh.	English.	Welsh.	English.
Basgawd	Basket.	Greidell	Grid in Gridiron.
Berfa	Barrow.	Grual	Gruel.
Botwm	Button.	Gwald (hem, border)	Welt.
Brân	Bran.		
Clwt	Clout, Rag.	Gwiced (little door)	Wicket.
Crochan	Crockery.		
Crog	Crook, Hook.	Gwn	Gown.
Cwch	Cock, in Cock-boat.	Gwyfr	Wire.
Cwysed	Gusset.	Masg (stitch in netting)	Mesh.
Cyl, Cyln	Kiln (Kill, provinc.).	Mattog	Mattock.
Dantaeth	Dainty.	Mop	Mop.
Darn	Darn.	Rhail (fence)	Rail.
Deentur	Tenter, in Tenter-hook.	Rhashg (slice)	Rasher.
Ffläim	Fleam, Cattle-lancet.	Rhuwch	Rug.
Fflaw	Flaw.	Sawduriaw	Solder.
Ffynnell (air-hole)	Funnel.	Syth (glue)	Size.
		Tacl	Tackle.
Gefyn (fetter)	Gyve.		

§ 71. *Latin of the first period.*—Of the Latin introduced by Cæsar and his successors, the few words remaining are those that relate to military affairs; *viz. street* (*strata*); *-coln* (as in *Lincoln=Lindi colonia*); *-cest-* (as in *Gloucester=glevæ castra*) from *castra*. The Latin words introduced between the time of Cæsar and Hengist may be called the *Latin of the first period*, or the *Latin of the Celtic period*.

§ 72. *The Anglo-Saxon.*—This is not noticed here, because, from being the staple of the present language, it is more or less the subject of the book throughout.

§ 73. *The Danish, or Norse.*—The pirates that pillaged Britain, under the name of Danes, were not exclusively the inhabitants of Denmark. Of the three Scandinavian nations, the Swedes took the least share, the Norwegians the greatest, in these invasions.

The language of the three nations was the same; the differences being differences of dialect. It was that which is now spoken in Iceland, having been once common to Scandinavia and Denmark.

The Danish that became incorporated with our language, under the reign of Canute and his sons, may be called the *direct* Danish element, in contradistinction to the *indirect* Danish of § 76.

The determination of the amount of Danish in English is difficult. It is not difficult to prove a word *Scandinavian*; but, then, we must also show that it is not German as well. A few years back the current opinion was against the doctrine that there was much Danish in England. At present, the tendency is rather the other way. The following facts are from Mr. Garnett.—" Phil. Trans." vol. i.

1. The Saxon name of the present town of *Whitby* in Yorkshire was *Streoneshalch*. The present name *Whitby, Hvitby*, or *Whitetown*, is Danish.

2. The Saxon name of the capital of Derbyshire was *Northweortheg*. The present name is Danish.

3. The termination -*by* = *town* is Norse.

4. On a monument in Aldburgh church, Holdernesse, in the East Riding of Yorkshire, referred to the age of Edward the Confessor, is found the following inscription:—

> *Ulf* het aræran cyrice *for hanum* and for Gunthara saula.
> "Ulf bid rear the church for him and for the soul of Gunthar."

Now, in this inscription, *Ulf*, in opposition to the Anglo-Saxon *Wulf*, is a Norse form; whilst *hanum* is a Norse dative, and by no means an Anglo-Saxon one.— Old Norse *hanum*, Swedish *honom*.

5. The use of *at* for *to* as the sign of the infinitive mood is Norse, not Saxon. It is the regular prefix in Icelandic, Danish, Swedish, and Feroic. It is also found in the northern dialects of the Old English, and in the particular dialect of Westmoreland at the present day.

6. The use of *sum* for *as*; e. g.,—*swa sum* we forgive oure detturs.

7. Isolated words in the northern dialects are Norse rather than Saxon.

Provincial.	*Common Dialect.*	*Norse.*
Braid	Resemble	Braas, *Swed.*
Eldin	Firing	Eld, *Dan.*
Force	Waterfall	Fors, *D. Swed.*
Gar	Make	Göra, *Swed.*
Gill	Ravine	Gil, *Iceland.*
Greet	Weep	Grata, *Iceland.*
Ket	Carrion	Kiöd = flesh, *Dan.*
Lait	Seek	Lede, *Dan.*
Lathe	Barn	Lade, *Dan.*
Lile	Little	Lille, *Dan.*

§ 74. *Roman of the second period.*—Of the Latin introduced under the Christianised Saxon sovereigns, many words are extant. The relate chiefly to ecclesiastical matters, just as the Latin of the Celtic period bore upon military affairs. *Mynster*, a minster, *monasterium; portic*, a porch, *porticus; cluster*, a cloister, *claustrum; munuc*, a monk, *monachus; bisceop*, a bishop, *episcopus; arcebisceop*, archbishop, *archiepiscopus; sanct*, a saint, *sanctus; profost*, a provost, *propositus; pall*, a pall, *pallium; calic*, a chalice, *calix; candel*, a candle, *candela; psalter*, a psalter, *psalterium; mæsse*, a mass, *missa; pistel*, an epistle, *epistola; prædic-ian*, to preach, *prædicare; prof-ian*, to prove, *probare*.

The following are the names of foreign plants and animals:—*camell*, a camel, *camelus; ylp*, elephant, *elephas; ficbeam*, fig-tree, *ficus; feferfuge*, feverfew, *febrifuga; peterselige*, parsley, *petroselinum*.

Others are the names of articles of foreign origin, as *pipor*, pepper, *piper; purpur*, purple, *purpura; pumic-stan*, pumicestone, *pumex*.

This is the Latin of the second, or Saxon period.

§ 75. *The Anglo-Norman element.*—For practical purposes we may say that the French or Anglo-Norman element appeared in our language after the battle of Hastings, A.D. 1066.

Previous, however, to that period we find notices of intercourse between the two countries.

1. The residence in England of Louis Outremer.

2. Ethelred II. married Emma, daughter of Richard Duke of Normandy, and the two children were sent to Normandy for education.

3. Edward the Confessor is particularly stated to have encouraged French manners and the French language in England.

4

4. Ingulphus of Croydon speaks of his own knowledge of French.

5. Harold passed some time in Normandy.

6. The French article *la*, in the term *la Drove*, occurs in a deed of A.D. 975.

The chief Anglo-Norman elements of our language are the terms connected with the feudal system, the terms relating to war and chivalry, and a great portion of the law terms—*duke, count, baron, villain, service, chivalry, warrant, esquire, challenge, domain*, &c.

§ 76. When we remember that the word *Norman* means *man of the north*, that it is a *Scandinavian*, and *not a French* word, that it originated in the invasions of the followers of Rollo and and other *Norwegians*, and that just as part of England was overrun by Pagan buccaneers called *Danes*, part of France was occupied by similar *Northmen*, we see the likelihood of certain Norse words finding their way into the French language, where they would be superadded to its original Celtic and Roman elements.

The extent to which this is actually the case has only been partially investigated. It is certain, however, that some French words are Norse or Scandinavian. Such, for instance, are several *names of geographical localities* either near the sea, or the river Seine, in other words, within that tract which was most especially occupied by the invaders. As is to be expected from the genius of the French language, these words are considerably altered in form. Thus,

NORSE.	ENGLISH.	FRENCH.
Toft	Toft	Tot.
Beck	Beck	Bec.
Flöt	Fleet*	Fleur, &c.

* Meaning *ditch*.

and in these shapes they appear in the Norman names *Yvetot, Caudebec,* and *Harfleur,* &c.

Now any words thus introduced from the Norse of Scandinavia into the French of Normandy, might, by the Norman Conquest of England, be carried further, and so find their way into the English.

In such a case, they would constitute its *indirect* Scandinavian element.

A list of these words has not been made; indeed the question requires far more investigation than it has met with. The names, however, of the islands *Guerns-ey, Jers-ey,* and *Aldern-ey,* are certainly of the kind in question—since the *-ey,* meaning *island,* is the same as the *-ey* in *Orkn-ey,* and is the Norse rather than the Saxon form.

§ 77. *Latin of the third period.*—This means the Latin which was introduced between the battle of Hastings and the revival of literature. It chiefly originated in the cloister, in the universities, and, to a certain extent, in the courts of law. It must be distinguished from the *indirect* Latin introduced as part and parcel of the Anglo-Norman. It has yet to be accurately analyzed.

§ 78. *Latin of the fourth period.*- This means the Latin which has been introduced between the revival of literature and the present time. It has originated in the writings of learned men in general, and is distinguished from that of the previous periods by:

1. Being less altered in form:
2. Preserving, with substantives, in many cases its original inflections; *axis, axes; basis, bases:*
3. Relating to objects and ideas for which the increase of the range of science in general has required a nomenclature.

§ 79. *Greek.*—Words derived *directly* from the Greek are in the same predicament as the Latin of the third period—*phænomenon, phænomena; criterion, criteria,* &c.; words which are only *indirectly* of Greek origin, being considered to belong to the language from which they were immediately introduced into the English. Such are *deacon, priest,* &c., introduced through the Latin. Hence a word like *church* proves no more in regard to a Greek element in English, than the word *abbot* proves in respect to a Syrian one.

§ 80. The Latin of the fourth period and the Greek agree in retaining, in many cases, original inflexions rather than adopting the English ones; in other words, they agree in being but *imperfectly incorporated.* The phænomenon of imperfect incorporation is reducible to the following rules:—

1. That it has a direct ratio to the date of the introduction, *i.e.*, the more recent the word the more likely it is to retain its original inflexion.

2. That it has a relation to the number of meanings belonging to the words: thus, when a single word has two meanings, the original inflexion expresses one, the English inflexion another—*genius,* genii, often (*spirits*), *geniuses* (*men of genius*).

3. That it occurs with substantives only, and that only in the expression of number. Thus, although the plural of substantives like *axis* and *genius* are Latin, the possessive cases are English. So also are the degrees of comparison for adjectives, like *circular,* and the tenses, &c. for verbs, like *perambulate.*

§ 81. The following is a list of the chief Latin substantives introduced during the latter part of the fourth period; and preserving the *Latin* plural forms—

LATIN OF FOURTH PERIOD.

FIRST CLASS.

Words wherein the Latin plural is the same as the Latin singular.

(a)
Sing.	Plur.
Apparatus	apparatus
Hiatus	hiatus
Impetus	impetus

(b)
Sing.	Plur.
Caries	caries
Congeries	congeries
Series	series
Species	species
Superficies	superficies

SECOND CLASS.

Words wherein the Latin plural is formed from the Latin singular by changing the last syllable.

(a).—*Where the singular termination* -a *is changed in the plural into* -æ:—

Sing.	Plur.	Sing.	Plur.
Formula	formulæ	Nebula	nebulæ
Lamina	laminæ	Scoria	scoriæ
Larva	larvæ		

(b).—*Where the singular termination* -us *is changed in the plural into* -i:—

Sing.	Plur.	Sing.	Plur.
Calculus	calculi	Polypus	polypi
Colossus	colossi	Radius	radii
Convolvulus	convolvuli	Ranunculus	ranunculi
Focus	foci	Sarcophagus	sarcophagi
Genius	genii	Schirrhus	schirrhi
Magus	magi	Stimulus	stimuli
Nautilus	nautili	Tumulus	tumuli
Œsophagus	œsophagi		

(c).—*Where the singular termination* -um *is changed in the plural into* -a:—

Sing.	Plur.	Sing.	Plur.
Animalculum	animalcula	Effluvium	effluvia
Arcanum	arcana	Emporium	emporia
Collyrium	collyria	Encomium	encomia
Datum	data	Erratum	errata
Desideratum	desiderata	Gymnasium	gymnasia

Sing.	Plur.	Sing.	Plur.
Lixiv*ium*	lixiv*ia*	Prem*ium*	prem*ia*
Lustr*um*	lustr*a*	Schol*ium*	schol*ia*
Mausole*um*	mausole*a*	Spectr*um*	spectr*a*
Medi*um*	medi*a*	Specul*um*	specul*a*
Memorand*um*	memorand*a*	Strat*um*	strat*a*
Menstru*um*	menstru*a*	Succedane*um*	succedane*a*
Moment*um*	moment*a*		

(*d*).—*Where the singular termination -is is changed in the plural into -es :—*

Sing.	Plur.	Sing.	Plur.
Amanuens*is*	amanuens*es*	Ellips*is*	ellips*es*
Analys*is*	analys*es*	Emphas*is*	emphas*es*
Antithes*is*	antithes*es*	Hypothes*is*	hypothes*es*
Ax*is*	ax*es*	Oas*is*	oas*es*
Bas*is*	bas*es*	Parenthes*is*	parenthes*es*
Cris*is*	cris*es*	Synthes*is*	synthes*es*
Diæres*is*	diæres*es*	Thes*is*	thes*es*

THIRD CLASS.

Words wherein the plural is formed by inserting -e between the last two sounds of the singular, so that the former number always contains a syllable more than the latter :—

Sing.			Plur.
Apex	*sounded*	apec-s	apices
Appendix	—	appendic-s	appendices
Calix	—	calic-s	calices
Cicatrix	—	cicatric-s	cicatrices
Helix	—	helic-s	helices
Index	—	indec-s	indices
Radix	—	radic-s	radices
Vertex	—	vertec-s	vertices
Vortex	—	vortec-s	vortices

In all these words the *c* of the singular number is sounded as *k*; of the plural, as *s*.

§ 82. The following is a list of the chief Greek

substantives lately introduced, and preserving the *Greek* plural forms—

FIRST CLASS.

Words where the singular termination -on is changed in the plural into -a :—

Sing.	Plur.	Sing.	Plur.
Aphelion	aphelia	Criterion	criteria
Perihelion	perihelia	Ephemeron	ephemera
Automaton	automata	Phænomenon	phænomena.

SECOND CLASS.

Words where the plural is formed from the original root by adding either -es or -a, but where the singular rejects the last letter of the original root.

Plurals in -es :—

Original root.	Plur.	Sing.
Apsid-	apsides	apsis
Cantharid-	cantharides	cantharis
Chrysalid-	chrysalides	chrysalis
Ephemerid-	ephemerides	ephemeris
Tripod-	tripodes	tripos.

Plurals in -a :—

Original root.	Plur.	Sing.
Dogmat-	dogmata	dogma
Lemmat-	lemmata	lemma
Miasmat-	miasmata	miasma.*

§ 83. *Miscellaneous elements.*—Of miscellaneous elements we have two sorts; those that are incorporated in our language, and are currently understood (*e. g.*, the Spanish word *sherry*, the Arabic word *alkali*, and the Persian word *turban*), and those that, even amongst the educated, are considered strangers. Of this latter kind

* This list is taken from Smart's valuable and logical English Grammar.

(amongst many others) are the oriental words *hummum, kaftan, gul*, &c.

Of the currently understood miscellaneous elements of the English language, the most important are from the French; some of which agree with those of the Latin of the fourth period, and the Greek, in preserving the *French* plural forms—as *beau, beaux, billets-doux*.

Italian.—Some words of Italian origin do the same; as *virtuoso, virtuosi*.

Hebrew.—The Hebrew words, *cherub* and *seraph* do the same; the form *cherub-im*, and *seraph-im* being not only plurals but Hebrew plurals.

Beyond the words derived from these five languages, none form their plural other than after the English method, *i. e.*, in *-s*; as *waltzes*, from the *German* word *waltz*.

§ 84. Hence we have a measure of the extent to which a language, which, like the English, at one and the same time requires names for many objects, comes in contact with the tongues of half the world, and has moreover, a great power of incorporating foreign elements, derives fresh words from varied sources; as may be seen from the following incomplete notice of the languages which have, in different degrees, supplied it with new terms.

Arabic.—Admiral, alchemist, alchemy, alcohol, alcove, alembic, algebra, alkali, assassin.

Persian.—Turban, caravan, dervise, &c.

Turkish.—Coffee, bashaw, divan, scimitar, janisary, &c.

Hindoo languages.—Calico, chintz, cowrie, curry, lac, muslin, toddy, &c.

Chinese.—Tea, bohea, congou, hyson, soy, nankin &c.

Malay.—Bantam (fowl), gamboge, rattan, sago, shaddock, &c.

Polynesian.—Taboo, tattoo.

Tungusian or some similar Siberian language.—Mammoth, the bones of which are chiefly from the banks of the Lena.

North American Indian.—Squaw, wigwam, pemmican.

Peruvian.—Charki = prepared meat; whence *jerked* beef.

Caribbean.—Hammock.

§. 85. A distinction is drawn between the *direct* and *indirect*, the latter leading to the *ultimate origin* of words.

Thus a word borrowed into the English from the French, might have been borrowed into the French from the Latin, into the Latin from the Greek, into the Greek from the Persian, &c., and so *ad infinitum.*

The investigation of this is a matter of literary curiosity rather than any important branch of philology.

The ultimate known origin of many common words sometimes goes back to a great date, and points to extinct languages—

Ancient Nubian.—Barbarous.
Ancient Egyptian.—Ammonia.
Ancient Syrian.—Cyder.
Ancient Lycian.—Pandar.
Ancient Lydian.—Mæander.
Ancient Persian.—Paradise.

§ 86. Again, a word from a given language may be introduced by more lines than one; or it may be introduced twice over; once at an earlier, and again at a later period. In such a case its form will, most probably, vary; and, what is more, its meaning as well.

Words of this sort may be called *di-morphic*, their *dimorphism* having originated in one of two reasons—a difference of channel or a difference of date. Instances of the first are, *syrup*, *sherbet*, and *shrub*, all originally from the *Arabic*, srb; but introduced differently, viz., the first through the Latin, the second through the Persian, and the third through the Hindoo. Instances of the second are words like *minster*, introduced during the Anglo-Saxon, as contrasted with *monastery*, introduced during the Anglo-Norman period. By the proper application of these processes, we account for words so different in present form, yet so identical in origin, as *priest* and *presbyter*, *episcopal* and *bishop*, &c.

§ 87. *Distinction.*—The history of the languages that have been spoken in a particular country, is a different subject from the history of a particular language. The history of the languages that have been spoken in the United States of America, is the history of *Indian* languages. The history of the languages of the United States is the history of a Germanic language.

§ 88. *Words of foreign simulating a vernacular origin.*—These may occur in any mixed language whatever; they occur, however, oftener in the English than in any other.

Let a word be introduced from a foreign language—let it have some resemblance in sound to a real English term: lastly, let the meanings of the two words be not absolutely incompatible. We may then have a word of foreign origin taking the appearance of an English one. Such, amongst others, are *beef-eater*, from *bœuffetier*; *sparrow-grass*, *asparagus*; *Shotover*, *Chateauvert*;[*] *Jerusalem*, *Girasole*;[†] *Spanish beefeater*, *spina*

---

[*] As in *Shotover Hill*, near Oxford.
[†] As in *Jerusalem artichoke*.

bifida; periwig, peruke; runagate, renegade; lutestring, lustrino ;* O yes, Oyez! ancient, ensign.†

Dog-cheap.—This has nothing to do with *dogs*. The first syllable is *god* = *good* transposed, and the second the *ch-p* in *chapman* (= *merchant*) *cheap,* and *Eastcheap.* In Sir J. Mandeville, we find *god-kepe* = *good bargain.*

Sky-larking.—Nothing to do with *larks* of any sort; still less the particular species, *alauda arvensis.* The word improperly spelt *l-a-r-k,* and banished to the slang regions of the English language, is the Anglo-Saxon *lác* = *game,* or *sport ;* wherein the *a* is sounded as in *father* (not as in *farther*). *Lek* = *game,* in the present Scandinavian languages.

Zachary Macaulay = *Zumalacarregui ; Billy Ruffian* = *Bellerophon ; Sir Roger Dowlas* = *Surajah Dowlah,* although so limited to the common soldiers and sailors, who first used them, as to be exploded vulgarisms rather than integral parts of the language, are examples of the same tendency towards the irregular accommodation of misunderstood foreign terms.

Birdbolt.—An incorrect name for the *gadus lota,* or *ell-pout,* and a transformation of *barbote.*

Whistle-fish.—The same for *gadus mustela,* or *weasel-fish.*

Liquorice = *glycyrrhiza.*

Wormwood = *weremuth,* is an instance of a word from the same language, in an antiquated shape, being equally transformed with a word of really foreign origin.

§ 89. Sometimes the transformation of the *name* has engendered a change in the object to which it applies, or, at least, has evolved new ideas in connection with it. How easy for a person who used the words *beef-eater,*

* A sort of silk. † *Ancient Cassio*—" Othello."

sparrow-grass, or *Jerusalem*, to believe that the officers designated by the former either eat or used to eat more beef than any other people; that the second word was the name for a *grass* or herb of which *sparrows* were fond; and that *Jerusalem* artichokes came from Palestine.

What has just been supposed has sometimes a real occurrence. To account for the name of *Shotover-hill*, I have heard that Little John *shot over* it. Here the confusion, in order to set itself right, breeds a fiction. Again, in chess, the piece now called the *queen*, was originally the *elephant*. This was in Persian, *ferz*. In French it became *vierge*, which, in time, came to be mistaken for a derivative, and *virgo* = *the virgin, the lady, the queen*.

§ 90. Sometimes, where the form of a word in respect to its *sound* is not affected, a false spirit of accommodation introduces an unetymological *spelling;* as *frontispiece*, from *frontispecium*, *sovereign*, from *sovrano*, *colleague* from *collega*, *lanthorn* (old orthography) from *lanterna*.

The value of forms like these consists in their showing that language is affected by false etymologies as well as by true ones.

* * * * * *

§ 91. In *lambkin* and *lancet*, the final syllables (-*kin* and -*et*) have the same power. They both express the idea of smallness or diminutiveness. These words are but two out of a multitude, the one (*lamb*) being of Saxon, the other (*lance*) of Norman origin. The same is the case with the superadded syllables: -*kin* being Saxon; -*et* Norman. Now to add a Saxon termination to a Norman word, or *vice versâ*, is to corrupt the English language.

This leads to some observation respecting the—

§ 92. *Introduction of new words and Hybridism.*—Hybridism is a term derived from *hybrid-a, a mongrel;* a Latin word *of Greek extraction.*

The terminations *-ize* (as in *criticize*), *-ism* (as in *criticism*), *-ic* (as in *comic*)—these, amongst many others, are Greek terminations. To add them to words not of Greek origin is to be guilty of hybridism. Hence, *witticism* is objectionable.

The terminations *-ble* (as in *penetrable*), *-bility* (as in *penetrability*), *-al* (as in *parental*)—these, amongst many others, are Latin terminations. To add them to words not of Latin origin is to be guilty of hybridism.

Hybridism is the commonest fault that accompanies the introduction of new words. The hybrid additions to the English language are most numerous in works on science.

It must not, however, be concealed that several well established words are hybrid; and that, even in the writings of the classical Roman authors, there is hybridism between the Latin and the Greek.

Nevertheless, the etymological view of every word of foreign origin is, not that it is put together in England, but that it is brought whole from the language to which it is vernacular. Now no derived word can be brought whole from a language unless, in that language, all its parts exist. The word *penetrability* is not derived from the English word *penetrable*, by the addition of *-ty*. It is the Latin word *penetrabilitas* imported.

In derived words all the parts must belong to one and the same language, or, changing the expression, *every derived word must have a possible form in the language from which it is taken.* Such is the rule against hybridism.

§ 93. A true word sometimes takes the appearance of

a hybrid without really being so. The *-icle,* in *icicle,* is apparently the same as the *-icle* in *radicle.* Now, as *ice* is Gothic, and *-icle* classical, hybridism is simulated. *Icicle,* however, is not a derivative but a compound; its parts being *is* and *gicel,* both Anglo-Saxon words.*

§ 94. *On incompletion of the radical.*—Let there be in a given language a series of roots ending in *-t,* as *sœmat.* Let a euphonic influence eject the *-t,* as often as the word occurs in the nominative case. Let the nominative case be erroneously considered to represent the root, or radical, of the word. Let a derivative word be formed accordingly, *i. e.,* on the notion that the nominative form and the radical form coincide. Such a derivative will exhibit only a part of the root; in other words, the radical will be incomplete.

Now all this is what actually takes place in words like *hœmo-ptysis (spitting of blood), sema-phore (a sort of telegraph).* The Greek imparisyllabics eject a part of the root in the nominative case; the radical forms being *hœmat-* and *sœmat-,* not *hœm-* and *sœm-.*

Incompletion of the radical is one of the commonest causes of words being coined faultily. It must not, however, be concealed, that even in the classical writers, we have in words like δίστομος examples of incompletion of the radical.

* * * * * *

§ 95. The preceding chapters have paved the way for a distinction between the *historical* analysis of a language, and the *logical* analysis of one.

Let the present language of England (for illustration's sake only) consist of 40,000 words. Of these let 30,000

---

* Be she constant, be she fickle,
Be she flame, or be she *ickle.*

SIR C. SEDLEY.

be Anglo-Saxon, 5,000 Anglo-Norman, 100 Celtic, 10 Latin of the first, 20 Latin of the second, and 30 Latin of the third period, 50 Scandinavian, and the rest miscellaneous. In this case the language is considered according to the historical origin of the words that compose it, and the analysis is an historical analysis.

But it is very evident that the English, or any other language, is capable of being contemplated in another view, and that the same number of words may be very differently classified. Instead of arranging them according to the languages whence they are derived, let them be disposed according to the meanings that they convey. Let it be said, for instance, that out of 40,000 words, 10,000 are the names of natural objects, that 1000 denote abstract ideas, that 1000 relate to warfare, 1000 to church matters, 500 to points of chivalry, 1000 to agriculture, and so on through the whole. In this case the analysis is not historical but logical; the words being classed not according to their *origin*, but according to their *meaning*.

Now the logical and historical analyses of a language generally in some degree coincide; that is, terms for a certain set of ideas come from certain languages; just as in English a large proportion of our chemical terms are Arabic, whilst a still larger one of our legal ones are Anglo-Norman.

CHAPTER II.

THE RELATION OF THE ENGLISH TO THE ANGLO-SAXON, AND THE STAGES OF THE ENGLISH LANGUAGE.

§ 96. THE relation of the present English to the Anglo-Saxon is that of a *modern* language to an *ancient* one: the words *modern* and *ancient* being used in a defined and technical sense.

Let the word *smiðum* illustrate this. *Smið-um*, the dative plural of *smið*, is equivalent in meaning to the English *to smiths*, or to the Latin *fabr-is*. *Smiðum*, however, is a single Anglo-Saxon word (a substantive, and nothing more); whilst its English equivalent is two words (*i. e.*, a substantive with the addition of a preposition). The letter *s*, in *smiths*, shows that the word is plural. The *-um*, in *smiðum*, does this and something more. It is the sign of the *dative case* plural. The *-um* in *smiðum*, is the part of a word. The preposition *to* is a separate word with an independent existence. *Smiðum* is the radical syllable *smið* + the subordinate inflectional syllable *-um*, the sign of the dative case. The combination *to smiths* is the substantive *smiths* + the preposition *to*, equivalent in power to the sign of a dative case, but different from it in form. As far, then, as the words just quoted is concerned, the Anglo-Saxon differs from the English by expressing an idea by a certain *modification of the form of the root*, whereas the modern English denotes the same idea by *the addition of a preposition ;* in other words, the Saxon *inflection* is superseded by a *combination* of words.

The sentences in italics are mere variations of the same general statement. 1. *The earlier the stage of a given language the greater the amount of its inflectional forms, and the later the stage of a given language, the smaller the amount of them.* 2. *As languages become modern they substitute prepositions and auxiliary verbs for cases and tenses.* 3. *The amount of inflection is in the inverse proportion to the amount of prepositions and auxiliary verbs.* 4. *In the course of time languages drop their inflections, and substitute in its stead circumlocutions by means of prepositions, &c.* The reverse never takes place. 5. *Given two modes of expression, the one inflectional* (smiðum), *the other circumlocutional** (to smiths), *we can state that the first belongs to an early, the second to a late, state of language.*

The present chapter, then showing the relation of the English to the Anglo-Saxon, shows something more. It exhibits the *general* relation of a modern to an ancient language. As the English is to the Anglo-Saxon, so are the Danish, Swedish, and Norwegian, to the old Norse; and so are the French, Italian, Spanish, Portuguese, Romanese and Wallachian to the Latin, and the Romaic to the ancient Greek.

§ 97. Contrasted with the English, the Anglo-Saxon has (among others) the following differences.

NOUNS.

1. *Gender.*—In Anglo-Saxon there were three genders, the masculine, the feminine, and the neuter. With *adjectives* each gender had its peculiar declension. With

---

* Or *periphrastic.*

substantives also there were appropriate terminations, though only to a certain degree.

2. The definite article varied with the gender of its substantive; þæt eage, the eye; se steorra, the star; seo tunge, the tongue.

3. *Number.*—The plural form in -*en* (as in *oxen*), rare in English, was common in Anglo-Saxon. It was the regular termination of a whole declension; e. g., *eágan*, eyes; *steorran*, stars; *tungan*, tongues. Besides this, the Anglo-Saxons had forms in -*u* and -*a* as *ricu*, kingdoms; *gifa*, gifts. The termination -*s*, current in the present English, was confined to a single gender and to a single declension, as *endas*, ends; *dagas*, days; *smiðas*, smiths.

4. *Case.*—Of these the Saxons had, for their substantives, at least three; viz., the nominative, dative, genitive. With the pronouns and adjectives there was a true accusative form; and with a few especial words an ablative or instrumental one. *Smið*, a smith; *smiðe*, to a smith; *smiðes*, of a smith. Plural, *smiðas*, smiths; *smiðum*, to smiths; *smiða*, of smiths: *he*, he; *hine*, him; *him*, to him; *his*, his: *se*, the; *þa*, the; *þy*, with the; *þam*, to the; *þæs*, of the.

5. *Declension.*—In *Anglo-Saxon* it was necessary to determine the declension of a substantive. There was the weak, or simple declension for words ending in a vowel (as, *eage, steorra, tunga*), and the strong declension for words ending in a consonant (*smið, spræc, leáf*). The letters *i* and *u* were dealt with as semivowels, semi-vowels being dealt with as consonants; so that words like *sunu* and *gifu* belonged to the same declension as *smið* and *sprǽc*.

6. *Definite and indefinite form of adjectives.*—In Anglo-Saxon each adjective had two forms, one *definite*

and one *indefinite*. There is nothing of this kind in English. We say *a good sword*, and *the good sword* equally. In Anglo-Saxon, however, the first combination would be *se gode sweord*, the second *án god sweord*, the definite form being distinguished from the indefinite by the addition of a vowel.

7. *Pronouns personal.*—The Anglo Saxon language had for the first two persons a *dual* number; inflected as follows:

	1st Person.			2nd Person.	
Nom.	Wit	*We two*	*Nom.*	Git	*Ye two.*
Acc.	Unc	*Us two*	*Acc.*	Ince	*You two*
Gen.	Uncer	*Of us two*	*Gen.*	Incer	*Of you two.*

Besides this, the demonstrative, possessive, and relative pronouns, as well as the numerals *twa* and *þreo*, had a fuller declension than they have at present.

VERBS.

8. *Mood.*—The subjunctive mood that in the present English (with one exception*) differs from the indicative only in the third person singular, was in Anglo-Saxon considerably different from the indicative.

Indicative Mood.

Pres. Sing. 1. Lufige.	*Plur.* 1. ⎫
2. Lufast.	2. ⎬ Lufiað.
3. Lufað.	3. ⎭

Subjunctive Mood.

Pres. Sing. 1. ⎫	*Plur.* 1. ⎫
2. ⎬ Lufige	2. ⎬ Lufion.
3. ⎭	3. ⎭

---

* That of the verb substantive, *if I were*, subjunctive, as opposed to *I was*, indicative.

The Saxon infinitive ended in -*an* (*lufian*), and besides this there was a so-called gerundial form, to *lufigenne*.

Besides these there were considerable differences in respect to particular words; but of these no notice is taken; the object being to indicate the differences between the *ancient* and *modern* stages of a language in respect to *grammatical structure*.

9. To bring about these changes a certain amount *of time* is, of course, necessary; a condition which suggests the difficult question as to the *rate* at which languages change. This is different for different languages; but as the investigation belongs to *general* philology rather than to the particular history of the English language, it finds no place here.

§ 98. The extent, however, to which external causes may accelerate or retard philological changes, is *not* foreign to our subject; the influence of the Norman Conquest, upon the previous Anglo-Saxon foundation, being a problem of some difficulty.

At the first glance it seems to have been considerable, especially in the way of simplifying the grammar. Yet the accuracy of this view is by no means unequivocal. The reasons against it are as follows:

a. In Friesland no such conquest took place. Yet the modern Frisian, as compared with the ancient, is nearly as simple in its grammatical structure, as the English is when compared with the Anglo-Saxon.

b. In Norway, Sweden, and Denmark, no such conquest took place. Yet the modern Danish and Swedish, as compared with the Old Norse, are nearly as simple in their grammatical structure, as the English is, when compared with the Anglo-Saxon.

The question requires more investigation than it has met with.

An extract from Mr. Hallam's "History of Literature" closes the present section, and introduces the next.

"Nothing can be more difficult, except by an arbitrary line, than to determine the commencement of the English language; not so much, as in those on the Continent, because we are in want of materials, but rather from an opposite reason, the possibility of showing a very gradual succession of verbal changes that ended in a change of denomination. We should probably experience a similar difficulty, if we knew equally well the current idiom of France or Italy in the seventh and eighth centuries. For when we compare the earliest English of the thirteenth century with the Anglo-Saxon of the twelfth, it seems hard to pronounce why it should pass for a separate language, rather than a modification or simplification of the former. We must conform, however, to usage, and say that the Anglo-Saxon was converted into English:—1. By contracting and otherwise modifying the pronunciation and orthography of words. 2. By omitting many inflections, especially of the noun, and consequently making more use of articles and auxiliaries. 3. By the introduction of French derivatives. 4. By using less inversion and ellipsis, especially in poetry. Of these, the second alone, I think, can be considered as sufficient to describe a new form of language; and this was brought about so gradually, that we are not relieved from much of our difficulty, as to whether some compositions shall pass for the latest offspring of the mother, or the earlier fruits of the daughter's fertility. It is a proof of this difficulty that the best masters of our ancient language have lately introduced the word Semi-Saxon, which is to cover everything from A. D. 1150 to A. D. 1250."—Chapter i. 47.

§ 99. This shows that by the middle of the 12th century, the Anglo-Saxon of the standard Anglo-Saxon authors, had undergone such a change as to induce the scholars of the present age to denominate it, not Saxon, but *Semi*-Saxon. It had ceased to be genuine Saxon, but had not yet become English.

Some, amongst others, of the earlier changes of the standard Anglo-Saxon are,

1. The substitution of *an* for *-as*, in the plural of

substantives, *munucan* for *munucas* (*monks*); and, conversely, the substitution of *-s* for *-n*, as *steorres* for *steorran* (*stars*).

2. The ejection or shortening of final vowels, *þæt ylc* for *þæt ylce*; *sone* for *sunu*; *name* for *nama*; *dages* for *dagas*.

3. The substitution of *-n* for *-m* in the dative case, *hwilon* for *hwilum*.

4. The ejection of the *-n* of the infinitive mood, *cumme* for *cuman* (*to come*), *nemne* for *nemnen* (*to name*).

5. The ejection of *-en* in the participle passive, *I-hote* for *gehaten* (*called, hight*).

6. The gerundial termination *-enne*, superseded by the infinitive termination *-en*; as *to lufian* for *to lufienne*, or *lufigenne*.

7. The substitution of *-en* for *-að* in the persons plural of verbs; *hi clepen* (*they call*) for *hi clypiað*, &c.

The preponderance (not the occasional occurrence) of forms like those above constitute *Semi-Saxon* in contradistinction to standard Saxon, classical Saxon, or Anglo-Saxon proper.

§ 100. *Old English stage.*—Further changes convert Semi-Saxon into Old English. Some, amongst others, are the following:—

1. The ejection of the dative plural termination *-um*, and the substitution of the preposition *to* and the plural sign *-s*; as *to smiths* for *smiðum*. Of the dative singular the *-e* is retained (*ende, worde*); but it is by no means certain that, although recognized in writing, it was equally recognized in pronunciation also.

2. The ejection of *-es* in the genitive singular whenever the preposition *of* came before it; *Godes love* (*God's love*), but the *love of God*, and not the *love of Godes*.

3. The syllable *-es* as a sign of the genitive case ex-

tended to all genders and to all declensions; *heart's* for *heortan*; *sun's* for *sunnan*.

4. The same in respect to the plural number; *sterres* for *steorran*; *sons* for *suna*.

5. The ejection of *-na* in the genitive plural; as *of tunges* for *tungena*.

6. The use of the word *the*, as an article, instead of *se*, &c.

The *preponderance* of the forms above (and not their mere occasional occurrence) constitutes *Old English* in contradistinction to Semi-Saxon.

§ 101. In the Old English the following forms predominate.

1. A fuller inflection of the demonstrative pronoun, or definite article; þan, þenne, þære, þam;—in contradistinction to the Middle English.

2. The presence of the dative singular in *-e*; *ende*, *smithe*.

3. The existence of a genitive plural in *-r* or *-ra*; *heora*, theirs; *aller*, of all. This, with substantives and adjectives, is less common.

4. The substitution of *heo* for *they*, of *heora* for *their*, of *hem* for *them*.

5. A more frequent use of *min* and *thin*, for *my* and *thy*;—in contradistinction to both Middle and Modern English.

6. The use of *heo* for *she*;—in contradistinction to Middle and Modern English and Old Lowland *Scotch*.

7. The use of broader vowels; as in *iclepud* or *iclepod* (for *icleped* or *yclept*); *geongost*, youngest; *ascode*, asked; *eldore*, elder.

8. The use of the strong preterits (*see* the chapter on the tenses of verbs), where in the present English the weak form is found—*wex*, *wop*, *dalf*, for *waxed*, *wept*, *delved*.

9. The omission not only of the gerundial termination -*enne*, but also of the infinitive sign -*en* after *to ; to honte, to speke ;*—in contradistinction to Semi-Saxon.

10. The substitution of -*en* for -*eþ* or -*eð*, in the first and second persons plural of verbs; *we wollen*, we will: *heo schullen*, they should.

11. The comparative absence of the articles *se* and *seo*.

12. The substitution of *ben* and *beeth*, for *synd* and *syndon* = *we, ye, they are*.

§ 102. Concerning the extent to which the Anglo-Norman was used, I retail the following statements and quotations.

1. "Letters even of a private nature were written in Latin till the beginning of the reign of Edward I., soon after 1270, when a sudden change brought in the use of French."—*Mr. Hallam, communicated by Mr. Stevenson* (*Literature of Europe*, i. 52, *and note*).

2. Conversation between the members of the Universities was ordered to be carried on either in Latin or French:—" *Si qua inter se proferant, colloquio Latino vel saltem Gallico perfruantur.*"—*Statutes of Oriel College, Oxford.*—Hallam, *ibid.* from Warton.

3. "The Minutes of the Corporation of London, recorded in the Town Clerk's Office, were in French, as well as the Proceedings in Parliament, and in the Courts of Justice."—*Ibid.*

4. "In Grammar Schools, boys were made to construe their Latin into French"—*Ibid.* " *Pueri in scholis, contra morem cæterarum nationum, et Normannorum adventu, derelicto proprio vulgari, construere Gallice compelluntur. Item quod filii nobilium ab ipsis cunabulorum crepundiis ad Gallicum idioma informantur. Quibus profecto rurales homines assimulari volentes, ut per hoc spectabiliores videantur, Francigenari satagunt omni nisu.*"—*Higden* (*Ed. Gale*, p. 210).

§ 103. The reigns of Edward III., and Richard II., may be said to form a transition from the *Old* to the *Middle ;* those of Mary and Elizabeth from the *Middle* to the *New, Recent* or *Modern English*. No very definite line of demarcation, however can be drawn.

§ 104. The *present* tendencies of the English may be determined by observation: and as most of them will be noticed in the etymological part of this volume, the few here indicated must be looked upon as illustrations only.

1. The distinction between the subjunctive and indicative mood is likely to pass away. We verify this by the very general tendency to say *if it is*, and *if he speaks*, rather than *if it be*, and *if he speak*.

2. The distinction between the participle passive and the past tense is likely to pass away. We verify this by the tendency to say *it is broke*, and *he is smote*, for *it is broken* and *he is smitten*.

3. Of the double forms, *sung* and *sang*, *drank* and *drunk*, &c., one only will be the permanent.

As stated above, these tendencies are but a few out of many, and have been adduced in order to indicate the subject rather than to exhaust it.

QUESTIONS.

1. Classify the Celtic elements of the English language.
2. Enumerate the chief periods during which words from the Latin were introduced into English, and classify the Latin elements accordingly.
3. What words were introduced *directly* by the Danes, Scandinavians, or Norsemen? What *indirectly?* Through what language did these latter come?
4. Give the dates of the Battle of Hastings, and of the reigns of Louis Outremer, Ethelred II., and Edward the Confessor. What was the amount of Norman-French elements in England anterior to the Conquest?
5. Give the languages from whence the following words were introduced into the English—*flannel jerked* (as to *beef*), *hammock, apparatus, waltz, Seraph, plaid, street, muslin.*
6. Distinguish between the *direct, indirect,* and *ultimate* origin of introduced words. What words have we in English which are supposed to have *originated* in the Ancient Ægyptian, the Syrian, and the languages of Asia Minor?
7. Under what different forms do the following words appear in English—*monasterium*, πρεσβύτερος, ἐπίσκοπος. Account for these differences. *Syrup, shrub,* and *sherbet,* all originate from the same word. Explain the present difference.
8. Give the *direct* origin (*i.e.*, the languages from which they were *immediately* introduced) of—*Druid, epistle, chivalry, eyder, mæander.* Give the *indirect* origin of the same.
9. Investigate the process by which a word like *sparrow-grass,* apparently of *English* origin, is, in reality, derived from the Latin word *asparagus.* Point out the incorrectness in the words *frontispiece, colleague,* and *lanthorn.*

10. To what extent may *Norse*, and to what extent may *Celtic* words, not found in the current language of English, be found in the provincial dialects?

11. What were the original names of the towns *Whitby* and *Derby?* From what language are the present names derived? Give the reason for your answer.

12. Show the extent to which the *logical* and *historical* analyses coincide in respect to the words introduced from the Roman of the second period, the Arabic, the Anglo-Norman, and the Celtic of the current English.

13. What are the plural forms of *criterion, axis, genius, index, dogma?* When is a word introduced from a foreign language *perfectly,* when *imperfectly* incorporated with the language into which it is imported? Is the following expression correct—*the cherubim that singeth aloft?* If not, why?

14. What is there exceptionable in the words *semaphore* (meaning a sort of telegraph), and *witticism.* Give the etymologies of the words *icicle, radicle,* and *radical.*

15. What are the singular forms of *cantharides, phænomena,* and *data?*

16. What are the stages of the English language? How does the present differ from the older ones?

17. Exhibit in detail the inflections of the Anglo-Saxon *a*) noun, and *b*) verb, which are not found in the present English. What is the import of the loss of inflections, and their replacement by separate words? What is the nature of such words in nouns? What in verbs?

18. Contrast the syntax of the Anglo-Saxon with the Modern English adjective. What is the English for the Anglo-Saxon words *wit, unc, incer?*

19. Express, in general terms, the chief points wherein a modern language differs from an ancient one: or, rather, the points wherein the different stages of the same language differ.

20. Investigate the influence of the Norman Conquest on the English. Explain the terms Semi-Saxon, Old English, and Middle English. Compare the stages of the English with those of the other Gothic tongues.

21. Give the Modern English for the following forms and expressions—*munucas, steorran, to lufienne.* What are the Anglo-Saxon forms of *munucan, steorres, i-hotte, clepen?* Translate the Latin word *omnium* (genitive plural of *omnis*) into *Old* English. Translate

the Greek ὁ, ἡ τὸ into Anglo-Saxon, Old English, and Modern English.

22. Investigate the extent to which the Anglo-Norman superseded the Anglo-Saxon subsequent to the Conquest. Is any further change in the grammatical structure of our language probable? If so, what do you consider will be the nature of it?

PART III.

SOUNDS, LETTERS, PRONUNCIATION, SPELLING.

CHAPTER I.

GENERAL NATURE AND CERTAIN PROPERTIES OF ARTICULATE SOUNDS.

§ 105. To two points connected with the subject of the following chapter, the attention of the reader is requested.

a. In the comparison of sounds the ear is liable to be misled by the eye. Thus—

The syllables *ka* and *ga* are similar syllables. The vowel is in each the same, and the consonant is but slightly different. Hence the words *ka* and *ga* are more allied to each other than the words *ka* and *ba*, *ka* and *ta*, &c., because the consonantal sounds of *k* and *g* are more allied than the consonantal sounds of *k* and *b*, *k* and *t*.

Comparing the syllables *ga* and *ka*, we see the affinity between the sounds, and we see it at the first glance. It lies on the surface, and strikes the ear at once.

It is, however, very evident that ways might be devised, or might arise from accident, of concealing the likeness between the two sounds, or, at any rate, of making it less palpable. One of such ways would be a faulty mode of spelling. If instead of *ga* we wrote *gha* the following would be the effect: the syllable would appear less simple than it really was; it would look as if it consisted of three parts instead of two, and consequently its affinity to *ka* would seem less than it really was. It is perfectly true that a little consideration would tell us that, as long as the sound remained the same, the relation of the two syllables remained the same also; and that, if the contrary appeared to be the case, the ear was misled by the eye. Still a little consideration would be required. Now in the English language we have (amongst others) the following modes of spelling that have a tendency to mislead;—

The sounds of *ph* and of *f*, in *Philip* and *fillip*, differ to the eye, but to the ear are identical. Here a difference is simulated.

The sounds of *th* in *thin*, and of *th* in *thine*, differ to the ear but to the eye seem the same. Here a difference is concealed.

Furthermore. These last sounds appear to the eye to be double or compound. This is not the case; they are simple single sounds, and not the sounds of *t* followed by *h*, as the spelling leads us to imagine.

b. Besides improper modes of spelling, there is another way of concealing the true nature of sounds. If I say that *ka* and *ga* are allied, the alliance is manifest; since I compare the actual *sounds*. If I say *ka* and *gee* are allied, the alliance is concealed; since I compare, not the actual sounds, but only the *names of the letters* that express those sounds. Now in the English language we have (amongst others) the following names of letters that have a tendency to mislead :—

The sounds *fa* and *va* are allied. The names *eff* and *vee* conceal this alliance.

The sounds *sa* and *za* are allied. The names *ess* and *zed* conceal the alliance.

In comparing sounds it is advisable to have nothing to do either with letters or names of letters. Compare the sounds themselves.

§ 106. In many cases it is sufficient, in comparing consonants, to compare syllables that contain those consonants; *e. g.*, in order to determine the relations of *p*, *b*, *f*, *v*, we say *pa, ba, fa, va;* or for those of *s* and *z*, we say *sa, za*. Here we compare *syllables*, each consonant being followed by a vowel. At times this is insufficient. We are often obliged to isolate the consonant from its vowel, and bring our organs to utter (or half utter) the imperfect sounds of *p', b', t', d'*.

§ 107. Let any of the *vowels* (for instance, the *a* in *father*) be sounded. The lips, the tongue, and the parts within the throat remain in the same position; and as long as these remain in the same position the sound is that of the vowel under consideration. Let, however, a change take place in the position of the organs of sound; let, for instance, the lips be closed, or the tongue be applied to the front part of the mouth: in that case the vowel sound is cut short. It undergoes a change. It terminates in a sound that is different, according to the state of those organs whereof the position has been changed. If, on the vowel in question, the lips be closed, there then arises an imperfect sound of *b* or *p*. If on the other hand, the tongue be applied to the front teeth, or to the forepart of the palate, the sound is one (more or less imperfect) of *t* or *d*. This fact illustrates the difference between the vowels and the consonants. It may be verified by pronouncing the *a* in *fate*, *ee* in *feet*, *oo* in *book*, *o* in *note*, &c.

It is a further condition in the formation of a vowel sound, that the passage of the breath be uninterrupted. In the sound of the *l'* in *lo* (isolated from its vowel) the sound is as continuous as it is with the *a* in *fate*. Between, however, the consonant *l* and the vowel *a* there is this difference: with *a*, the passage of the breath is uninterrupted; with *l*, the tongue is applied to the palate, breaking or arresting the passage of the breath.

§ 108. The primary division of our articulate sounds is into vowels and consonants. The latter are again divided into liquids (*l*, *m*, *n*, *r*) and mutes (*p*, *b*, *f*, *v*, *t*, *d*, *k*, *g*, *s*, *z*, &c.).

§ 109. *Sharp and flat.*—Take the sounds of *p*, *f*, *t*, *k*, *s*. Isolate them from their vowels, and pronounce them. The sound is the sound of a whisper.

Let *b*, *v*, *d*, *g*, *z*, be similarly treated. The sound is no whisper, but one at the natural tone of our voice.

Now *p*, *f*, *t*, *k*, *s* (with some others that will be brought forward anon) are *sharp*, whilst *b*, *v*, &c., are *flat*. Instead of *sharp*, some say *hard*, and instead of *flat*, some say *soft*. The terms *sonant* and *surd* are, in a scientific point of view, the least exceptionable. They have, however, the disadvantage of being pedantic. The *tenues* of the classics (as far as they go) are sharp, the *mediæ* flat.

§ 110. *Continuous and explosive.*—Isolate the sounds of *b*, *p*, *t*, *d*, *k*, *g*. Pronounce them. You have no power of prolonging the sounds, or of resting upon them. They escape with the breath, and they escape at once.

It is not so with *f*, *v*, *sh*, *zh*. Here the breath is transmitted by degrees, and the sound can be drawn out and prolonged for an indefinite space of time. Now *b*, *p*, *t*, &c., are explosive; *f*, *v*, &c., continuous.

§ 111. Concerning the vowels, we may predicate *a*) that they are all continuous, *b*) that they are all flat.

Concerning the liquids, we may predicate *a*) that they are all continuous, *b*) that they are all flat.

Concerning the mutes, we may predicate *a*) that one half of them is flat, and the other half sharp, and *b*) that some are continuous, and that others are explosive.

112.—The letter *h* is no *articulate* sound, but only a breathing

CHAPTER II.

SYSTEM OF ARTICULATE SOUNDS.

§ 113.—The attention of the reader is now directed to the following *foreign* vowel sounds.

1. The *é fermé*, of the French.—This is a sound allied to, but different from, the *a* in *fate*, and the *ee* in *feet*. It is intermediate to the two.

2. The *u* of the French, *ü* of the Germans, *y* of the Danes.—This sound is intermediate to the *ee* in *feet*, and the *oo* in *book*.

3. The *o chiuso*, of the Italians.—Intermediate to the *o* in *note*, and the *oo* in *book*.

For these sounds we have the following sequences: *a* in *fate*, *é fermé*, *ee* in *feet*, *ü* in *übel* (German), *oo* in *book*, *o chiuso*, *o* in *note*. And this is the true order of alliance among the vowels; *a* in *fate*, and *o* in *note*, being the extremes; the other sounds being transitional or intermediate. As the English orthography is at once singular and faulty, it exhibits the relationship but imperfectly.

§ 114. *The system of the mutes.*—Preliminary to the consideration of the system of the mutes, let it be observed:—

1. that the *th* in *thin* is a simple single sound, different from the *th* in *thine*, and that it may be expressed by the sign þ.
2. That the *th* in *thine* is a simple single sound, different

from the *th* in *thin*, and that it may be expressed by the sign ð.

3. That the *sh* in *shine* is a simple single sound, and that it may be expressed by the sign σ* (Greek σῖγμα).
4. That the *z* in *azure, glazier* (French *j*) is a simple single sound, and that it may be expressed by the sign ζ* (Greek ζῆτα).
5. That in the Laplandic, and possibly in many other languages, there are two peculiar sounds, different from any in English, German, and French, &c., and that they may respectively be expressed by the sign κ and the sign γ* (Greek κάππα and γάμμα).

§ 115. With these preliminary notices we may exhibit the system of the sixteen mutes; having previously determined the meaning of two fresh terms, and bearing in mind what was said concerning the words *sharp* and *flat, continuous* and *explosive*.

Lene and *aspirate*.—From the sound of *p* in *pat*, the sound of *f* in *fat* differs in a certain degree. This difference is not owing to a difference in their sharpness or flatness. Each is sharp. Neither is it owing to a difference in their continuity or explosiveness; although *f* is continuous, whilst *p* is explosive. This we may ascertain by considering the position of *s*. The sound of *s* is *continuous*; yet *s*, in respect to the difference under consideration, is classed not with *f* the continuous sound but with *p* the explosive one. This difference, which has yet to be properly elucidated, is expressed by a particular term; and *p* is called *lene*, *f* is called *aspirate*.

As *f* is to *p* so is *v* to *b*.
As *v* is to *b* so is þ to *t*.

* This by no means implies that such was the power of σ, ζ, γ, κ, in Greek. They are merely convenient symbols.

As þ is to *t* so is ð to *d*.
As ð is to *d* so is κ to *k*.
As κ is to *k* so is γ to *g*.
As γ is to *g* so is σ to *s*.
As σ is to *s* so is ζ to *z*.

Hence *p, b, t, d, k, g, s, z*, are *lene; f, v,* þ, ð, κ, γ, σ, ζ, are *aspirate*. Also *p, f, t,* þ, *k*, κ, *s*, σ, are *sharp*, whilst *b, v, d,* ð, *g*, γ, *z*, ζ, are *flat;* so that there is a double series of relationship capable of being expressed as follows:—

Lene.		Aspirate.		Sharp.		Flat.	
Sharp.	Flat.	Sharp.	Flat.	Lene.	Aspirate.	Lene.	Aspirate.
p	*b*	*f*	*v*	*p*	*f*	*b*	*v*
t	*d*	þ	ð	*t*	þ	*d*	ð
k	*g*	κ	γ	*k*	κ	*g*	γ
s	*z*	σ	ζ	*s*	σ	*z*	ζ

All the so-called aspirates are continuous; and, with the exception of *s* and *z*, all the lenes are explosive.

§ 116. I believe that in the fact of each mute appearing in a four-fold form (*i. e.*, sharp, or flat, lene, or aspirate), lies the essential character of the mutes as opposed to the liquids.

§ 117. Y and *w*.—These sounds, respectively intermediate to γ and *i* (the *ee* in *feet*), and to *v* and *u* (*oo* in *book*), form a transition from the vowels to the consonants.

§ 118. The French word *roi*, and the English words *oil, house*, are specimens of a fresh class of articulations; *viz.*, of *compound vowel* sounds or diphthongs. The diphthong *oi* is the vowel *o* + the *semivowel y*. The diphthongal sound in *roi* is the vowel *o* + the semivowel *w*. In *roi* the semivowel element precedes; in *oil* it follows.

§ 119. The words quoted indicate the nature of the diphthongal system.

1. Diphthongs with the semivowel *w*, a) *preceding*, as in the French word *roi*, b) *following*, as in the English word *new*.

2. Diphthongs with the semivowel *y*, a) *preceding*, as is common in the languages of the Lithuanic and Slavonic stocks, b) *following*, as in the word *oil*.

3. Triphthongs with a semivowel both *preceding* and *following*.

The diphthongs in English are four; *ow* as in *house*, *ew* as in *new*, *oi* as in *oil*, *i* as in *bite, fight*.

§ 120. *Chest, jest.*—Here we have *compound consonantal* sounds. The *ch* in *chest* = *t* + *sh*; the *j* in *jest* = *d* + *zh*. I believe that in these combinations one or both the elements, viz., *t* and *sh*, *d* and *zh*, are modified; but I am unable to state the exact nature of this modification.

§ 121. *Ng.*—The sound of the *ng* in *sing, king, throng*, when at the end of a word, or of *singer, ringing*, &c., in the middle of a word, is not the natural sound of the combination *n* and *g*, each letter retaining its natural power and sound; but a simple single sound, for which the combination *ng* is a conventional mode of expression.

§ 122. Compared with *a* in *fate*, and the *o* in *note*, *a* in *father*, and the *aw* in *bawl*, are *broad*; the vowels of *note* and *fate* being *slender*.

§ 123. In *fat*, the vowel is, according to common parlance, *short*; in *fate*, it is *long*. Here we have the introduction of two fresh terms. For the words *long* and *short*, I substitute *independent* and *dependent*. If from the word *fate* I separate the final consonantal sound, the syllable *fa* remains. In this syllable the *a* has precisely the sound that it had before. It remains unaltered. The removal of the consonant has in nowise modified its sound or power. It is not so, however, with the vowel in the word *fat*. If from this I remove the consonant following, and so leave the *a* at the end of the syllable, instead of in the middle, I must do one of two things: I must sound it either as the *a* in *fate*, or else as the *a* in *father*. Its (so-called) short sound it cannot retain, unless it be supported by a consonant following. For this reason it is *dependent*. The same is the case with all the so-called short sounds, *viz.*, the *e* in *bed*, *i* in *fit*, *u* in *bull*, *o* in *not*, *u* in *but*.

§ 124. It is not every vowel that is susceptible of every modification. *I* (*ee*) and *u* (*oo*) are incapable of becoming *broad*. The *e* in *bed*, although both broad and slender, is incapable of becoming *independent*. For the *u* in *but*, and for the *ö* of certain foreign languages, I have no satisfactory systematic position.

§ 125. *Vowel System.*

Broad.		Slender.	
Independent.	Independent.		Dependent.
a, in *father* . .	*a*, in *fate.* . . .		*a*, in *fat.*
. . . .	*é* in *fermé, long* . .		*é*, in *fermé, short.*
e, in *mein*, Germ .	. . . . .		*e*, in *bed.*
. . . .	*ee*, in *feet* . . .		*i*, *pit.*
. . . .	*ü*, of the German, *long* .		the same, *short.*
. . . .	*oo*, in *book* . . .		*ou*, in *could.*
. . . .	*o* in *chiuso* . . .		the same, *short.*
aw, in *bawl* . ·	*o*, in *note* . . .		*o*, in *not.*

From these the semivowels *w* and *y* make a transition to the consonants *v* and the so-called aspirate of *g*, respectively.

§ 126. *System of Consonants.*

Liquids.	Mutes.				Semivowels.
	Lene.		Aspirate.		
	Sharp.	Flat.	Sharp.	Flat.	
m	p	v	f	v	w
n	t	d	þ	ð	.
l	k	g	κ	γ	y
r	s	z	σ	ζ	.

CHAPTER III.

OF CERTAIN COMBINATIONS OF ARTICULATE SOUNDS.

§ 127. CERTAIN combinations of articulate sounds are incapable of being pronounced. The following rule is one that, in the forthcoming pages, will frequently be referred to. *Two* (*or more*) mutes, *of different degrees of sharpness and flatness, are incapable of coming together in the same syllable.* For instance, *b, v, d, g, z*, &c., being flat, and *p, f, t, k, s*, &c., being sharp, such combinations as *abt, avt, apd, afd, agt, akd, atz, ads*, &c., are unpronounceable. *Spell*, indeed, they may be; but all attempts at *pronunciation* end in a *change* of the combination. In this case either the flat letter is really changed to its sharp equivalent (*b* to *p*, *d* to *t*, &c.) or *vice versâ* (*p* to *b*, *t* to *d*). The combinations *abt* and *agt*, to be pronounced, must become either *apt* or *abd*, or else *akt* or *agd*.

The word *mutes* in the third sentence of this section must be dwelt on. It is only with the *mutes* that there is an impossibility of pronouncing the heterogeneous combinations above-mentioned. The liquids and the vowels are flat; but the liquids and vowels, although flat, may be followed by a sharp consonant. If this were not the case, the combinations *ap, at, alp, alt*, &c., would be unpronounceable.

The semivowels, also, although flat, admit of being followed by a sharp consonant.

§ 128. *Unstable combinations.*—That certain sounds in combination with others have a tendency to undergo farther changes, may be collected from the observation of our own language, as we find it spoken by those around us, or by ourselves. The diphthong *ew* is a sample of what may be called an unsteady or *unstable* combination. There is a natural tendency to change it either into *oo* or *yoo;* perhaps also into *yew*. Hence *new* is sometimes sounded *noo,* sometimes *nyoo,* and sometimes *nyew*.

§ 129. *Effect of the semivowel* y *on certain letters when they precede it.*—Taken by itself the semivowel *y*, followed by a vowel (*ya, yee, yo, you,* &c.), forms a stable combination. Not so, however, if it be preceded by a consonant, of the series *t* or *s*, as *tya, tyo; dya, dyo; sya, syo*. There then arises an unstable combination. *Sya* and *syo* we pronounce as *sha* and *sho; tya* and *tyo* we pronounce as *cha* and *ja* (*i. e., tsh, dzh*). This we may verify from our pronunciation of words like *sure, picture, verdure* (*shoor, pictshoor, verdzhoor*), having previously remarked that the *u* in those words is not sounded as *oo* but as *yoo*. The effect of the semivowel *y*, taken with the instability of the combination *ew*, accounts for the tendency to pronounce *dew* as if written *jew*.

§ 130. *Double consonants rare.*—It cannot be too clearly understood that in words like *pitted, stabbing, massy,* &c., there is no real reduplication of the sounds of *t, b,* and *s,* respectively. Between the words *pitted* (as with the small-pox) and *pitied* (as being an object of pity) there is a difference in spelling only. In speech the words are identical. *The reduplication of the consonant is, in English and the generality of languages, a conventional mode of expressing in writing the shortness or dependence, of the vowel preceding.*

§ 131. Real reduplications of consonants, *i. e.*, reduplications of their *sound*, are, in all languages, extremely rare. In English they occur only under one condition. In *compound* and *derived* words, where the original root *ends*, and the superadded affix *begins* with the same letter, there is a reduplication of the sound and not otherwise. In the word *soulless*, the *l* is doubled to the ear as well as to the eye; and it is a false pronunciation to call it *souless* (*soless*). In the "Deformed Transformed" it is made to rhyme with *no less*, improperly:—

> "Clay, not dead but soulless,
>   Though no mortal man would choose thee,
> An immortal no less
>   Deigns not to refuse thee."

In the following words, all of which are compounds, we have true specimens of the doubled consonant.

n is doubled in *unnatural, innate, oneness.*
l — *soulless, civil-list, palely.*
k — *book-case.*
t — *seaport-town.*

It must not, however, be concealed, that, in the mouths even of correct speakers, one of the doubled sounds is often dropped.

§ 132. *True aspirates rare.*—The criticism applied to words like *pitted*, &c., applies also to words like *Philip, thin, thine*, &c. There is therein no sound of *h*. How the so-called aspirates differ from their corresponding lenes has not yet been determined. That it is *not* by the addition of *h* is evident. *Ph* and *th* are conventional modes of spelling simple single sounds, which might better be expressed by simple single signs.

In our own language the *true* aspirates, like the true reduplications, are found only in compound words; and there they are often slurred in the pronunciation.

We find *p* and *h* in the words *haphazard, upholder.*
— *b* and *h* — *abhorrent, cub-hunting.*
— *f* and *h* — *knife-handle, off hand.*
— *v* and *h* — *stave-head.*
— *d* and *h* — *adhesive, childhood.*
— *t* and *h* — *nuthook.*
— *th* and *h* — *withhold.*
— *k* and *h* — *inkhorn, bakehouse.*
— *g* and *h* — *gig-horse.*
— *s* and *h* — *race-horse, falsehood.*
— *z* and *h* — *exhibit, exhort.*
— *r* and *h* — *perhaps.*
— *l* and *h* — *wellhead, foolhardy.*
— *m* and *h* — *Amherst.*
— *n* and *h* — *unhinge, inherent, unhappy.*

CHAPTER IV.

EUPHONY AND THE PERMUTATION OF LETTERS.

§ 133. 1. Let there be two syllables of which the one ends in *m*, and the other begins with *r*, as we have in the syllables *num-* and *-rus* of the Latin word *numerus*.

2. Let an ejection of the intervening letters bring these two syllables into immediate contact, *numrus*. The *m* and *r* form an unstable combination. To remedy this there is a tendency to insert an intervening sound.

In English, the form which the Latin word *numerus* takes is *number;* in Spanish, *nombre*. The *b* makes no part of the original word, but has been inserted for the sake of *euphony;* or, to speak more properly, by a euphonic process. The word euphony is derived from εὖ (*well*), and φωνή (*fóna*, a voice).

§ 134. In the words *give* and *gave* we have a change of tense expressed by a change of vowel. In the words *price* and *prize* a change of meaning is expressed by a change of consonant. In *clothe* and *clad* there is a change both of a vowel and of a consonant. In the words *to use* and *a use* there is a similar change, although it is not expressed by the spelling. To the ear the verb *to use* ends in *z*, although not to the eye. All these are instances of the *permutation* of letters.

Permutation of Vowels.

a	to	ĕ,	as	*man, men.*
a	to	oo,	as	*stand, stood.*
a	to	u,	as	*dare, durst.*
a	to	ē,	as	*was, were.*
ea	to	o,	as	*speak, spoken.*
ea=ĕ	to	ea=ē,	as	*breath, breathe.*
ee	to	ĕ,	as	*deep, depth.*
ea	to	o,	as	*bear, bore.*
i	to	a,	as	*spin, span.*
i	to	u,	as	*spin, spun.*
ī=ei	to	o,	as	*smite, smote.*
i=ei	to	ĭ,	as	*smite, smitten.*
i	to	a,	as	*give, gave.*
i=e:	to	a,	as	*rise, raise.*
ĭ	to	e,	as	*sit, set.*
ow	to	ew,	as	*blow, blew.*
o	to	e,	as	*strong, strength.*
oo	to	ee,	as	*tooth, teeth.*
o	to	i,	as	*top, tip.*
o	to	e,	as	*old, elder; tell, told.*
ŏ	to	e,	as	*brother, brethren.*
ŏ=oo	to	i,	as	*do, did.*
o=oo	to	o=ŭ	as	*do, done.*
oo	to	o,	as	*choose, chose.*

Permutation of Consonants.

f	to	v,	*life, live; calf, calves.*
þ	to	ð,	*breath, to breathe.*
þ	to	d,	*seethe, sod; clothe, clad.*
d	to	t,	*build, built.*
s	to	z,	*use, to use.*
s	to	r,	*was, were; lose, forlorn.*

In *have* and *had* we have the *ejection* of a sound; in *work* and *wrought*, the *transposition* of one.

Permutation of Combinations.

ie=i	to	*ow,*	as	*grind, ground.*
ow	to	*i=ci,*	as	*mouse, mice; cow, kine.*
ink	to	*augh,*	as	*drink, draught.*
ing	to	*ough,*	as	*bring, brought.*
y (formerly *g*),		*ough,*	as	*buy, bought.*
igh=ci	to	*ough,*	as	*fight, fought.*
eek	to	*ough,*	as	*seek, sought.*

It must be noticed that the list above is far from being an exhaustive one. The expression too of the changes undergone has been rendered difficult on account of the imperfection of our orthography. The whole section has been written in illustration of the meaning of the word *permutation*, rather than for any specific object in grammar.

CHAPTER V.

ON THE FORMATION OF SYLLABLES.

§ 135. In respect to the formation of syllables, I am aware of no more than one point that requires any especial consideration.

In certain words, of more than one syllable, it is difficult to say to which syllable an intervening consonant belongs. For instance, does the *v* in *river*, and the *e* in *fever*, belong to the first or the second syllable? Are the words to be divided thus, *ri-ver, fe-ver?* or thus, *riv-er, fev-er?*

The solution of the question lies by no means on the surface.

In the first place, the case is capable of being viewed in two points of view—an etymological and a phonetic one.

That the *c* and *r* in *become, berhymed,* &c., belong to the second syllable, we determine at once by taking the words to pieces; whereby we get the words *come* and *rhymed* in an isolated independent form. But this fact, although it settles the point in etymology, leaves it as it was in phonetics; since it in nowise follows, that, because the *c* in the *simple* word *come* is exclusively attached to the letter that succeeds, it is, in the *compound* word *become*, exclusively attached to it also.

To the following point of structure in the consonantal sounds the reader's attention is particularly directed.

1. Let the vowel *a* (as in *fate*) be sounded.—2. Let it be followed by the consonant *p*, so as to form the syllable *āp*. To form the sound of *p*, it will be found that the lips close on the sound of *a*, and arrest it. Now, if the lips be left to themselves they will not *remain* closed on the sound, but will open again; in a slight degree indeed, but in a degree sufficient to cause a kind of vibration, or, at any rate, to allow an escape of the remainder of the current of breath by which the sound was originally formed. To re-open in a slight degree is the natural tendency of the lips in the case exhibited above.

Now, by an effort, let this tendency to re-open be counteracted. Let the remaining current of breath be cut short. We have, then, only this, *viz.*, so much of the syllable *āp* as can be formed by the *closure* of the lips. All that portion of it that is caused by their reopening is deficient. The resulting sound seems truncated, cut short, or incomplete. It is the sound of *p*, *minus* the remnant of breath. All of the sound *p* that is now left is formed, not by the *escape* of the breath, but by the *arrest* of it.

The *p* in *āp* is a *final* sound. With initial sounds the case is different. Let the lips be *closed*, and let an attempt be made to form the syllable *pa* by suddenly opening them. The sound appears incomplete; but its incompleteness is at the *beginning* of the sound, and not at the end of it. In the natural course of things there would have been a current of breath *preceding*, and this current would have given a vibration, now wanting. All the sound that is formed here is formed, not by the *arrest* of breath, but by the *escape* of it.

I feel that this account of the mechanism of the apparently simple sound *p*, labours under all the difficulties that attend the *description* of a sound; and for this reason I again request the reader to satisfy himself either of its truth or of its inaccuracy, before he proceeds to the conclusions that will be drawn from it.

The account, however, being recognized, we have in the sound of *p*, two elements:—

1. That formed by the current of air and the closure of the lips, as in *ap*. This may be called the sound of breath *arrested*.

2. That formed by the current of air, and the opening of the lips, as in *pa*. This may be called the sound of breath *escaping*.

Now what may be said of *p* may be said of all the other consonants, the words *tongue, teeth*, &c., being used instead of *lips*, according to the case.

Let the sound of breath *arrested* be expressed by π, and that of breath *escaping* be expressed by ϖ, the two together form p ($\pi + \varpi = p$).

Thus *ap* (as quoted above) is $p - \varpi$, or π; whilst *pa* (sounded similarly is $p - \pi$, or ϖ.

In the formation of syllables, I consider that the sound of breath arrested belongs to the first, and the sound of breath escaping to the second syllable; that if each sound were expressed by a separate sign, the word *happy* would be divided thus, *haπ-ϖy*; and that such would be the case with all consonants between two syllables. The *whole* consonant belongs neither to one syllable nor the other. Half of it belongs to each. The reduplication of the *p* in *happy*, the *t* in *pitted*, &c., is a mere point of spelling.

CHAPTER VI.

ON QUANTITY.

§ 136. THE dependent vowels, as the *a* in *fat*, *i* in *fit*, *u* in *but*, *o* in *not*, have the character of being uttered with rapidity, and they pass quickly in the enunciation, the voice not resting on them. This rapidity of utterance becomes more evident when we contrast with them the prolonged sounds of the *a* in *fate*, *ee* in *feet*, *oo* in *book*, or *o* in *note;* wherein the utterance is retarded, and wherein the voice rests, delays, or is prolonged. The *f* and *t* of *fate* are separated by a longer interval than the *f* and *t* of *fat;* and the same is the case with *fit*, *feet*, &c.

Let the *n* and the *t* of *not* be each as 1, the *o* also being as 1; then each letter, consonant or vowel, shall constitute ⅓ of the whole word.

Let, however, the *n* and the *t* of *not* be each as 1, the *o* being as 2. Then, instead of each consonant constituting ⅓ of the whole word, it shall constitute but ¼.

Upon the comparative extent to which the voice is prolonged, the division of vowels and syllables into *long* and *short* has been established: the *o* in *note* being long, the *o* in *not* being short. And the longness or shortness of a vowel or syllable is said to be its *quantity*.

§ 137. Attention is directed to the word *vowel*. The longness or shortness of a *vowel* is one thing. The longness or shortness of a *syllable* another. This difference is important in prosody; especially in comparing the English with the classical metres.

The vowel in the syllable *see* is long; and long it remains, whether it stand as it is, or be followed by a consonant, as in *see-n*, or by a vowel, as in *see-ing*.

The vowel in the word *sit* is short. If followed by a vowel it becomes unpronounceable, except as the *ea* in *seat* or the *i* in *sight*. By a consonant, however, it *may* be followed. Such is the case in the word quoted—*sit*. Followed by a *second* consonant, it still retains its shortness, *e. g.*, *sits*. Whatever the comparative length of the *syllables*, *see* and *seen*, *sit* and *sits*, may be, the length of their respective *vowels* is the same.

Now, if we determine the character of the syllable by the character of the vowel, all syllables are short wherein there is a short vowel, and all are long wherein there is a long one. Hence, measured by the quantity of the vowel, the word *sits* is short, and the syllable *see-* in *seeing* is long.

§ 138. But it is well known that this view is not the view commonly taken of the syllables *see* (in *seeing*) and *sits*. It is well known, that, in the eyes of a classical scholar, the *see* (in *seeing*) is short, and that in the word *sits* the *i* is long.

The classic differs from the Englishman thus,—*He measures his quantity, not by the length of the vowel, but by the length of the syllable taken altogether.* The perception of this distinction enables us to comprehend the following statements.

a. That vowels long by nature may *appear* to become short by position, and *vice versâ*.

b. That, by a laxity of language, the *vowel* may be said to have changed its quantity, whilst it is the *syllable* alone that has been altered.

c. That if one person measures his quantities by the vowels, and another by the syllables, what is short to the one, shall be long to the other, and *vice versâ*. The same is the case with nations.

d. That one of the most essential differences between the English and the classical languages is that the quantities (as far as they go) of the first are measured by the vowel, those of the latter by the syllable. To a Roman the word *monument* consists of two short syllables and one long one; to an Englishman it contains three short syllables.

CHAPTER VII.

ON ACCENT.

§ 139. In the word *tyrant* there is an emphasis, or stress, upon the first syllable. In the word *presume* there is an emphasis, or stress, on the second syllable. This emphasis, or stress, is called *accent*. The circumstance of a syllable bearing an accent is sometimes expressed by a mark ('); in which case the word is said to be accentuated, *i. e.*, to have the accent signified in writing.

Words accented on the last syllable—*Brigáde, preténce, harpoón, relieve, detér, assúme, besóught, beréft, befóre, abroád, abóde, abstrúse, intermíx, superádd, cavaliér.*

Words accented on the last syllable but one—*An'chor, ar'gue, hásten, fáther, fóxes, smíling, húsband, márket, vápour, bárefoot, archángel, bespátter, disáble, terrífic.*

Words accented on the last syllable but two—*Reg'ular, an'tidote, for'tify, suscéptible, incontrovértible.*

Words accented on the last syllable but three (rare)—*Réceptacle, régulating, tálkativeness, ábsolutely, líminary, inévitable,* &c.

§ 140. A great number of words are distinguished by the difference of accent alone.

An *áttribute*.	To *attríbute*.
The month *Áugust*.	An *augúst* person.
A *com'pact*.	*Compáct* (close).

To con'jure (magically).	Conjúre (enjoin).
Des'ert, wilderness.	Desért, merit.
Inválid, not valid.	Inválid, a sickly person.
Mínute, 60 seconds.	Minúte, small.
Súpine, part of speech.	Supíne, careless, &c.

§ 141. In *ty'rant* and *presúme*, we deal with single words; and in each *word* we determine which *syllable* is accented. Contrasted with the sort of accent that follows, this may be called a *verbal* accent.

In the line,

> Better for *us*, perhaps, it might appear,
> (Pope's "Essay on Man," 1. 169.)

the pronoun *us* is strongly brought forward. An especial stress or emphasis is laid upon it, denoting that *there are other beings to whom it might not appear*, &c. This is collected from the context. Here there is a *logical* accent. "When one word in a sentence is distinguished by a stress, as more important than the rest, we may say that it is *emphatical*, or that an *emphasis* is laid upon it. When one syllable in a word is distinguished by a stress, and more audible than the rest, we say that it is accented, or that an accent is put upon it. Accent, therefore, is to syllables what emphasis is to sentences; it distinguishes one from the crowd, and brings it forward to observation."—Nares' "Orthoepy," part ii. chap. 1.

CHAPTER VIII.

ORTHOGRAPHY.

§ 142. ORTHOEPY, a word derived from the Greek *orthon* (*upright*), and *epos* (*a word*), signifies the right utterance of words. Orthoepy determines words, and deals with a language as it is *spoken;* orthography determines the correct spelling of words, and deals with a language as it is *written*. This latter term is derived from the Greek words *orthos* (*upright*), and *graphē*, or *grafæ* (*writing*). Orthography is less essential to language than orthoepy; since all languages are spoken, whilst but a few languages are written. Orthography presupposes orthoepy. Orthography addresses itself to the eye, orthoepy to the ear. Orthoepy deals with the articulate sounds that constitute syllables and words; orthography treats of the signs by which such articulate sounds are expressed in writing. A *letter* is the sign of an articulate (and, in the case of *h*, of an inarticulate) sound.

§ 143. A full and perfect system of orthography consists in two things:—1. The possession of a sufficient and consistent alphabet. 2. The right application of such an alphabet. This position may be illustrated more fully.

§ 144. First, in respect to a sufficient and consistent alphabet—Let there be in a certain language, simple single articulate sounds, to the number of forty, whilst the simple single signs, or letters, expressive of them, amount to no more than *thirty*. In this case the alphabet is insufficient. It is not full enough: since ten of the simple single articulate sounds have no corresponding signs whereby they may be expressed. In our own language, the sounds (amongst others) of *th* in *thin*, and of *th* in *thine*, are simple and single, whilst there is no sign equally simple and single to spell them with.

§ 145. An alphabet, however, may be sufficient, and yet imperfect. It may err on the score of inconsistency. Let there be in a given language two simple single sounds, (for instance) the *p* in *pate*, and the *f* in *fate*. Let these sounds stand in a given relation to each other. Let a given sign, for instance, פ (as is actually the case in Hebrew), stand for the *p* in *pate;* and let a second sign be required for the *f* in *fate*. Concerning the nature of this latter sign, two views may be taken. One framer of the alphabet, perceiving that the two sounds are mere modifications of each other, may argue that no new sign (or letter) is at all necessary, but that the sound of *f* in *fate* may be expressed by a mere modification of the sign (or letter) פ, and may be written thus פ, or thus פ' or פ', &c.; upon the principle that like sounds should be expressed by like signs. The other framer of the alphabet, contemplating the difference between the two sounds, rather than the likeness, may propose, not a mere modification of the sign פ, but a letter altogether new, such as *f*, or φ, &c., upon the principle that sounds of a given degree of dissimilitude should be expressed by signs of a different degree of dissimilitude.

Hitherto the expression of the sounds in point is a matter of convenience only. No question has been raised as to its consistency or inconsistency. This begins under conditions like the following:—Let there be in the language in point the sounds of the *t* in *tin*, and of the *th* in *thin;* which (it may be remembered) are precisely in the same relation to each other as the *p* in *pate* and the *f* in *fate*. Let each of these sounds have a sign or letter expressive of it. Upon the nature of these signs, or letters, will depend the nature of the sign or letter required for the *f* in *fate*. If the letter expressing the *th* in *thin* be a mere modification of the letter expressing the *t* in *tin*, then must the letter expressive of the *f* in *fate* be a mere modification of the letter expressing the *p* in *pate*, and *vice versâ*. If this be not the case, the alphabet is inconsistent.

In the English alphabet we have (amongst others) the following inconsistency:—The sound of the *f* in *fate*, in a certain relation to the sound of the *p* in *pate*, is expressed by a totally distinct sign; whereas, the sound of the *th* in *thin* (similarly related to the *t* in *tin*) is expressed by no new sign, but by a mere modification of *t*; viz., *th*.

§ 146. A third element in the faultiness of an alphabet is the fault of erroneous representation. The best illustration of this we get from the Hebrew alphabet, where the sounds of ת and ט, mere *varieties* of each other, are represented by distinct and dissimilar signs, whilst ת and ת, sounds *specifically* distinct, are expressed by a mere modification of the same sign, or letter.

§ 147. *The right application of an alphabet.*—An alphabet may be both sufficient and consistent, accurate in its representation of the alliances between articulate sounds, and in no wise redundant; and yet, withal, it may be so wrongly applied as to be defective. Of defect in the use or application of the letters of an alphabet, the three main causes are the following:—

a. Unsteadiness in the power of letters.—Of this there are two kinds. In the first, there is one sound with two (or more) ways of expressing it. Such is the sound of the letter *f* in English. In words of Anglo-Saxon origin it is spelt with a single simple sign, as in *fill;* whilst in Greek words it is denoted by a combination, as in *Philip.* The reverse of this takes place with the letter *g;* here a single sign has a double power; in *gibbet* it is sounded as *j*, and in *gibberish* as *g* in *got.*

b. The aim at secondary objects.—The natural aim of orthography, of spelling, or of writing, is to express the *sounds* of a language. Syllables and words it takes as they meet the ear, it translates them by appropriate signs, and so paints them, as it were, to the eye. That this is the natural and primary object is self-evident; but beyond this natural and primary object there is, with the orthographical systems of most languages, a secondary one, *viz.,* the attempt to combine with the representation of the sound of a given word, the representation of its history and origin.

The sound of the *c*, in *city*, is the sound that we naturally spell with the letter *s*, and if the expression of this sound was the *only* object of our orthographists, the word would be spelt accordingly (*sity*). The following facts, however, traverse this simple view of the matter. The word is a derived word; it is transplanted into our own language from the Latin, where it is spelt with a *c* (*civitas*); and to change this *c* into *s* conceals the origin and history of the word. For this reason the *c* is retained, although, as far as the mere expression of sounds (the primary object in orthography) is concerned, the letter is a superfluity. In cases like the one adduced the orthography is bent to a secondary end, and is traversed by the etymology.

c. Obsoleteness.—It is very evident that modes of spelling which at one time may have been correct, may, by a change of pronunciation, become incorrect; so that orthography becomes obsolete whenever there takes place a change of speech without a correspondent change of spelling.

§ 148. From the foregoing sections we arrive at the theory of a full and perfect alphabet and orthography, of which a few (amongst many others) of the chief conditions are as follow:—

1. That for every simple single sound, incapable of being represented by a combination of letters, there be a simple single sign.

2. That sounds within a determined degree of likeness be represented by signs within a determined degree of likeness; whilst sounds beyond a certain degree of likeness be represented by distinct and different signs, *and that uniformly.*

3. That no sound have more than one sign to express it.

4. That no sign express more than one sound.

5. That the primary aim of orthography be to express the sounds of words, and not their histories.

6. That changes of speech be followed by corresponding changes of spelling.

With these principles in our mind we may measure the imperfections of our own and of other alphabets.

§ 149. Previous to considering the sufficiency or insufficiency of the English alphabet, it is necessary to enumerate the elementary articulate sounds of the language. The vowels belonging to the English language are the following *twelve*:—

1.	That of	*a* in *father.*		7.	That of *e* in *bed.*
2.	—	*a* — *fat.*		8.	— *i* — *pit.*
3.	—	*a* — *fate.*		9.	— *ee* — *feet.*
4.	—	*aw* — *bawl.*		10.	— *u* — *bull.*
5.	—	*o* — *not.*		11.	— *oo* — *fool.*
6.	—	*o* — *note.*		12.	— *u* — *duck.*

The diphthongal sounds are *four*.

1. That of ou in *house*.
2. — ew — *new*.
3. — oi — *oil*.
4. — i — *bite*.

This last sound being most incorrectly expressed by the single letter *i*.

The consonantal sounds are, 1. the two semivowels; 2. the four liquids; 3. fourteen out of the sixteen mutes; 4. *ch* in *chest*, and *j* in *jest*, compound sibilants; 5. *ng*, as in *king*; 6. the aspirate *h*. In all, twenty-four.

1. w	as in	*wet*.	13. *th*	as in	*thin*.
2. y	—	*yet*.	14. *th*	—	*thine*.
3. m	—	*man*.	15. *g*	—	*gun*.
4. n	—	*not*.	16. *k*	—	*kind*.
5. l	—	*let*.	17. *s*	—	*sin*.
6. r	—	*run*.	18. *z*	—	*zeal*.
7. p	—	*pate*.	19. *sh*	—	*shine*.
8. b	—	*ban*.	20. *z*	—	*azure, glazier*.
9. f	—	*fan*.	21. *ch*	—	*chest*.
10. v	—	*van*.	22. *j*	—	*jest*.
11. t	—	*tin*.	23. *ng*	—	*king*.
12. d	—	*din*.	24. *h*	—	*hot*.

§ 150. Some writers would add to these the additional sound of the *é fermé* of the French: believing that the vowel in words like *their* and *rein* has a different sound from the vowel in words like *there* and *rain*. For my own part I cannot detect such a difference either in my own speech or that of my neighbours; although I am far from denying that in certain *dialects* of our language such may have been the case. The following is an extract from the "Danish Grammar for Englishmen," by Professor Rask, whose eye, in the matter in question, seems to have misled his ear; "The *fermé*, or *close é*, is very frequent in Danish, but scarcely perceptible in English; unless in such words as *their, vein, veil*, which appear to sound a little different from *there, rain, vale*."

§ 151. The vowels being twelve, the diphthongs four, and the consonantal sounds twenty-four, we have altogether as many as forty sounds, some being so closely allied to each other as to be mere modifications, and others being combinations rather than simple sounds; all, however, agreeing in requiring to be expressed by letters or by combinations of letters, and to be distinguished from each other. This enables us to appreciate—

§ 152. *The insufficiency of the English alphabet.*—

a. In respect to the vowels.—Notwithstanding the fact that the sounds of the *a* in *father, fate,* and *fat,* and of the *o* and the *aw* in *note, not,* and *bawl,* are modifications of *a* and *o* respectively, we have still *six* vowel sounds specifically distinct, for which (*y* being a consonant rather than a vowel) we have but *five* signs. The *u* in *duck*, specifically distinct from the *u* in *bull*, has no specifically distinct sign to represent it.

b. In respect to the consonants.—The *th* in *thin*, the *th* in *thine*, the *sh* in *shine*, the *z* in *azure*, and the *ng* in *king*, five sounds specifically distinct, and five sounds perfectly simple require corresponding signs, which they have not.

§ 153. *Its inconsistency.*—The *f* in *fan*, and the *v* in *van*, sounds in a certain degree of relationship to *p* and *b*, are expressed by sounds as unlike as *f* is unlike *p*, and as *v* is unlike *b*. The sound of the *th* in *thin*, the *th* in *thine*, the *sh* in *shine*, similarly related to *t, d,* and *s*, are expressed by signs as like *t. d.* and *s*, respectively, as *th* and *sh*.

The compound sibilant sound of *j* in *jest* is spelt with

the single sign *j*, whilst the compound sibilant sound in *chest* is spelt with the combination *ch*.

§ 154. *Erroneousness.*—The sound of the *ee* in *feet* is considered the long (independent) sound of the *e* in *bed;* whereas it is the long (independent) sound of the *i* in *pit*.

The *i* in *bite* is considered as the long (independent) sound of the *i* in *pit;* whereas it is a diphthongal sound.

The *u* in *duck* is looked upon as a modification of the *u* in *bull;* whereas it is a specifically distinct sound.

The *ou* in *house* and the *oi* in *oil* are looked upon as the compounds of *o* and *i* and of *o* and *u* respectively; whereas the latter element of them is not *i* and *u*, but *y* and *w*.

The *th* in *thin* and the *th* in *thine* are dealt with as one and the same sound; whereas they are sounds specifically distinct.

The *ch* in *chest* is dealt with as a modification of *c* (either with the power of *k* or of *s*); whereas its elements are *t* and *sh*.

§ 155. *Redundancy.*—As far as the representation of sounds is concerned the letter *c* is superfluous. In words like *citizen* it may be replaced by *s;* in words like *cat* by *k*. In *ch,* as in *chest,* it has no proper place. In *ch,* as in *mechanical,* is may be replaced by *k*.

Q is superfluous, *cw* or *kw* being its equivalent.

X also is superfluous, *ks, gz,* or *z,* being equivalent to it.

The diphthongal forms *æ* and *œ,* as in *Æneas* and *Crœsus,* except in the way of etymology, are superfluous and redundant.

§ 156. *Unsteadiness.*—Here we have (amongst many

other examples), 1. The consonant *c* with the double power of *s* and *k*; 2. *g* with its sound in *gun* and also with its sound in *gin*; 3. *x* with its sounds in *Alexander, apoplexy, Xenophon*.

In the foregoing examples a single sign has a double power; in the words *Philip* and *filip*, &c.; a single sound has a double sign.

In respect to the degree wherein the English orthography is made subservient to etymology, it is sufficient to repeat the statement that as many as three letters *c*, *œ*, and *æ* are retained in the alphabet for *etymological purposes only*.

§ 157. The defects noticed in the preceding sections are *absolute* defects, and would exist, as they do at present, were there no language in the world except the English. This is not the case with those that are now about to be noticed; for them, indeed, the word *defect* is somewhat too strong a term. They may more properly be termed inconveniences.

Compared with the languages of the rest of the world the use of many letters in the English alphabet is *singular*. The letter *i* (when long or independent) is, with the exception of England, generally sounded as *ee*. With Englishmen it has a diphthongal power. The inconvenience of this is the necessity that it imposes upon us, in studying foreign languages, of unlearning the sound which we give it in our own, and of learning the sound which it bears in the language studied. So it is (amongst many others) with the letter *j*. In English this has the sound of *dzh*, in French of *zh*, and in German of *y*. From singularity in the use of letters arises inconvenience in the study of foreign tongues.

In using *j* as *dzh* there is a second objection. It is not only inconvenient, but it is theoretically incorrect.

The letter *j* was originally a modification of the vowel *i*. The Germans, who used it as the semivowel *y*, have perverted it from its original power less than the English have done, who sound it *dzh*.

With these views we may appreciate in the English alphabet and orthography—

Its convenience or inconvenience in respect to learning foreign tongues.—The sound given to the *a* in *fate* is singular. Other nations sound it as *a* in *father*.

The sound given to the *e*, long (or independent), is singular. Other nations sound it either as *a* in *fate*, or as *é fermé*.

The sound given to the *i* in *bite* is singular. Other nations sound it as *ee* in *feet*.

The sound given to the *oo* in *fool* is singular. Other nations sound it as the *o* in *note*, or as the *ó chiuso*.

The sound given to the *u* in *duck* is singular. Other nations sound it as the *u* in *bull*.

The sound given to the *ou* in *house* is singular. Other nations, more correctly, represent it by *au* or *aw*.

The sound given to the *w* in *wet* is somewhat singular, but is also correct and convenient. With many nations it is not found at all, whilst with those where it occurs it has the sound (there or thereabouts) of *v*.

The sound given to *y* is somewhat singular. In Danish it has a vowel power. In German the semi-vowel sound is spelt with *j*.

The sound given to *z* is not the sound which it has in German and Italian, but its power in English is convenient and correct.

The sound given to *ch* in *chest* is singular. In other languages it has generally a guttural sound; in French that of *sh*. The English usage is more correct than the French, but less correct than the German.

The sound given to *j* (as said before) is singular.

§ 158. *The historical propriety or impropriety of certain letters.*—The use of *i* with a diphthongal power is not only singular and inconvenient, but also *historically incorrect*. The Greek *iota*, from whence it originates, has the sound of *i* and *ee*, as in *pit* and *feet*.

The *y*, sounded as in *yet*, is historically incorrect. It grew out of the Greek υ, a vowel, and no semivowel. The Danes still use it as such, that is, with the power of the German *ü*.

The use of *j* for *dzh* is historically incorrect.

The use of *c* for *k* in words derived from the Greek as *mechanical, ascetic,* &c., is historically incorrect. The form *c* is the representative of γ and σ and not of the Greek *kappa*.

§ 159. *On certain conventional modes of spelling.*—In the Greek language the sounds of *o* in *not* and of *o* in *note* (although allied) are expressed by the unlike signs (or letters) ο and ω, respectively. In most other languages the difference between the sounds is considered too slight to require for its expression signs so distinct and dissimilar. In some languages the difference is neglected altogether. In many, however, it is expressed, and that by some modification of the original letter.

Let the sign (¯) denote that the vowel over which it stands is long, or independent, whilst the sign (˘) indicates shortness, or dependence. In such a case, instead of writing *not* and *nωt*, like the Greeks, we may write *nŏt* and *nōt*, the sign serving for a fresh letter. Herein the expression of the nature of the sound is natural, because the natural use of (¯) and (˘) is to express length or shortness, dependence or independence. Now, supposing the broad sound of *o* to be already represented, it is very evident that, of the other two sounds of *o*, the one must be long (independent), and the other short (dependent); and as it is only necessary to express one of these conditions, we may, if we choose, use the sign (ˉ) alone; its presence denoting length, and its absence shortness (independence or dependence).

As signs of this kind, one mark is as good as another; and instead of (ˉ) we may, if we chose, substitute such a mark as (′) and write *nŏt* = *nŏt*—*nwt* = *nōte*; provided only that the sign (′) expresses no other condition or affection of a sound. This use of the mark (′), as a sign that the vowel over which it is placed is long (independent), is common in many languages. But is this use of (′) natural? For a reason that the reader has anticipated, it is not natural, but conventional. Neither is it convenient. It is used elsewhere not as the sign of *quantity*, but as the sign of *accent*; consequently, being placed over a letter, and being interpreted according to its natural meaning, it gives the idea, not that the syllable is long, but that it is emphatic or accented. Its use as a sign of quantity then, would be an orthographical expedient, or an inconvenient conventional mode of spelling.

The English language abounds in orthographical expedients; the modes of expressing the quantity of the vowels being particularly numerous. To begin with these:—

The reduplication of a vowel where there is but one syllable (as in *feet, cool*), is an orthographical expedient. It merely means that the syllable is long (or independent).

The juxtaposition of two different vowels, where there is but one syllable (as in *plain, moan*), is an orthographical expedient. It generally means the same as the reduplication of a vowel, *i. e.*, that the syllable is long (independent).

The addition of the *e* mute, as in *plane, whale* (whatever may have been its origin), is, at present, but an orthographical expedient. It denotes the lengthening of the syllable.

The reduplication of the consonant after a vowel, as in *spotted, torrent*, is in most cases but an orthographical expedient. It merely denotes that the preceding vowel is short (dependent).

The use of *ph* for *f* in *Philip*, is an orthographical expedient, founded upon etymological reasons.

The use of *th* for the simple sound of the first consonant in *thin* and *thine*, is an orthographical expedient. The combination must be dealt with as a single letter.

Caution.—The letter *x* and *q* are not orthographical expedients. They are orthographical *compendiums*, $x = ks$, and $q = kw$.

CHAPTER IX.

HISTORICAL SKETCH OF THE ENGLISH ALPHABET

§ 160. The preceding chapter has exhibited the theory of a full and perfect alphabet; it has shown how far the English alphabet falls short of such a standard; and, above all, it has exhibited some of the conventional modes of spelling which the insufficiency of alphabets, combined with other causes, has engendered. The present chapter gives a *history* of our alphabet, whereby many of its defects are *accounted for*. These defects, it may be said, once for all, the English alphabet shares with those of the rest of the world; although, with the doubtful exception of the French, it possesses them in a higher degree than any.

With few, if any exceptions, *all the modes of writing in the world originate*, directly or indirectly, from the Phœnician.

At a certain period the alphabet of Palestine, Phœnicia, and the neighboring languages of the Semitic tribes, consisted of *twenty-two* separate and distinct letters.

Now the chances are, that, let a language possess as few elementary articulate sounds as possible, an alphabet of only *twenty-two* letters will be insufficient.

Hence it may safely be asserted, that the original Semitic alphabet was *insufficient* for even the *Semitic* languages.

§ 161. In this state it was imported into Greece.

Now, as it rarely happens that any two languages have precisely the same elementary articulate sounds, so it rarely happens that an alphabet can be transplanted from one tongue to another, and be found to suit. When such is the case, alterations are required. The extent to which these alterations are made at all, or (if made) made on a right principle varies with different languages. Some *adapt* an introduced alphabet well: others badly.

Of the *twenty-two* Phœnician letters the Greeks took but *twenty-one*. The eighteenth letter, *tsadi* צ, was never imported into Europe.

Compared with the Semitic, the *Old* Greek alphabet ran thus:—

	Hebrew.	Greek.		Hebrew.	Greek.
1.	א	A.	13.	מ	M.
2.	ב	B.	14.	נ	N.
3.	ג	Γ.	15.	ס	Σ?
4.	ד	Δ.	16.	ע	O.
5.	ה	E.	17.	פ	Π.
6.	ו	Digamma.	18.	צ	—
7.	ז	Z.			A letter called
8.		H.	19.	ק	koppa, afterwards ejected.
9.	ט	Θ.			
10.		I.	20.	ר	P.
11.	כ	K.	21.	ש	M afterwards Σ?
12.	ל	Λ.	22.	ת	T.

The *names* of the letters were as follows:

	Hebrew.	Greek.		Hebrew.	Greek.
1.	Aleph	Alpha.	7.	Zayn	Zæta,
2.	Beth	Bæta.	8.	Heth	Hæta.
3.	Gimel	Gamma.	9.	Teth	Thœta.
4.	Daleth	Delta.	10.	Yod	Iŏta.
5.	He	E, *psilon.*	11.	Kaph	Kappa.
6.	Vaw	*Digamma.*	12.	Lamed	Lambda.

Hebrew.	Greek.		Hebrew.	Greek.
13. Mem	. . Mu.		18. Tsadi	———
14. Nun	. . . Nu.		19. Kof	. . Koppa, *Archaic.*
15. Sameeh	. Sigma?		20. Resh	. Rho.
16. Ayn	. . . O.		21. Sin	. . San, *Doric.*
17. Pi.	. . . Phi.		22. Tau	. . Tau.

The alphabet of Phœnicia and Palestine being adapted to the language of Greece, the first change took place in the manner of writing. The Phœnicians wrote from right to left; the Greeks from left to right. Besides this, the following principles were recognised;—

a. Letters for which there was no use were left behind. This was the case, as seen above, with the eighteenth letter, *tsadi*.

b. Letters expressive of sounds for which there was no precise equivalent in Greek, were used with other powers. This was the case with letters 5, 8, 16, and probably with some others.

c. Letters of which the original sound, in the course of time, became changed, were allowed, as it were, to drop out of the alphabet. This was the case with 6 and 19.

d. For such simple single elementary articulate sounds as there was no sign or letter representant, new signs, or letters, were invented. This principle gave to the Greek alphabet the new signs φ, χ, υ, ω.

e. The new signs were not mere modifications of the older ones, but totally new letters.

All this was correct in principle; and the consequence is, that the Greek alphabet, although not originally meant to express a European tongue at all, expresses the Greek language well.

§ 162. But it was not from the Greek that our own alphabet was immediately derived; although ultimately it is referable to the same source as the Greek, *viz.*, the Phœnician.

It was the *Roman* alphabet which served as the basis to the English.

And it is in the changes which the Phœnician alphabet underwent in being accommodated to the Latin language that we must investigate the chief peculiarities of the present alphabet and orthography of Great Britain and America.

Now respecting the Roman alphabet, we must remember that it was *not* taken *directly* from the Phœnician; in this important point differing from the Greek.

Nor yet was it taken, *in the first instance*, from the Greek.

It had a *double* origin.

The operation of the principles indicated in § 161 was a work of the time; and hence the older and more unmodified Greek alphabet approached in character its Phœnician prototype much more than the later, or modified. As may be seen, by comparing the previous alphabets with the common alphabets of the Greek Grammar, the letters 6 and 19 occur in the earlier, whilst they are missing in the later, modes of writing. On the other hand, the *old* alphabet has no such signs as ϕ, χ, v, ω, ψ, and ξ.

Such being the case, it is easy to imagine what would be the respective conditions of two Italian languages which borrowed those alphabets, the one from the earlier, the other from the later Greek. The former would contain the equivalents to *vaw* (6), and *kof* (19); but be destitute of ϕ, χ, &c.: whereas the latter would have ϕ, χ, &c., but be without either *vaw* or *kof*.

Much the same would be the case with any single

Italian language which took as its basis the *earlier*, but adopted, during the course of time, modifications from the *later* Greek. It would exhibit within itself characters common to the two stages.

This, or something very like it, was the case with Roman. For the first two or three centuries the alphabet was Etruscan; Etruscan derived *directly* from the Greek, and from the *old* Greek.

Afterwards, however, the later Greek alphabet had its influence, and the additional letters which it contained were more or less incorporated; and that without effecting the ejection of any earlier ones.

§ 163. With these preliminaries we may investigate the details of the Roman alphabet, when we shall find that many of them stand in remarkable contrast with those of Greece and Phœnicia. At the same time where they differ with them, they agree with the English.

Order.	Roman.	English.	Greek.	Hebrew.
1.	A	A	Alpha	Aleph.
2.	B	B	Bæta	Beth.
3.	C	C	Gamma	Gimel.
4.	D	D	Delta	Daleth.
5.	E	E	Epsilon	He.
6.	F	F	*Digamma*	Vaw.
7.	G	G	——	——
8.	H	H	Hæta	Heth.
9.	I	I	Iôta	Iod.
10.	J	J	Iôta	Iod.
11.		K	*Kappa*	Kaf.
12.	L	L	Lamda	Lamed.
13.	M	M	Mu	Mem.
14.	N	N	Nu	Nun.
15.	O	O	Omicron	Ayn.
16.	P	P	Pi	Phi.
17.	Q	Q	*Koppa*	Kof.
18.	R	R	Rho	Resh.

Order.	Roman.	English.	Greek.	Hebrew.
19	S	S	San.	Sin.
20.	T	T	Tau.	Tau.
21.	U	U	Upsilon	—
22.	V	V	Upsilon	—
23.		W	Upsilon	—
24.	X	X	Xi	Samech.*
25.	Y	Y	Upsilon	—
26.	Z	Z	Zæta	Zain.

§ 164. The differences of this table are referable to one of the following four heads:—*a*. Ejection. *b*. Addition. *c*. Change of power. *d*. Change of order.

a. Ejection.—In the first instance, the Italians ejected as unnecessary, letters 7,† 9, and 11: *zayn* (*zæta*), *teth* (*thæta*), and *kaf* (*kappa*). Either the sounds which they expressed were wanting in their language; or else they were expressed by some other letter. The former was probably the case with 7 and 9, *zæta* and *thæta*; the latter with 11, *kappa*.

b. Addition.—Out of the Greek *iota*, two; out of the Greek *upsilon*, four modifications have been evolved; viz., *i* and *j* out of *i*, and *u*, *v*, *w*, *y*, out of *v*.

c. Change of power.—Letter 3, in Greek and Hebrew had the sound of the *g* in *gun*; in Latin that of *k*. The reason for this lies in the structure of the Etruscan language. In that tongue the *flat* sounds were remarkably deficient; indeed, it is probable, that that of *g* was wanting. Its *sharp* equivalent, however, the sound of *k*, was by no means wanting; and the Greek *gamma* was used to denote it. This made the equivalent to *k*, the third letter of the alphabet, as early as the time of the Etruscans.

But the *Romans* had both sounds, the *flat* as well as

---

* As a name, *Sigma*=*Samech*.
† Of the Hebrew and Greek tables.

7

the *sharp*, *g* as well as *k*. How did they express them?
Up to the second Punic War they made the rounded
form of the Greek Γ, out of which the letter C has arisen,
do double work, and signify *k* and *g* equally, just as
in the present English *th* is sounded as the Greek Θ,[*]
and as *dh* ;[†] in proof whereof we have in the Duillian
column, MACESTRATOS = MAGISTRATOS, and CARTHACI-
NIENSES = CARTHAGINIENSES.

Thus much concerning the power and places of the
Latin *c*, as opposed to the Greek γ. But this is not all.
The use of *gamma*, with the power of *k*, made *kappa*
superfluous, and accounts for its ejection in the *Etruscan*
alphabet; a fact already noticed.

Furthermore, an addition to the Etruscan alphabet
was required by the existence of the sound of *g*, in Latin,
as soon as the inconvenience of using *c* with a double
power became manifest. What took place then? Even
this. The third letter was modified in form, or became a
new letter, *c* being altered into *g*; and the new letter took
its place in the alphabet.

Where was this? As the *seventh* letter between *f*
(*digamma*) and *h* (*hæta*).

Why? Because it was there where there was a
vacancy, and where it replaced the Greek *zæta*, or the
Hebrew *zayin*, a letter which, *at that time*, was not
wanted in Latin.

d. Change of order.—As far as the letters *c* and *g*
are concerned, this has been explained; and it has been
shown that change of order and change of power are
sometimes very closely connected. All that now need
be added is, that those letters which were *last* introduced
from the Greek into the Roman alphabet, were placed at
the end.

[*] In *thin*. [†] In *thine*.

This is why *u*, *v*, *w*, and *y* come after *t*—the last letter of the original Phœnician, and also of the *older* Greek.

This, too, is the reason for *z* coming last of all. It was restored for the purpose of spelling Greek words. But as its original place had been filled up by *g*, it was tacked on as an appendage, rather than incorporated as an element.

X in *power*, coincided with the Greek *xi*; in *place*, with the Greek *khi*. Its *position* seems to have determined its *form*, which is certainly that of X rather than of Ξ. The full investigation of this is too lengthy for the present work.

§ 165. It should be observed, that, in the Latin, the letters have no longer any *names* (like *beth*, *bæta*), except such as are derived from their powers (*be*, *ce*).

§ 166. The principles which determined the form of the Roman alphabet were, upon the whole, correct; and, hence, the Roman alphabet, although not originally meant to express an Italian tongue at all, expressed the language to which it was applied tolerably.

On the other hand, there were both omissions and alterations which have had a detrimental effect upon the orthography of those other numerous tongues to which Latin has supplied the alphabet. Thus—

a. It is a matter of regret, that the differences which the Greeks drew between the so-called *long* and *short e* and *o*, was neglected by the Latins; in other words, that ω was omitted entirely, and η changed in power. Had this been the case, all the orthographical expedients by which we have to express the difference between the *o* in *not*, and the *o* in *note*, would have been prevented—*not, note, moat—bed, bead, heel, glede*, &c.

b. It is a matter of regret, that such an unnecessary

compendium as $q = cu$, or cw, should have been retained from the old Greek alphabet; and, still more so, that the equally superfluous $x = cs$, or ks, should have been re-admitted.

c. It is a matter of regret, that the Greek Θ was not treated like the Greek ζ. Neither were wanted at first; both afterwards. The manner, however, of their subsequent introduction was different. *Zeta* came in as a simple single letter, significant of a simple single sound. *Theta*, on the contrary, although expressive of an equally simple sound, became *th*. This was a combination rather than a letter; and the error which it engendered was great.

It suggested the idea, that a simple sound was a compound one—which was wrong.

It further suggested the idea, that the sound of Θ differed from that of τ, by the addition of *h*—which was wrong also.

§ 167. The Greek language had a system of sounds different from the Phœnician; and the alphabet required modifying accordingly.

The Roman language had a system of sounds different from the Greek and the alphabet required modifying accordingly.

This leads us to certain questions concerning the Anglo-Saxon. Had *it* a system of sounds different from the Roman? If so, what modifications did the alphabet require? Were such modifications effected? If so, how? Sufficiently or insufficiently? The answers are unsatisfactory.

§ 168. The Anglo-Saxon had, even in its earliest stage, the following sounds, for which the Latin alphabet had no equivalent signs or letters—

1. The sound of the *th* in *thin*.

2. The sound of the *th* in *thine*.

It had certainly these: probably others.

§ 169. Expressive of these, two new signs were introduced, *viz.*, Þ = *th* in *thin*, and ð = *th* in *thine*.

W, also evolved out of *u*, was either an original improvement of the Anglo-Saxon orthographists, or a mode of expression borrowed from one of the allied languages of the Continent. Probably the latter was the case; since we find the following passage in the Latin dedication of Otfrid's "Krist:"—" Hujus enim linguæ barbaries, ut est inculca et indisciplinabilis, atque insueta capi regulari freno grammaticæ artis, sic etiam in multis dictis scriptu est difficilis propter literarum aut congeriem, aut incognitam sonoritatem. Nam interdum tria *u u u* ut puto quærit in sono; priores duo consonantes, ut mihi videtur, tertium vocali sono manente."

This was, as far as it went, correct, so that the Anglo-Saxon alphabet, although not originally meant to express a Gothic tongue at all, answered the purpose to which it was applied tolerably.

§ 170. Change, however, went on; and the orthography which suited the earlier Anglo-Saxon would not suit the later; at any rate, it would not suit the language which had become or was becoming, *English;* wherein the sounds for which the Latin alphabet had no equivalent signs increase. Thus there is at present—

1. The sound of the *sh* in *shine*.
2. The sound of the *z* in *azure*.

How are these to be expressed? The rule has hitherto been to denote simple single sounds, by simple single signs, and where such signs have no existence already, to *originate new ones*.

To *combine existing letters*, rather than to coin a new one, has only been done rarely. The Latin substitution of the combination *th* for the simple single ð, was exceptionable. It was a precedent, however, which now begins to be followed generally.

§ 171. It is this precedent which accounts for the absence of any letter in English, expressive of either of the sounds in question.

§ 172. Furthermore, our alphabet has not only not increased in proportion to our sound-system, but it has *decreased*. The Anglo-Saxon Þ = the *th* in *thin*, and ð = the *th* in *thine*, have become obsolete; and a difference in pronunciation, which our ancestors expressed, *we* overlook.

The same precedent is at the bottom of this; a fact which leads us to—

§ 173. *The Anglo-Norman alphabet.*—The Anglo-Saxon language was *Gothic;* the alphabet, *Roman*.

The Anglo-Norman language was *Roman;* the alphabet, *Roman* also.

The Anglo-Saxon took his speech from one source; his writing from another.

The Anglo-Norman took both from the same.

In adapting a Latin alphabet to a Gothic language, the Anglo-Saxon allowed himself more latitude than the Anglo-Norman. We have seen that the new signs Þ and ð were Anglo-Saxon.

Now the sounds which these letters represent did not occur in the Norman-French, consequently the Norman-French alphabet neither had nor needed to have signs to express them; until after the battle of Hastings, *when it became the Anglo-Norman of England.*

Then, the case became altered. The English language influenced the Norman orthography, and the Norman orthography the English language; and the result was, that the simple single correct and distinctive signs of the Anglo-Saxon alphabet, became replaced by the incorrect and indistinct combination *th*.

This was a loss, both in the way of theoretical correctness and perspicuity.

Such is the general view of the additions, ejections, changes of power, and changes of order in the English alphabet. The extent, however, to which an alphabet is faulty, is no measure of the extent to which an orthography is faulty; since an insufficient alphabet may, by consistency in its application, be more useful than a full and perfect alphabet unsteadily applied.

§ 174. One of our orthographical expedients, *viz.*, the reduplication of the consonant following, to express the shortness (dependence) of the preceding vowel, is as old as the classical languages: *terra*, $\vartheta\acute{a}\lambda a\sigma\sigma a$. Nevertheless, the following extract from the "Ormulum" (written in the thirteenth century) is the fullest recognition of the practice that I have met with.

>And whase wilenn shall þis boc,
>   Efft oþerr siþe writenn,
>Himm bidde icc þatt hett write rihht,
>   Swa sum þiss boc himm tæcheþþ;
>All þwerrt utt affterr þatt itt iss
>   Opp þiss firrste bisne,
>Wiþþ all swilc rime als her iss sett,
>   Wiþþ alse fele wordess:
>And tatt he loke well þatt he
>   *An boc-staff write twiggess*,*
>Eggwhær þær itt uppo þiss boc
>   Iss writenn o þatt wise:
>Loke he well þatt hett write swa,
>   Forr he ne magg noht elless,
>On Englissh writenn rihht te word,
>   þatt wite he well to soþe.

---

* Write one letter twice.

§ 175. *The order of the alphabet.*—In the history of our alphabet, we have had the history of certain changes in the arrangement, as well as of the changes in the number and power of its letters. The following question now presents itself: *viz.*, Is there in the order of the letters any *natural* arrangement, or is the original as well as the present succession of letters arbitrary and accidental? The following facts suggest an answer in the affirmative.

The order of the Hebrew alphabet is as follows:—

Name.	Sound.	Name.	Sound.
1. Aleph	Either a vowel or a breathing.	12. Lamed	L.
2. Beth	B.	13. Mem	M.
3. Gimel	G, as in *gun*.	14. Nun	N.
4. Daleth	D.	15. Samech	a variety of S.
5. He	Either a vowel or an aspirate.	16. Ayn	Either a vowel or—?
6. Vaw	V.	17. Pe	P.
7. Zayn	Z.	18. Tsadi	TS.
8. Kheth	a variety of K.	19. Kof	a variety of K.
9. Teth	a variety of T.	20. Resh	R.
10. Yod	I.	21. Sin	S.
11. Caph	K.	22. Tau	T.

Let *beth, vaw,* and *pe* (*b, v, p*) constitute a series called series P. Let *gimel, kheth,* and *kof* (*g, kh, k*) constitute a series called series K. Let *daleth, teth,* and *tau,* (*d, t', t*) constitute a series called series T. Let *aleph, he,* and *ayn* constitute a series called the vowel series. Let the first four letters be taken in their order.

    1. Aleph . . . . of the vowel series.
    2. Beth . . . . of series P.
    3. Gimel . . . . of series K.
    4. Daleth . . . . of series T.

Herein the consonant of series B comes next to the letter of the vowel series; that of series K follows; and in the last place, comes the letter of series T. After this the order changes; *daleth* being followed by *he* of the vowel series.

  5. *He* . . . . of the vowel series.
  6. *Vau* . . . . of series P.
  7. *Zayn* . . . . ———
  8. *Kheth* . . . . of series K.
  9. *Teth* . . . . of series T.

In this second sequence the *relative* positions of *v*, *kh*, and *t*, are the same in respect to each other, and the same in respect to the vowel series. The sequence itself is broken by the letter *zayn*, but it is remarkable that the principle of the sequence is the same. Series P follows the vowel, and series T is farthest from it. After this the system becomes but fragmentary. Still, even now, *pe*, of series P, follows *ayn; tau*, of series T, is farthest from it, and *kof*, of series K, is intermediate.

If this be the case, and, if the letters, so to say, *circulate*, the alterations made in their order during the transfer of their alphabet from Greece to Rome, have had the unsatisfactory effect of concealing an interesting arrangement, and of converting a real, though somewhat complex regularity, into apparent hazard and disorder.

QUESTIONS.

1. Explain the terms *sharp, explosive, true aspirate, apparent aspirate, broad, dependent*.

2. Exhibit the difference between the quantity of *syllables* and the quantity of *vowels*.

3. Accentuate the following words,—*attribute* (*adjective*), *survey* (*verb*), *August* (*the month*).

4. Under what conditions is the *sound* of consonants doubled?

5. Exhibit, in a tabular form, the relations of the *a*) mutes, *b*) the vowels, underlining those which do not occur in English.

6. What is the power of *ph* in *Philip?* what in *haphazard?* Illustrate the difference fully.

7. Investigate the changes by which the words *picture, nature*, derived from the Latin *pictura* and *natura*, are sounded *pictshur* and *natshur*.

8. How do you sound the combination *apd?* Why?

9. In what points is the English alphabet *insufficient, redundant*, and *inconsistent?*

10. Why is *z* (*zeta*), which is the sixth letter in the Greek, the last in the English alphabet?

PART IV.

ETYMOLOGY.

CHAPTER I.

ON THE PROVINCE OF ETYMOLOGY.

§ 175. THE word etymology, derived from the Greek, in the current language of scholars and grammarians, has a double meaning. At times it is used in a wide, and at times in a restricted sense.

If in the English language we take such a word as *fathers*, we are enabled to divide it into two parts; in other words, to reduce it into two elements. By comparing it with the word *father*, we see that the *s* is neither part nor parcel of the original word. Hence the word is capable of being analysed; *father* being the original primitive word, and *s* the secondary superadded termination. From the word *father*, the word *fathers* is *derived*, or (changing the expression) deduced, or descended. What has been said of the word *fathers* may also be said of *fatherly, fatherlike, fatherless*, &c. Now, from the word *father*, all these words (*fathers, fatherly, fatherlike,* and *fatherless*) differ in form and in meaning. To become such a word as *fathers*, &c., the word *father* is *changed*. Of changes of this sort, it is the province of etymology to take cognizance.

§ 177. Compared with the form *fathers*, the word *father* is the older form of the two. The word *father* is a word current in this the nineteenth century. The same word is found much earlier, under different forms, and in different languages. Thus, in the Latin language, the form was *pater;* in Greek, πατήρ. Now, with *father* and *fathers*, the change takes place within the same language, whilst the change that takes place between *pater* and *father* takes place within different languages. Of changes of this latter kind it is, also, the province of etymology to take cognizance.

§ 178. In its widest signification, etymology takes cognizance *of the changes of the form of words*. However, as the etymology that compares the forms *fathers* and *father* is different from the etymology that compares *father* and *pater*, we have, of etymology, two sorts: one dealing with the changes of form that words undergo in one and the same language (*father, fathers*), the other dealing with the changes that words undergo in passing from one language to another (*pater, father*).

The first of these sorts may be called etymology in the limited sense of the word, or the etymology of the grammarian. In this case it is opposed to orthoepy, orthography, syntax, and the other parts of grammar. This is the etymology of the ensuing pages.

The second may be called etymology in the wide sense of the word, *historical* etymology, or *comparative* etymology.

§ 179. It must be again repeated that the two sorts of etymology agree in one point, viz., in taking cognizance of the *changes of forms that words undergo*. Whether the change arise from grammatical reasons, as *father, fathers,* or from a change of language taking place in the lapse of time, as *pater, father,* is a matter of indifference.

In the Latin *pater,* and in the English *father,* we have one of two things, either two words descended or derived from each other, or two words descended or derived from a common original source.

In *fathers* we have a formation deduced from the radical word *father.*

With these preliminaries we may understand Dr. Johnson's explanation of the word etymology.

"Etymology, *n. s.* (*etymologia,* Lat.) ἔτυμος (*etymos*) *true, and* λόγος (*logos*) *a word.*

"1. *The descent or derivation of a word from its original; the deduction of formations from the radical word; the analysis of compounds into primitives.*

"2. *The part of grammar which delivers the inflections of nouns and verbs."*

CHAPTER II.

ON GENDER.

§ 180. How far is there such a thing as *gender* in the English language? This depends upon the meaning that we attach to the word.

In the Latin language we have the words *taurus* = *bull*, and *vacca* = *cow*. Here the natural distinction of sex is expressed by *wholly* different words. With this we have corresponding modes of expression in English: *e. g.*,

Male.	Female.	Male.	Female.
Bachelor	Spinster.	Horse	Mare.
Boar	Sow.	Ram	Ewe.
Boy	Girl.	Son	Daughter.
Brother	Sister.	Uncle	Aunt.
Buck	Doe.	Father	Mother, &c.

The mode, however, of expressing different sexes by *wholly* different words is not a matter of *gender*. The words *boy* and *girl* bear no *etymological* relation to each other; neither being derived from the other, nor in any way connected with it.

§ 181. Neither are words like *cock-sparrow*, *man-servant*, *he-goat*, &c., as compared with *hen-sparrow*, *maid-servant*, *she-goat*, &c., specimens of *gender*. Here a difference of sex is indicated by the addition of a fresh term, from which is formed a compound word.

§ 182. In the Latin words *genitrix* = *a mother*, and

genitor = *a father*, we have a nearer approach to *gender*. Here the difference of sex is expressed by a difference of termination; the words *genitor* and *genitrix* being in a true etymological relation, *i. e.*, either derived from each other, or from some common source. With this we have, in English corresponding modes of expression: *e. g.*

Male.	Female.	Male.	Female.
Actor	Actress.	Lion	Lioness.
Arbiter	Arbitress.	Peer	Peeress.
Baron	Baroness.	Poet	Poetess.
Benefactor	Benefactress.	Sorcerer	Sorceress.
Count	Countess.	Songster	Songstress.
Duke	Duchess.	Tiger	Tigress.

§ 183. This, however, in strict grammatical language, is an approach to gender rather than *gender* itself; the difference from true grammatical gender being as follows:—

Let the Latin words *genitor* and *genitrix* be declined:—

Sing. Nom.	Genitor	Genitrix.
Gen.	Genitor-*is*	Genitric-*is*.
Dat.	Genitor-*i*	Genitric-*i*.
Acc.	Genitor-*em*	Genitric-*em*.
Voc.	Genitor	Genitrix.
Plur. Nom.	Genitor-*es*	Genitric-*es*.
Gen.	Genitor-*um*	Genitric-*um*.
Dat.	Genitor-*ibus*	Genitric-*ibus*.
Acc.	Genitor-*es*	Genitric-*es*.
Voc.	Genitor-*es*	Genitric-*es*.

The syllables in italics are the signs of the cases and numbers. Now these signs are the same in each word, the difference of meaning (or sex) not affecting them.

§ 184. Contrast, however, with the words *genitor*

and *genitrix* the words *domina* = *a mistress*, and *dominus* = *a master*.

Sing. Nom.	Domin-*a*	Domin-*us*.
Gen.	Domin-*æ*	Domin-*i*.
Dat.	Domin-*æ*	Domin-*o*.
Acc.	Domin-*am*	Domin-*um*.
Voc.	Domin-*a*	Domin-*e*.
Plur. Nom.	Domin-*æ*	Domin-*i*.
Gen.	Domin-*arum*	Domin-*orum*.
Dat.	Domin-*abus*	Domin-*is*.
Acc.	Domin-*as*	Domin-*os*.
Voc.	Domin-*æ*	Domin-*i*.

Here the letters in italics, or the signs of the cases and numbers, are different; the difference being brought about by the difference of gender. Now it is very evident that, if *genitrix* be a specimen of gender, *domina* is something more.

§ 185. It may be laid down as a sort of definition, that *there is no gender where there is no affection of the declension:* consequently, that, although we have, in English, words corresponding to *genitrix* and *genitor*, we have no true genders until we find words corresponding to *dominus* and *domina*.

§ 186. The second element in the notion of gender, although I will not venture to call it an essential one, is the following:—In the words *domina* and *dominus*, *mistress* and *master*, there is a *natural* distinction of sex : the one being masculine, or male, the other feminine, or female. In the words *sword* and *lance* there is *no natural* distinction of sex. Notwithstanding this, the word *hasta*, in Latin, is as much of the feminine gender as *domina*, whilst *gladius* = *a sword* is, like *dominus*, a masculine noun. From this we see that, in languages wherein there are true genders, a fictitious or conventional sex is attributed even to inanimate objects; in other words, *sex* is a natural distinction, *gender* a grammatical one.

§ 187. In § 185 it is written, that "although we have, in English, words corresponding to *genitrix* and *genitor*, we have no true genders until we find *words corresponding to dominus and domina*."—The sentence was intentionally worded with caution. Words like *dominus* and *domina*, that is, words where the declension is affected by the sex, *are* to be found *even in English*.

The pronoun *him*, from the Anglo-Saxon and English *he*, as compared with the pronoun *her*, from the Anglo-Saxon *heó*, is affected in its declension by the difference of sex, and is a true, though fragmentary, specimen of gender. The same is the case with the form *his* as compared with *her*.

The pronoun *it* (originally *hit*), as compared with *he*, is a specimen of gender.

The relative *what*, as compared with the masculine *who*, is a specimen of gender.

The forms *it* (for *hit*) and *he* are as much genders as *hoc* and *hic*, and the forms *hoc* and *hic* are as much genders as *bonum* and *bonus*.

§ 188. The formation of the neuter gender by the addition of *-t*, in words like *wha-t*, *i-t*, and *tha-t*, occurs in other languages. The *-t* in *tha-t* is the *-d* in *istu-d*, Latin, and the *-t* in *ta-t*, Sanskrit.

§ 189. In the Mœso-Gothic and Scandinavian, the *adjectives* form the neuters in *-t*, in Old High German in *-z* (*ts*), and in Modern German in *-s* (derived from *-z*)—Mœso-Gothic, *blind-ata*; Icel., *blind-t*; Old High German, *plint-ez*, M. G. *blind-es* = *cœc-um*.

Caution.— *Which*, is *not* the neuter of *who*.

§ 190. Just as there are in English fragments of a gender modifying the declension, so are there, also, fragments of the second element of gender; *viz.*, the attribution of sex to objects naturally destitute of it. *The sun in* his *glory, the moon in* her *wane*, are examples of this. A sailor calls his ship *she*. A husbandman, according to Mr. Cobbett, does the same with his *plough* and working implements:—"In speaking of a *ship* we say *she* and *her*. And you know that our country-folks in Hampshire call almost every thing *he* or *she*. It is curious to observe that country labourers give the feminine appellation to those things only which are more closely identified with themselves, and by the qualities or conditions of which their own efforts, and their character as workmen, are affected. The mower calls his *scythe* a *she*, the ploughman calls his *plough* a *she*; but a prong, or a shovel, or a harrow, which passes promiscuously from hand to hand, and which is appropriated to no particular labourer, is called a *he*."— "English Grammar," Letter v.

§ 191. Now, although Mr. Cobbett's statements may account for a sailor calling his ship *she*, they will not account for the custom of giving to the sun a masculine, and to the moon a feminine, pronoun, as is done in the expressions quoted in the last section; still less will it account for the circumstance of the Germans reversing the gender, and making the *sun* feminine, and the *moon* masculine.

§ 192. Let there be a period in the history of a language wherein the *sun* and *moon* are dealt with, not as inanimate masses of matter, but as animated divinities. Let there, in other words, be a time when dead things are personified, and when there is a *mythology*. Let an object like the *sun* be deemed a *male*, and an object like the *moon*, a *female*, deity. We may then understand the origin of certain genders.

The Germans say the *sun in* her *glory;* the *moon in* his *wane.* This difference between the usage of the two languages, like so many others, is explained by the influence of the classical languages upon the English.—
"*Mundilfori had two children; a son, Máni (Moon), and a daughter, Söl (Sun).*"—Such is an extract out of an Icelandic mythological work, *viz.*, the prose Edda. In the classical languages, however, *Phœbus* and *Sol* are masculine, and *Luna* and *Diana* feminine. Hence it is that, although in Anglo-Saxon and Old-Saxon the *sun* is *feminine*, it is in English *masculine*.

Philosophy, charity, &c., or the names of abstract qualities personified, take a conventional sex, and are feminine from their being feminine in Latin.

As in all these words there is no change of form, the consideration of them is a point of rhetoric, rather than of etymology.

§ 193. The remainder of this chapter is devoted to miscellaneous remarks upon the true and apparent genders of the English language.

1. With the false genders like *baron, baroness*, it is a general rule that the feminine form is derived from the masculine, and not the masculine from the feminine; as *peer, peeress*. The words *widower, gander*, and *drake* are exceptions. For the word *wizard*, from *witch*, see the section on augmentative forms.

2. The termination -*ess*, in which so large a portion of our feminine substantives terminate, is not of Saxon but of classical origin, being derived from the termination -*ix*, *genitrix*.

3. The words *shepherdess, huntress*, and *hostess* are faulty; the radical part of the word being Germanic, and

the secondary part classical: indeed, in strict English Grammar, the termination -*ess* has no place at all. It is a classic, not a Gothic, element.

4. The termination -*inn*, is current in German, as the equivalent to -*ess*, and as a feminine affix (*freund = a friend*; *freundinn = a female friend*). In English it occurs only in a fragmentary form;—*e. g.*, in *vixen*, a true feminine derivative from *fox = füchsinn*, German.

Bruin = the bear, may be either a female form, as in Old High German *përo = a he-bear*, *pirinn = a she-bear*; or it may be the Norse form *björn = a bear*, male or female.

Caution.—Words like *margravine* and *landgravine* prove nothing, being scarcely naturalised.

5. The termination -*str*, as in *webster*, *songster*, and *baxter*, was originally a feminine affix. Thus, in Anglo-Saxon,

Sangere, *a male singer*		Sangüstre, *a female singer*.
Bacere, *a male baker*		Bacestre, *a female baker*.
Fiðelere, *a male fiddler*	were opposed to	Fiðelstre, *a female fiddler*.
Vebbere, *a male weaver*		Vëbbëstre, *a female weaver*.
Rædere, *a male reader*		Rædestre, *a female reader*.
Seamere, *a male seamer*		Seamestre, *a female seamer*.

The same is the case in the present Dutch of Holland: *e. g.*, *spookster = a female fortune-teller*; *baxster = a baking-woman*; *waschster = a washerwoman*. The word *spinster* still retains its original feminine force.

6. The words *songstress* and *seamstress*, besides being, as far as concerns the intermixture of languages, in the predicament of *shepherdess*, have, moreover, a double feminine termination; 1st. -*str*, of Germanic, 2nd. -*ess*, of classical, origin.

7. In the word *heroine* we have a Greek termination, just as -*ix* is a Latin, and -*inn* a German one. It must

not, however, be considered as derived from *hero*, by any process of the English language, but be dealt with as a separate importation from the Greek language.

8. The form *deaconness* is not wholly unexceptionable; since the termination -*ess* is of Latin, the root *deacon* of Greek origin: this Greek origin being rendered all the more conspicuous by the spelling, *deacon* (from *diaconos*), as compared with the Latin *decanus*.

9. *Goose, gander.*—One peculiarity in this pair of words has already been indicated. In the older forms of the word *goose*, such as χὴν, Greek; *anser*, Latin; *gans*, German, as well as in the derived form *gander*, we have the proofs that, originally, there belonged to the word the sound of the letter *n*. In the forms ὀδοὺς, ὀδόντος, Greek; *dens, dentis*, Latin; *zahn*, German; *tooth*, English, we find the analogy that accounts for the ejection of the *n*, and the lengthening of the vowel preceding. With respect, however, to the *d* in *gander*, it is not easy to say whether it is inserted in one word or omitted in the other. Neither can we give the precise power of the -*er*. The following forms occur in the different Gothic dialects. *Gans*, fem.; *ganazzo*, masc., Old High German—*gôs*, f.; *gandra*, m., Anglo-Saxon—*gás*, Icelandic, f.; *guas*, Danish, f.; *gassi*, Icelandic, m.; *gasse*, Danish, m.—*ganser, ganserer, gansart, gänserich, gander*, masculine forms in different New German dialects.

10. Observe, the form *gänserich*, has a masculine termination. The word *täuberich*, in provincial New German, has the same form and the same power. It denotes a *male dove; taube*, in German, signifying a *dove*. In *gänserich* and *täuberich*, we find preserved the termination -*rich* (or *rik*), with a masculine power. Of this termination we have a remnant, in English, preserved in the curious word *drake*. To *duck* the word *drake* has no ety-

mological relation whatsoever. It is derived from a word with which it has but one letter in common; *viz.*, the Latin *anas* = *a duck*. Of this the root is *anat-*, as seen in the genitive case *anatis*. In Old High German we find the form *anetrekho* = *a drake*; in provincial New High German there is *enterich* and *äntrecht*, from whence come the English and Low German form, *drake*.

11. *Peacock, peahen.*—In these compounds, it is not the word *pea* that is rendered masculine or feminine by the addition of *cock* and *hen*, but it is the words *cock* and *hen* that are modified by prefixing *pea*.

CHAPTER III.

THE NUMBERS.

§ 194. In the Greek language the word *patær* signifies a *father*, denoting *one*, whilst *patere* signifies *two fathers*, denoting a pair, and thirdly, *pateres* signifies *fathers*, speaking of any number beyond two. The three words, *patær*, *patere*, and *pateres*, are said to be in different numbers, the difference of meaning being expressed by a difference of form. These numbers have names. The number that speaks of *one* is the *singular*, the number that speaks of *two* is the *dual* (from the Latin word *duo* = *two*), and the number that speaks of *more than two* is the *plural*.

All languages have numbers, but all languages have not them to the same extent. The Hebrew has a dual, but it is restricted to nouns only. It has, moreover, this peculiarity; it applies, for the most part, only to things which are naturally double, as *the two eyes, the two hands*, &c. The Latin has no dual number, except the *natural* one in the words *ambo* and *duo*.

§ 195. The question presents itself,—to what extent have we numbers in English? Like the Greek, Hebrew, and Latin, we have a singular and a plural. Like the Latin, and unlike the Greek and Hebrew, we have no dual.

§ 196. Different from the question, *to what degree have we numbers?* is the question,—*over what extent of* our language have we numbers? This distinction has already been foreshadowed or indicated. The Greeks, who said *typtô = I beat, typtelon = ye two beat, typtomen = we beat*, had a dual number for their verbs as well as their nouns; while the Hebrew dual was limited to the nouns only. In the Greek, then, the dual number is spread over a greater extent of the language than in the Hebrew.

There is no dual in the *present* English. It has been seen, however, that in the Anglo-Saxon there *was* a dual. But the Anglo-Saxon dual, being restricted to the personal pronouns (*wit = we two; git = ye two*), was not co-extensive with the Greek dual.

There is no dual in the present German. In the ancient German there *was* one.

In the present Danish and Swedish there is no dual. In the Old Norse and in the present Icelandic a dual number is to be found.

From this we learn that the dual number is one of those inflections that languages drop as they become modern.

§ 197. The numbers, then, in the present English are two, the singular and the plural. Over what extent of language have we a plural? The Latins say *bonus pater = a good father; boni patres = good fathers*. In the Latin, the adjective *bonus* changes its form with the change of number of the substantive that it accompanies. In English it is only the substantive that is changed. Hence we see that in the Latin language the numbers were extended to adjectives, whereas in English they are confined to the substantives and pronouns. Compared with the Anglo-Saxon, the present English is in the same relation as it is with the Latin. In the Anglo-Saxon there were plural forms for the adjectives.

§ 198. Respecting the formation of the plural, the current rule is, that it is formed from the singular by adding *s*, as *father, fathers*. This, however, is by no means a true expression. The letter *s* added to the word *father*, making it *fathers*, is *s* to the *eye* only. To the *ear* it is *z*. The word sounds *fatherz*. If the *s* retained its sound the spelling would be *fatherce*. In *stags, lads*, &c., the sound is *stagz, ladz*. The rule, then, for the formation of the English plurals, rigorously, though somewhat lengthily expressed, is as follows.— *The plural is formed from the singular, by adding to words ending in a vowel, a liquid or flat mute, the flat lene sibilant (z); and to words ending in a sharp mute, the sharp lene sibilant (s): e.g.* (the sound of the word being expressed), *pea, peaz; tree, treez; day, dayz; hill, hillz; hen, henz; gig, gigz; trap, traps; pit, pits; stack, stacks.*

§ 199. Upon the formation of the English plural some further remarks are necessary.

a. In the case of words ending in *b, v, d*, the *th* in *thine* = ð, or *g*, a change either of the final flat consonant, or of the sharp *s* affixed, was *not a matter of choice but of necessity;* the combinations *abs, avs, ads, aðs, ags*, being unpronounceable.

b. Whether the first of the two mutes should be accommodated to the second (*aps, afs, ats, aþs, aks*), or the second to the first (*abz, avz, adz, aðz, agz*), is determined by *the habit of the particular language* in question; and, with a few *apparent* exceptions it is the rule of the English language to accommodate the second sound to the first, and not *vice versâ*.

c. Such combinations as *peas, trees, hills, hens*, &c., (the *s* preserving its original power, and being sounded as is written *peace, treece, hillce, hence*), being pronounceable, the change from *s* to *z*, in words so ending, is *not* a matter determined by the necessity of the case, but by the habit of the English language.

d. Although the vast majority of our plurals ends, not in *s*, but in *z*, the original addition was not *z*, but *s*. This we infer from three facts: 1. From the spelling; 2. from the fact of the sound of *z* being either rare or non-existent in Anglo-Saxon; 3. from the sufficiency of the causes to bring about the change.

It may now be seen that some slight variations in the form of our plurals are either mere points of orthography, or else capable of being explained on very simple euphonic principles.

§ 200. *Boxes, churches, judges, lashes, kisses, blazes, princes.*—Here there is the addition, not of the mere letter *s*, but of the syllable -*es*. As *s* cannot be immediately added to *s*, the intervention of a vowel becomes necessary; and that all the words whose plural is formed in -*es* really end either in the sounds of *s*, or in the allied sounds of *z*, *sh*, or *zh*, may be seen by analysis; since *x* = *ks*, *ch* = *tsh*, and *j* or *ge* = *dzh*, whilst *ce*, in *prince*, is a mere point of orthography for *s*.

Monarchs, heresiarchs.—Here the *ch* equals not *tsh*, but *k*; so that there is no need of being told that they do not follow the analogy of *church*, &c.

Cargoes, echoes.—From *cargo* and *echo*, with the addition of *e*; an orthographical expedient for the sake of denoting the length of the vowel *o*.

Beauty, beauties; key, keys.—Like the word *cargoes*, &c., these forms are points, not of etymology, but of orthography.

Pence.—The peculiarity of this word consists in having a *flat* liquid followed by the sharp sibilant *s* (spelt *ce*), contrary to the rule given above. In the first place, it is a contracted form from *pennies;* in the second place, its sense is collective rather than plural; in the third place, the use of the sharp sibilant *lene* distinguishes it from *pens*, sounded *penz*. That its sense is *collective* rather than *plural*, we learn from the word *sixpence*, which, compared with *sixpences*, is no plural, but a singular form.

Dice.—In respect to its form, peculiar for the reason that *pence* is peculiar.—We find the sound of *s* after a vowel, where that of *z* is expected. This distinguishes *dice* for play, from *dies* (*diz*) for coining. *Dice*, perhaps, like *pence*, is collective rather than plural.

In *geese*, *lice*, and *mice*, we have, apparently, the same phenomenon as in *dice*, viz., a sharp sibilant (*s*) where a *flat* one (*z*) is expected. The *s*, however, in these words is not the sign of the plural, but the last letter of the original word.

Alms.—This is no true plural form. The *s* belongs to the original word, Anglo-Saxon, *almesse;* Greek, ἐλεημοσύνη; just as the *s* in *goose* does. How far the word, although a true singular in its form, may have a collective signification, and require its verb to be plural, is a point not of etymology, but of syntax. The same is the case with the word *riches*, from the French *richesse*. In *riches* the last syllable being sounded as *ez*, increases its liability to pass for a plural.

News, means, pains.—These, the reverse of *alms* and *riches*, are true plural forms. How far, in sense, they are singular is a point not of etymology, but of syntax.

Mathematics, metaphysics, politics, ethics, optics, physics.—The following is an exhibition of my hypothesis respecting these words, to which I invite the reader's criticism. All the words in point are of Greek origin, and all are derived from a Greek adjective. Each is the name of some department of study, of some art, or of some science. As the words are Greek, so also are the sciences which they denote, either of Greek origin, or else such as flourished in Greece. Let the arts and sciences of Greece be expressed in Greek, rather by a substantive and an adjective combined, than by a simple substantive; for instance, let it be the habit of the language to say *the musical art*, rather than *music*. Let the Greek for *art* be a word in the feminine gender; *e. g.*, τέχνη (*tekhnæ*), so that the *musical art* be ἡ μουσίκη τέχνη (*hæ mousikæ tekhnæ*). Let, in the progress of language (as was actually the case in Greece), the article and substantive be omitted, so that, for the *musical art*, or for *music*, there stand only the feminine adjective, μουσίκη. Let there be, upon a given art or science, a series of books, or treatises; the Greek for *book*, or *treatise*, being a neuter substantive, βίβλιον (*biblion*). Let the substantive meaning *treatise* be, in the course of language, omitted, so that whilst the science of physics is called φυσίκη (*fysikæ*), *physic*, from ἡ φυσίκη τέχνη, a series of treatises (or even chapters) upon the science shall be called φύσικα (*fysika*) or *physics*. Now all this was what happened in Greece. The science was denoted by a feminine adjective singular, as φυσίκη (*fysicæ*), and the treatises upon it, by the neuter adjective plural, as φύσικα (*fysika*). The treatises of Aristotle are generally so named. To apply this, I conceive, that in the middle ages a science of Greek origin might have its name drawn from two sources, *viz.*, from the name of the art or science, or from the name of the books wherein it was treated. In the first case it had a singular form, as *physic, logic*; in the second place a plural form, as *mathematics, metaphysics, optics*.

In what number these words, having a collective sense, require their verbs to be, is a point of syntax.

§ 201. The plural form *children* (*child-er-en*) requires particular notice.

In the first place it is a double plural; the *-en* being the *-en* in *oxen*, whilst the simpler form *child-er* occurs in the old English, and in certain provincial dialects.

Now, what is the *-er* in *child-er*?

In Icelandic, no plural termination is commoner than that in *-r*; as *geisl-ar* = *flashes*, *tung-ur* = *tongues*, &c. Nevertheless, it is not the Icelandic that explains the plural form in question.

Besides the word *childer*, we collect from the Old High German the following forms in *-r*:—

Hus-ir,	*Houses*,
Chalp-ir,	*Calves*,
Lemp-ir,	*Lambs*,
Plet-ir,	*Blades of grass*,
Eig-ir,	*Eggs*,

and others, the peculiarity of which is the fact of their all being *of the neuter gender*.

Now, the theory respecting this form which is propounded by Grimm is as follows:—

1. The *-r* represents an earlier *-s*.

2. Which was, originally, no sign of a plural number, but merely a neuter derivative affix, common to the singular as well as to the plural number.

3. In this form it appears in the Mœso-Gothic: *ag-is* = *fear* (whence *ague* = *shivering*), *hat-is* = *hate*, *riqv-is* = *smoke* (*reek*). In none of these words is the *-s* radical, and in none is it limited to the singular number.

To these doctrines, it should be added, that the reason why a singular derivational affix should become the sign of the plural number, lies, most probably, in the *collective* nature of the words in which it occurs: *Husir* = *a collection of houses*, *eiger* = *a collection of eggs*, *eggery* or *cyry*. In words like *yeoman-r-y* and *Jew-r-y*, the *-r* has, probably, the same origin, and is *collective*.

In Wicliffe we find the form *lamb-r-en*, which is to *lamb* as *children* is to *child*.

§ 202. *The form in -en.*—In the Anglo-Saxon no termination of the plural number is more common than *-n: tungan*, tongues; *steorran*, stars. Of this termination we have evident remains in the words *oxen, hosen, shoon, eyne*, words more or less antiquated. This, perhaps, is *no* true plural. In *welk-in* = *the clouds*, the original singular form is lost.

§ 203. *Men, feet, teeth, mice, lice, geese.*—In these we have some of the oldest words in the language. If these were, to a certainty, true plurals, we should have an appearance somewhat corresponding to the so-called *weak* and *strong* tenses of verbs; *viz.*, one series of plurals formed by a change of the vowel, and another by the addition of the sibilant. The word *kye*, used in Scotland for *cows*, is of the same class. The list in Anglo-Saxon of words of this kind is different from that of the present English.

Sing.	*Plur.*	
Freónd	Frý'nd	*Friends.*
Feónd	Fynd	*Foes.*
Niht	Niht	*Nights.*
Bóc	Béc	*Books.*
Burh	Byrig	*Burghs.*
Bróc	Bréc	*Breeches.*
Turf	Tý'rf	*Turves.*

§ 204. *Brethren.*—Here there are two changes. 1. The alteration of the vowel. 2. The addition of *-en*. Mr. Guest quotes the forms *brethre* and *brothre* from the Old English. The sense is collective rather than plural.

Peasen = *pulse.*—As *children* is a double form of one

sort ($r + en$), so is *peasen* a double form of another ($s + en$); *pea, pea-s, pea-s-en*. Wallis speaks to the *singular* power of the form in *-s*;—"Dicunt nonnulli *a pease*, pluraliter *peasen*; at melius, singulariter *a pea*, pluraliter *pease*."—P. 77. He might have added, that, theoretically, *pease* was the proper singular form; as shown by the Latin *pis-um*.

Pullen = poultry.

<blockquote>
Lussurioso.—What? three-and-twenty years in law?

Vendice.—I have known those who have been five-and-fifty, and all about *pullen* and pigs.—"Revenger's Tragedy," iv. 1.
</blockquote>

If this were a plural form, it would be a very anomalous one. The *-en*, however, is no more a sign of the plural than is the *-es* in *rich-es* (*richesse*.) The proper form is in *-ain* or *-eyn*.

<blockquote>
A false theefe,

That came like a false fox, my *pullain* to kill and mischeefe.

"Gammer Gurton's Needle," v. 2.
</blockquote>

Chickens.—A third variety of the double inflection ($en + s$), with the additional peculiarity of the form *chicken* being used, at present, almost exclusively in the singular number, although, originally, it was, probably, the plural of *chick*. So Wallis considered it:—"At olim etiam per *-en* vel *-yn* formabant pluralia; quorum pauca admodum adhuc retinemus. Ut, *an ox*, *a chick*, pluralitur *oxen, chicken* (sunt qui dicunt in singulari *chicken*, et in plurali *chickens*)." *Chick, chick-en, chick-en-s.*

Fern.—According to Wallis the *-n* in *fer-n* is the *-en* in *oxen*, in other words a plural termination:—"A *fere* (*filix*) pluraliter *fern* (verum nunc plerumque *fern* utroque numero dicitur, sed et in plurali *ferns*); nam *fere* et *feres* prope obsoleta sunt." Subject to this view, the word *fer-n-s* would exhibit the same phenomenon as the word *chicke n-s.* It is doubtful, however, whether Wallis's view be correct. A reason for believing the *-n* to be radical is presented by the Anglo-Saxon form *fearn,* and the Old High German, *varam.*

Women.—Pronounced *wimmen,* as opposed to the singular form *woomman.* Probably an instance of accommodation.

Houses.—Pronounced *houz-ez.* The same peculiarity in the case of *s* and *z,* as occurs between *f* and *v* in words like *life, lives,* &c.

Paths, youths.—Pronounced *padhz, yoodhz.* The same peculiarity in the case of þ and ð, as occurs between s and z in the words *house, houses.* "Finita in *f* plerumque alleviantur in plurali numero, substituendo *v ;* ut *wife, wives,* &c. Eademque alleviatio est etiam in *s* et *th,* quamvis retento charactere, in *house, cloth, path.*"

§ 205. The words sounded *houz-ez, padh-z, yoodh-z,* taken along with the extract from Wallis, lead us to an important class of words.—§ 199 *b.*

§ 206. Certain words ending in *f,* like *loaf, wife,* &c.

The regular plural of these would be *loafs, wifes,* pronounced *loafce, wifce,* &c.

But this is not the case. The sound added to the final *f* is the sound of *z,* not that of *s.*

And the plurals are sounded *loavz, wivz* (*wivez, weivz*).

Furthermore, the sound of the final *f* is changed to that of *v ;* in other words, the *first* of the two letters is accommodated to the second, in violation to the rule of § 199 *b.*

Can this be explained? Perhaps it can. In the Swedish language the letter *f* has the sound of *v ;* so that *staf* is sounded *stav.*

Again, in the allied languages the words in question

end in the *flat* (not the *sharp*) mute,—*weib, laub, calb, halb, stab*, &c. = *wife, leaf, calf, half, staff.*

This makes it probable that, originally, the *f* in *wife, loaf*, &c., was sounded as *v;* so that the singular forms were *wive, loav.*

If so, the *plural is* perfectly normal; it being the *singular* form on which the irregularity lies.

CHAPTER IV.

ON THE CASES.

§ 207. The extent to which there are, in the English language, cases, depends on the meaning which we attach to the word case. In the term *a house of a father*, the idea expressed by the words *of a father*, is an idea of relation between them and the word *house*. This idea is an idea of property or possession. The relation between the words *father* and *house* may be called the *possessive* relation. This relation, or connexion, between the two words, is expressed by the preposition *of*.

In the term *a father's house*, the idea is, there or thereabouts, the same; the relation or connexion between the two words being the same. The expression, however, differs. In *a father's house* the relation, or connexion, is expressed, not by a preposition, but by a change of form, *father* becoming *father's*.

He gave the house to a father.—Here the words *father* and *house* stand in another sort of relationship, the relationship being expressed by the preposition *to*. The idea *to a father* differs from the idea *of a father*, in being expressed in one way only; *viz.*, by the preposition. There is no second mode of expressing it by a change of form, as was done with *father's*.

The father taught the child.—Here there is neither preposition nor change of form. The connexion between the words *father* and *child* is expressed by the arrangement only.

§ 208. Now if the relation alone between two words constitute a case, the words *a child, to a father, of a father,* and *father's*, are all equally cases; of which one may be called the accusative, another the dative, a third the genitive, and so on.

Perhaps, however, the relationship alone does not constitute a case. Perhaps there is a necessity of either the addition of a preposition (as in *of a father*), or of a change in form (as in *father's*). In this case (although *child* be not so) *father's, of a father,* and *to a father,* are all equally cases.

Now it has long been remarked, that if the use of a preposition constitute a case, there must be as many cases in a language as there are prepositions, and that "*above a man, beneath a man, beyond a man, round about a man, within a man, without a man,* shall be cases as well as *of a man, to a man,* and *with a man.*"

§ 209. For etymological purposes, therefore, it is necessary to limit the meaning of the word case; and, as a sort of definition, it may be laid down that *where there is no change of form there is no case*. With this remark, the English language may be compared with the Latin.

		Latin.	English.
Sing.	Nom.	Pater	a father.
	Gen.	Patris	a father's.
	Dat.	Patri	to a father.
	Acc.	Patrem	a father.
	Abl.	Patre	from a father.

Here, since in the Latin language there are five changes of form, whilst in English there are but *two*, there are (as far, at least, as the word *pater* and *father* are concerned) three more cases in Latin than in English.

It does not, however, follow that because in the particular word *father* we have but two cases, there may not be other words wherein there are more than two.

§ 210. Neither does it follow, that because two words may have the *same form* they are necessarily in the *same case;* a remark which leads to the distinction between *a real and an accidental identity of form.*

In the language of the Anglo-Saxons the genitive cases of the words *smið, ende,* and *dæg,* were respectively, *smiðes, endes,* and *dæges;* whilst the nominative plurals were, *smiðas, endas,* and *dægas.*

But when a change took place, by which the vowel of the last syllable in each word was ejected, the result was, that the forms of the genitive singular and the nominative plural, originally different, became one and the same; so that the identity of the two cases is an accident.

This fact relieves the English grammarian from a difficulty. The nominative plural and the genitive singular are, in the present language of England, identical; the apostrophe in *father's* being a mere matter of orthography. However, there was *once* a difference. This modifies the previous statement, which may now stand thus:— *for a change of case there must be a change of form existing or presumed.*

§ 211. *The number of our cases and the extent of language over which they spread.*—In the English language there is undoubtedly a *nominative* case. This occurs in substantives, adjectives, and pronouns (*father, good, he*) equally. It is found in both numbers.

§ 212. *Accusative.*—Some call this the *objective* case. The words *him* and *them* (whatever they may have been

THE CASES. 157

originally) are now (to a certain extent) true accusatives. The accusative case is found in pronouns only. *Thee, me, us,* and *you* are, to a certain extent, true accusatives. These are accusative thus far: 1. They are not derived from any other case. 2. They are distinguished from the forms *I, my,* &c. 3. Their meaning is accusative. Nevertheless, they are only imperfect accusatives. They have no sign of case, and are distinguished by negative characters only.

One word in the present English is probably a true accusative in the strict sense of the term, *viz.,* the word *twain = two.* The *-n* in *twai-n* is the *-n* in *hine = him* and *hwone = whom.* This we see from the following inflection:—

	Neut.	Masc.	Fem.
N. and Acc.	Twá,	Twégen,	Twá.
Abl. and Dat.		Twäm,	Twæ'm.
Gen.		Twegra,	Twega.

Although nominative as well as accusative, I have little doubt as to the original character of *twégen* being accusative. The *-n* is by no means radical; besides which, it *is* the sign of an accusative case, and is *not* the sign of a nominative.

§ 213. *Dative.*—In the antiquated word *whilom* (*at times*), we have a remnant of the old dative in *-m.* The *sense* of the word is abverbial; its form, however, is that of a dative case.

§ 214. *Genitive.*—Some call this the possessive case. It is found in substantives and pronouns (*father's, his*), but not in adjectives. It is formed like the nominative plural, by the addition of the lene sibilant (*father, fathers; buck, bucks*); or if the word end in *-s,* by that of *-es* (*boxes, judges,* &c.) It is found in both numbers:

the men's hearts; the children's bread. In the plural number, however, it is rare; so rare, indeed, that wherever the plural ends in *s* (as it almost always does), there is no genitive. If it were not so, we should have such words as *fatherses, foxeses, princeses,* &c.

§ 215. *Instrumental.*—The following extracts from Rask's "Anglo-Saxon Grammar," teach us that there exist in the present English two powers of the word spelt *t-h-e*, or of the so-called definite article—"The demonstrative pronouns are þæt, se, seó (*id, is, ea*), which are also used for the article; and þis, þes, þeós (*hoc, hic, hæc*). They are thus declined:—

		Neut.	Masc.	Fem.	Neut.	Masc.	Fem.
Sing	N.	þæt	se	seó	þis	þes	þeós.
	A.	þæt	þone	þá	þis	þisne	þás.
	Abl.	þy'	þæ're		þise	þisse	
	D.	þám	þæ're		þisum	þisse.	
	G.	þæs	þæ're		þises	þisse.	
Plur. N. and A.		þá			þás.		
Abl. and D.		þám			þisum.		
G.		þára.			þissa.		

"The indeclinable þe is often used instead of þæt, se, seó, in all cases, but especially with a relative signification, and, in later times, as an article. Hence the English article *the*.

"þy' seems justly to be received as a proper *ablativus instrumenti*, as it occurs often in this character, even in the masculine gender; as, *mid, þy' áþe = with that oath* ("Inæ Leges," 53). And in the same place in the dative, *on þæ'm áþe = in that oath.*"—Pp. 56, 57.

Hence the *the* that has originated out of the Anglo-Saxon þy is one word; whilst the *the* that has originated out of the Anglo-Saxon þe, another. The latter is the common article: the former the *the* in expressions like *all the more, all the better* = *more by all that, better by all that*, and the Latin phrases *eo majus, eo melius*.

That *why* is in the same case with the instrumental *the* (= þy) may be seen from the following Anglo-Saxon inflexion of the interrogative pronoun:—

	Neut.	*Masc.*
N.	Hwæt	Hwá
A.	Hwæt	Hwone (hwæne)
Abl.		Hwí
D.		Hwám (hwæ'm)
G.		Hwæs.

Hence, then, in *the* and *why* we have instrumental ablatives, or, simply, *instrumentals*.

§ 216. *The determination of cases.*—How do we determine cases? In other words, why do we call *him* and *them* accusatives rather than datives or genitives? By one of two means; *viz.*, either by the *sense* or the *form*.

Suppose that in the English language there were ten thousand dative cases and as many accusatives. Suppose, also, that all the dative cases ended in *-m*, and all the accusatives in some other letter. It is very evident that, whatever might be the meaning of the words *him* and *them* their form would be dative. In this case the meaning being accusatives, and the form dative, we should doubt which test to take.

My own opinion is, that it would be convenient to determine cases by the *form* of the word *alone*; so that, even if a word had a dative sense only once, where it had an accusative sense ten thousand times, such a word should be said to be in the dative case. Now the words *him* and *them* (to which we may add *whom*) were once dative cases;* -*m* in Anglo-Saxon being the sign of the dative case. In the time of the Anglo-Saxons their sense coincided with their form. At present they are dative forms with an accusative meaning. Still, as the word *give* takes after it a dative case, we have, even now, in the sentence, *give it him, give it them*, remnants of the old dative sense. To say *give it to him, to them*, is unnecessary and pedantic: neither do I object to the expression, *whom shall I give it?* If ever the *formal* test become generally recognised and consistently adhered to, *him, them*, and *whom* will be called datives with a latitude of meaning; and then the only true and unequivocal accusatives in the English language will be the forms *you, thee, us, me*, and *twain*.

§ 217. *Analysis of cases.*—In the word *children's* we are enabled to separate the word into three parts. 1. The root *child*. 2. The plural signs *r* and *en*. 3. The sign of the genitive case, *s*. In this case the word is said to be analysed, since we not only take it to pieces, but also give the respective powers of each of its elements; stating which denotes the case, and which the number. Although it is too much to say that the analysis of every case of every number can be thus effected, it ought always to be attempted.

§ 218. *The true nature of the genitive form in 's.*—It is a common notion that the genitive form *father's* is contracted from *father his*. The expression in our liturgy, *for Jesus Christ his sake*, which is merely a pleonastic one, is the only foundation for this assertion. As the idea, however, is not only one of the commonest, but also one of the greatest errors in etymology, the following

* This explains the words, "Whatever they may have been originally," and "to a certain extent," in § 212.

three statements are given for the sake of contradiction to it.

1. The expression the *Queen's Majesty* is not capable of being reduced to the *Queen his Majesty*.

2. In the form *his* itself, the *s* has precisely the power that it has in *father's*, &c. Now *his* cannot be said to arise out of *he + his*.

3. In the Slavonic, Lithuanic, and classical tongues, the genitive ends in *s*, just as it does in English; so that even if the words *father his* would account for the English word *father's*, it would not account for the Sanskrit genitive *pad-as*, of a foot; the Zend *dughdhar-s*, of a daughter; the Lithuanic *dugter-s* · the Greek ὀδόντ-ος; the Latin *dent-is*, &c.

CHAPTER V.

THE PERSONAL PRONOUNS.

§ 219. *I, we, us, me, thou, ye.*—These constitute the true personal pronouns. From *he, she,* and *it,* they differ in being destitute of gender.

These latter words are demonstrative rather than personal, so that there are in English true personal pronouns for the first two persons only.

§ 220. The usual declension of the personal pronouns is exceptionable. *I* and *me, thou* and *ye,* stand in no etymological relations to each other. The true view of the words is, that they are not irregular but defective. *I* has no *oblique,* and *me* no nominative case. And so it is with the rest.

§ 221. *You.*—As far as the practice of the present mode of speech is concerned, the word *you* is a *nominative* form; since we say *you move, you are moving, you were speaking.*

Why should it not be treated as such? There is no absolute reason why it should not. The Anglo-Saxon form for *you* was eow, for *ye,* ge. Neither bears any sign of case at all, so that, form for form, they are equally and indifferently nominative and accusative. Hence, it, perhaps, is more logical to say that a certain form (*you*), is used *either* as a nominative or accusative, than to say that the accusative case is used instead of a nominative. It is clear that *you* can be used instead of *ye* only so far as it is nominative in power.

Ye.—As far as the evidence of such expressions as *get on with ye* is concerned, the word *ye* is an accusative form. The reasons why it should or should not be treated as such are involved in the previous paragraph.

§ 222. *Me.*—carrying out the views just laid down, and admitting *you* to be a nominative, or *quasi*-nominative case, we may extend the reasoning to the word *me*, and call it also a secondary or equivocal nominative; inasmuch as such phrases as *it is me* it = *is I* are common.

Now to call such expressions incorrect English is to assume the point. No one says that *c'est moi* is bad French, and that *c'est je* is good.

§ 223. *Caution.*—Observe, however, that the expression *it is me* = *it is I* will not justify the use of *it is him*, *it is her* = *it is he* and *it is she*. *Me, ye, you*, are what may be called *indifferent forms, i. e.*, nominative as much as accusative, and accusative as much as nominative. *Him* and *her*, on the other hand, are not indifferent. The *-m* and *-r* are respectively the signs of cases other than the nominative.

§ 224. Again: the reasons which allow the form *you* to be considered as a nominative plural, on the strength of its being used for *ye*, will not allow it to be considered a nominative singular on the strength of its being used for *thou*.

§ 225. In phrases like *you are speaking*, &c., even when applied to a single individual, the idea is really plural; in other words, the courtesy consists in treating *one* person as *more than one*, and addressing him as such, rather than in using a plural form in a singular sense. It is certain that, grammatically considered, *you = thou* is a plural, since the verb with which it agrees is plural:—*you are speaking*, not *you art speaking*.

CHAPTER VI.

ON THE TRUE REFLECTIVE PRONOUN IN THE GOTHIC LANGUAGES, AND ON ITS ABSENCE IN ENGLISH.

§ 226. A TRUE reflective pronoun is wanting in English. In other words, there are no equivalents to the Latin forms *sui, sibi, se.*

Nor yet are there any equivalents to the forms *suus, sua, suum:* since *his* and *her* are the equivalents to *ejus* and *illius*, and are not adjectives but genitive cases.

At the first view, this last sentence seems unnecessary. It might seem superfluous to state, that, if there were no such primitive form as *se*, there could be no such secondary form as *suus.*

Such, however, is not the case. *Suus* might exist in the language, and yet *se* be absent; in other words, the derivative form might have continued whilst the original one had become extinct.

Such is really the case with the *Old* Frisian. The reflective personal form, the equivalent to *se*, is lost, whilst the reflective possessive form, the equivalent to *suus*, is found. In the *Modern* Frisian, however, both forms are lost.

CHAPTER VII.

THE DEMONSTRATIVE PRONOUNS, &C.

§ 227. The demonstrative pronouns are, 1. *He, it.* 2. *She.* 3. *This, that.* 4. *The.*

He, she, and *it,* generally looked on as personal, are here treated as demonstrative pronouns, for the following reasons.

1. The personal pronouns form an extremely natural class, if the pronouns of the two first persons be taken by themselves. This is not the case if they be taken along with *he, it,* and *she.*

2. The idea expressed by *he, it,* and *she* is naturally that of demonstrativeness. In the Latin language *is, ea, id; ille, illa, illud; hic, hæc, hoc,* are demonstrative pronouns in sense, as well as in declension.

3. The plural forms *they, them,* in the present English, are the plural forms of the root of *that,* a true demonstrative pronoun; so that even if *he, she,* and *it* could be treated as personal pronouns, *they* could not.

4. The word *she* has grown out of the Anglo-Saxon *seó.* Now *seó* was in Anglo-Saxon the feminine form of the definite article; the definite article itself being originally a demonstrative pronoun.

§ 228. Compared with the Anglo-Saxon the present English stands as follows:—

She.—The Anglo-Saxon form *heó,* being lost to the language, is replaced by the feminine article *seó.*

DEMONSTRATIVE PRONOUNS.

§ 229. *Her.*—This is a case, not of the present *she*, but of the Anglo-Saxon *heó:* so that *she* may be said to be defective in the oblique cases, and *her* to be defective in the nominative.

Him.—A dative form, which has replaced the Anglo-Saxon *hine.* When used as a dative, it was neuter as well as masculine.

His.—Originally neuter as well as masculine. Now as a neuter, replaced by *its*—"et quidem ipsa vox *his*, ut et interrogativum *whose*, nihil aliud sunt quam *hee's, who's*, ubi *s* omnino idem præstat quod in aliis possessivis. Similiter autem *his* pro *hee's* eodem errore quo nonnunquam *bin* pro *been;* item *whose* pro *who's* eodem errore quo *done, gone, knowne, growne,* &c., pro *doen, goen, knowen*, vel *do'n, go'n, know'n, grow'n;* utrobique contra analogiam linguæ; sed usu defenditur."—Wallis, c. v.

It.—Changed from the Anglo-Saxon *hit*, by the ejection of *h*. The *t* is no part of the original word, but a sign of the neuter gender, forming it regularly from *he*. The same neuter sign is preserved in the Latin *id* and *illud*.

Its.—In the course of time the nature of the neuter sign *t*, in *it*, the form being found in but a few words, became misunderstood. Instead of being looked on as an affix, it passed for part of the original word. Hence was formed from *it* the anomalous genitive *its* superseding the Saxon *his*. The same was the case with—

Hers.—The *r* is no part of the original word, but the sign of the dative case. These formations are of value in the history of cases.

§ 230. *Theirs.*—In the same predicament with *hers* and *its;* either the case of an adjective, or a case formed from a case.

Than or *then,* and *there.*—Although now adverbs,

they were once demonstrative pronouns, in a certain case and in a certain gender, viz., *than* and *then* masculine accusative and singular, *there* feminine dative and singular.

§ 231. An exhibition of the Anglo-Saxon declension is the best explanation of the English. Be it observed, that the cases marked in italics are found in the present language.

I.
Se, seó (= she).

Of this word we meet two forms only, both of the singular number, and both in the nominative case; viz., masc., *se;* fem. *seó* (= the). The neuter gender and the other cases of the article were taken from the pronoun þæt (= that).

II.
þæt (= that, the), and þis (= this).

	Neut.	Masc.	Fem.	Neut.	Masc.	Fem.
Sing. Nom.	þæt	—	—	þis	þes	þeós.
Acc.	þæt	þone	þá	þis	þisne	þás.
Abl.	þy	þy	þæ're.	þise	þise	þisse.
Dat.	þám	þám	þæ're.	þisum	þisum	þisse.
Gen.	þæs	þæs	þæ're.	þises	þises	þisse.

Plur. Nom. Acc.	þá.		þás.
Abl. Dat.	þám.		þisum.
Gen.	á ra.		þissa.

III.
Hit (= it), (he = he), heó (= she).

Sing. Nom.	hit	he	heó.
Acc.	hit	hine	hí.
Dat.	him	him	hire.
Gen.	his	his	hire.

Plur. Nom. Acc.	hí.
Dat.	him (heom).
Gen.	hira (heora).

IV.
þe (the)—Undeclined, and used for all cases and genders.

§ 232. *These.*—Here observe—

1st. That the *s* is no inflection, but a radical part of the word, like the *s* in *geese*.

2nd. That the Anglo-Saxon form is þás.

These facts create difficulties in respect to the word *these.* Mr. Guest's view is, perhaps, the best; *viz.*, that the plural element of the word is the final *-e*, and that this *-e* is the old English and Anglo-Saxon adjective plural; so that *thes-e* is formed from *this*, as *gode* (= *boni*) is from *god* (= *bonus*).

The nominative plural in the Old English adjective ended in *e-*; as,

Singular.			Plural.		
M.	*F.*	*N.*	*M.*	*F.*	*N.*
God,	god,	god,		gode.	

In Old English MSS. this plural in *-e* is general. It occurs not only in adjectives and pronouns as a regular inflection, but even as a plural of the genitive *his*, that word being treated as a nominative singular; so that *hise* is formed from *his*, as *sui* from *suus*, or as *eji* might have been formed from *ejus;* provided that in the Latin language this last word had been mistaken for a nominative singular. The following examples are Mr. Guest's.

1. In those lay a gret multitude of *syke* men, *blinae*, crokid, and *drye*.—*Wicliffe*, Jon. v.

2. In all the orders foure is non that can
So much of dalliance and faire language,
He hadde ymade ful many a marriage—
His tippet was ay farsed ful of knives,
And pinnes for to given *faire* wives.
Chau., Prol.

3. And *al* the cuntre of Judee wente out to him, and *alle* men of Jerusalem.—*Wicliffe*, Mark i.

9

4. He ghyueth lif to *alle* men, and brething, and *alle* thingis; and made of von *al* kynde of men to inhabit on *al* the face of the erthe.— *Wicliffe*, Dedis of Apostlis, xvii.

5. That fadres sone which *alle* thinges wrought;
And *all*, that wrought is with a skilful thought,
The Gost that from the fader gan procede,
Hath souled hem.
Chau., The Second Nonnes Tale.

6. And *alle* we that ben in this aray
And maken *all* this lamentation,
We losten *alle* our husbondes at that toun.
Chau., The Knightes Tales.

7. A *good* man bryngeth forth *gode* thingsis of *good* tresore.— *Wicliffe*, Matt. xii.

8. So every *good* tree maketh *gode* fruytis, but an yvel tree maketh yvel fruytes. A *good* tree may not mak yvel fruytis, neither an yvel tree may make *gode* fruytis. Every tree that maketh not *good* fruyt schal be cut down.— *Wicliffe*, Matt. vii.

9. Men loveden more darknessis than light for her werkes weren *yvele*, for ech man that doeth *yvel*, hateth the light.— *Wicliffe*, John iii.

10. And *othere* seedis felden among thornes wexen up and strangliden hem, and *othere* seedis felden into good lond and gaven fruyt, sum an hundred fold, *another* sixty fold, an *other* thritty fold, &c.— *Wicliffe*, Matt. xiii.

11. Yet the while he spake to the puple lo *his* mother and *hise* brethren stonden withoute forth.— *Wicliffe*, Mat. xii.

12. And *hise* disciplis camen and taken *his* body.— *Wicliffe*, Matt. xiv.

13. When *thise* Bretons tuo were fled out of *this* lond
Ine toke his feaute of alle, &c.
Rob Brunne, p. 3.

14. *This* is thilk disciple that bereth witnessyng of *these* thingis, and wroot them.— *Wicliffe*, John xxi.

15. Seye to us in what powers thou doist *these* thingis, and who is he that gaf to thee *this* power.— *Wicliffe*, Luke xx.

DEMONSTRATIVE PRONOUNS.

§ 233. *Those.*—Perhaps the Anglo-Saxon þá with *s* added. Perhaps the þás from þis with its power altered. Rask, in his Anglo-Saxon Grammar, writes "from þis we find, in the plural, þæs for þás. From which afterwards, with a distinction in signification, *these* and *those*." The English form *they* is illustrated by the Anglo-Saxon form ðage = þá. The whole doctrine of the forms in question has yet to assume a satisfactory shape.

The present declension of the demonstrative pronouns is as follows :—

A.
She.—Defective in the oblique cases.

B.
He.

	Masc.	Neut.	Fem.
Nom.	He	It (from *hit*)	—
Acc.	Him	It	Her.
Dat.	Him	—	Her.
Gen.	His	—	Her.
Secondary Gen.	—	Its	Hers.

No plural form.

C.
I.
That.

	Neut.	Masc.	Fem.
Sing. Nom.	That	—	—
Acc.	That	Than,* then*	—
Dat.	—	—	There.*
Instrumental		Thence.	
Plur. Nom.	...	They.†	
Acc.	...	Them.†	
Gen.	...	Their.†	
Secondary Gen.	...	Theirs.†	

* Used as adverbs.   † Used as the plurals of *he*, *she*, and *it*.

II.
Singular, This.   *Plural*, These.

III.
Those.

IV.
The—Undeclined.

CHAPTER VIII.

THE RELATIVE, INTERROGATIVE, AND CERTAIN OTHER PRONOUNS.

§ 234. In the relative and interrogative pronouns, *who, what, whom, whose,* we have, expressed by a change of form, a neuter gender, *what;* a dative case *whom;* and a genitive case, *whose:* the true power of the *s* (*viz.*, as the sign of a case) being obscured by the orthographical addition of the *e* mute.

To these may be added, 1. the adverb *why,* originally the ablative form *hvi* (*quo modo? quâ viâ?*). 2. The adverb *where,* a feminine dative, like *there.* 3. *When,* a masculine accusative (in Anglo-Saxon *hwæne*), and analogous to *then.*

The two sounds in the Danish words *hvi, hvad,* &c., and the two sounds in the English, *what, when* (Anglo-Saxon, *hwæt, hwæne*) account for the forms *why* and *how.* In the first the *w* alone, in the second the *h* alone, is sounded. The Danish for *why* is *hvi,* pronounced *vi.*

§ 235. The following remarks (some of them not strictly etymological) apply to a few of the remaining pronouns.

Same.—Wanting in Anglo-Saxon, where it was replaced by the word *ylca, ylce.* Probably derived from the Norse.

Self.—In *myself, thyself, herself, ourselves, yourselves,* a substantive (or with a substantival power), and preceded by a genitive case. In *himself* and *themselves* an adjective (or with an adjectival power), and preceded by an accusative case. *Itself* is equivocal, since we cannot say whether its elements are *it* and *self*, or *its* and *self;* the *s* having been dropped in utterance. It is very evident that either the form like *himself*, or the form like *thyself*, is exceptionable; in other words, that the use of the word is inconsistent. As this inconsistency is as old as the Anglo-Saxons, the history of the word gives us no elucidation. In favour of the forms like *myself* (*self* being a substantive), are the following facts:—

1. The plural word *selves*, a substantival, and not an adjectival form.

2. The Middle High German phrases *min lip, din lip, my body, thy body*, equivalent in sense to *myself, thyself*.

3. The circumstance that if *self* be dealt with as a substantive, such phrases as *my own self, his own great self*, &c., can be used; whereby the language is a gainer.

" Vox *self*, pluraliter *selves*, quamvis etiam pronomen a quibusdam censeatur (quoniam ut plurimum per Latinum *ipse* redditur), est tamen plane nomen substantivum, cui quidem vix aliquod apud Latinos substantivum respondet; proxime tamen accedet vox *persona* vel *propria persona* ut *my self, thy self, our selves, your selves*, &c. (*ego ipse, tu ipse, nos ipsi, vos ipsi*, &c.), ad verbum *mea persona, tua persona*, &c. Fateor tamen *himself, itself, themselves*, vulgo dici pro *his-self, its-self, theirselves;* at (interposito *own*) *his own self*, &c., *ipsius propria persona*, &c."—Wallis. c. vii.

4. The fact that many persons actually say *hisself* and *theirselves*.

Whit.—As in the phrase *not a whit.* This enters in the compound pronouns *aught* and *naught.*

One.—As in the phrase *one does so and so.* From the French *on.* Observe that this is from the Latin *homo,* in Old French *hom, om.* In the Germanic tongues *man* is used in the same sense: *man sagt* = *one says* = *on dit.* *One,* like *self* and *other,* is so far a substantive, that it is inflected. Gen. sing. *one's own self:* plural, *my wife and little ones are well.*

Derived pronouns.—*Any,* in Anglo-Saxon, *ænig.* In Old High German we have *einic* = *any,* and *einac* = *single.* In Anglo-Saxon *ânega* means *single.* In Middle High German *einec* is always single. In New High German *einig* means, 1. *a certain person* (*quidam*), 2. *agreeing; einzig,* meaning *single.* In Dutch *enech* has both meanings. This indicates the word *án, one,* as the root of the word in question.

Compound pronouns.—*Which,* as has been already stated more than once, is most incorrectly called the neuter of *who.* Instead of being a neuter, it is a compound word. The adjective *leiks, like,* is preserved in the Mœso-Gothic words *galeiks* and *missaleiks.* In Old High German the form is *lih,* in Anglo-Saxon *lic.* Hence we have Mœso-Gothic *hvêleiks;* Old High German, *huëlih;* Anglo-Saxon, *huilic* and *hvile;* Old Frisian, *hwelik;* Danish, *hvilk-en;* German, *welch;* Scotch, *whilk;* English, *which.* The same is the case with—

1. *Such.*—Mœso-Gothic, *svaleiks;* Old High German, *sôlih;* Old Saxon, *sulic;* Anglo-Saxon, *svile;* German, *solch;* English, *such.* Rask's derivation of the Anglo-Saxon *svile* from *swa-ylc,* is exceptionable.

2. *Thilk.*—An old English word, found in the provincial dialects, as *thick, thuck, theck,* and hastily derived by Tyrwhitt, Ritson, and Weber, from *së ylca,* is found

in the following forms: Mœso-Gothic, *þéleiks;* Norse, *þvilikr.*

3. *Ilk.*—Found in the Scotch, and always preceded by the article; *the ilk,* or *that ilk,* meaning *the same.* In Anglo-Saxon this word is *ylca,* preceded also by the article *se ylca, seó ylce, þæt ylce.* In English, as seen above, the word is replaced by *same.* In no other Gothic dialect does it occur. According to Grimm, this is no simple word, but a compound one, of which some such wore as *ei* is the first, and *lic* the second element.

Aught.—In Mœso-Gothic is found the particle, *aiv, ever,* but only in negative propositions; *ni* (*not*) preceding it. Its Old High German form is *éo, io;* in Middle High German, *ie;* in New High German, *je;* in Old Saxon, *io;* in Anglo-Saxon, *â;* in Norse, *æ.* Combined with this particle the word *whit* (*thing*) gives the following forms: Old High German, *éowiht;* Anglo-Saxon, *âwiht;* Old Frisian, *âwet;* English *aught.* The word *naught* is *aught* preceded by the negative particle.

Each.—The particle *gi* enters, like the particle in the composition of pronouns. Old High German, *éogaliher,* every one; *éocalih,* all; Middle High German, *iegelich;* New High German, *jeglich;* Anglo-Saxon, *ælc;* English, *each;* the *l* being dropped, as in *which* and *such. Ælc,* as the original of the English *each* and the Scotch *ilka,** must by no means be confounded with the word *ylce, the same.*

Every in Old English, *everich, everech, everilk one,* is *ælc,* preceded by the particle *ever.* (Grimm. D. G. iii. 54.)

Either.—Old High German, *éogahuédar;* Middle High German, *iegewéder;* Anglo-Saxon, *æghvæðer, ægðer;* Old Frisian, *eider.*

---
* Different from *ilk.*

Neither.—The same with the negative article prefixed. *Neither : either : : naught : aught.*

§ 236. *Other, whether.*—These words, although derived forms, being simpler than some that have preceded, might fairly have been dealt with before. They make, however, a transition from the present to the succeeding chapter, and so find a place here.

A. *First,* it may be stated of them that the idea which they express is not that *of one out of many,* but that of *one out of two.*

1. In Sanscrit there are two forms,[a]) *kataras,* the same word as *whether,* meaning *which out of two;*[b]) *katamas, which out of many.* So also *êkateras, one out of two; êkatamas, one out of many.* In Greek the Ionic form κότερος (πότερος); in Latin, *uter, neuter, alter;* and in Mœso-Gothic, *hvathar,* have the same form and the same meaning.

2. In the Scandinavian language the word *anden,* Dano-Saxon, *annar,* Iceland. corresponds to the English word *second,* and not the German *zweite:* e. g., *Karl den Anden, Charles the Second.* Now *anthar* is the older form *of other.*

B. *Secondly,* it may be stated of them, that the termination *-er* is the same termination that we find in the comparative degree.

1. The idea expressed by the comparative degree is the comparison, not of *many* but of *two* things; *this is better than that.*

2. In all the Indo-European languages where there are pronouns in *-ter,* there is also a comparative degree in *-ter.* See next chapter.

3. As the Sanscrit form *kataras* corresponds with the comparative degree, where there is the comparison of *two things with each other;* so the word *katamas* is a super-

lative form; and in the superlative degree lies the comparison of *many* things with each other.

Hence *other* and *whether* (to which may be added *either* and *neither*) are pronouns with the comparative form.

Other has the additional peculiarity of possessing the plural form *others*. Hence, like *self*, it is, in the strictest sense, a substantival pronoun.

CHAPTER IX.

ON CERTAIN FORMS IN -ER.

§ 237. PREPARATORY to the consideration of the degrees of comparison, it is necessary to make some remarks upon a certain class of words, which, with considerable differences of signification, all agree in one fact, *viz.*, all terminate in -*er*, or *t-er*.

1. Certain pronouns, as *ei-th-er*, *n-ei-th-er*, *whe-th-er*, or *o-th-er*.

2. Certain prepositions and adverbs, as *ov-er*, *und-er*, *af-t-er*.

3. Certain adjectives, with the form of the comparative, but the power of the positive degree; as *upp-er und-er*, *inn-er*, *out-er*, *hind-er*.

4. All adjectives of the comparative degree; as *wis-er*, *strong-er*, *bett-er*, &c.

Now what is the idea common to all these words, expressed by the sign -*er*, and connecting the four divisions into one class? It is not the mere idea of comparison; although it is the comparative degree, to the expression of which the affix in question is more particularly applied. Bopp, who has best generalised the view of these forms, considers the fundamental idea to be that of *duality*. In the comparative degree we have a relation between one object and *some* other object like it, or a relation between two single elements of comparison: *A is wiser than B.* In the superlative degree we have a relation between one object and *all* others like it, or a relation between one single and one complex element of comparison: *A is wiser than B, C, D,* &c.

"As in comparatives a relation between *two,* and in superlatives a relation between *many,* lies at the bottom, it is natural that their suffixes should be transferred to other words, whose chief notion is individualised through that of duality or plurality."—"Vergleichende Grammatik," § 292, Eastwick's and Wilson's Translation.

The most important proofs of the view adduced by Bopp are,—

1. The Sanskrit form *kataras* = *which of* two *persons?* is a comparative form; whilst *katamas* = *which of more than two persons?* a superlative form. Similarly, *êkataras* = *one of two persons; êkatamas* = *one of more than two persons.*

2. The Greek forms, ἑκάτερος = *each* (or *either*) *out of two persons;* whilst ἕκαστος = *each or any out of more than two persons.*

§ 238. The more important of the specific modifications of the general idea involved in the comparison of two objects are,—

1. Contrariety: as in *inner, outer, under, upper, over.* In Latin the words for *right* and *left* end in *-er,*—*dexter, sinister.*

2. Choice in the way of an alternative; as *either, neither, whether, other.*

§ 239. *Either, neither, other, whether.*—It has just been stated that the general fundamental idea common to all these forms is that of *choice between one of two objects in the way of an alternative.* Thus far the termination *-er* in *either,* &c., is the termination *-er* in the true comparatives, *brav-er, wis-er,* &c. *Either* and *neither* are common pronouns. *Other,* like *one,* is a pronoun capable of taking the plural form of a substantive (*others*), and also that of the genitive case (*the other's money, the other's bread*). *Whether* is a pronoun in the almost obsolete form *whether* (= *which*) *of the two do you prefer*, and a conjunction in sentences like *whether will you do this or not?* The use of the form *others* is recent. " *They are taken out of the way as all other.*" —Job. " *And leave their riches for other.*"—Psalms.

CHAPTER X.

THE COMPARATIVE DEGREE.

§ 240. THERE are four leading facts here,—

1. *The older form in -s.* In English we say old-*er*, bett-*er*, sweet-*er*; in Old High German they similarly said, alt-*iro*, bets-*iro*, suats-*iro*; but in Mœso-Gothic the forms were ald-*iza*, bat-*iza*, sut-*iza*.

2. *Adverbs* are susceptible of comparison; *e.g.*—*Come as soon as you can, but do not come sooner than is convenient.*

3. The Anglo-Saxon comparison of the adverbs is different from that of the adjectives; there being one form in -*re* and -*este*, another in -*or* and -*ost* respectively. Now the first of these was the form taken by adjectives: as *se scearp-re sword* = *the sharper sword*, and *se scearp-este sword* = *the sharpest sword*. The second, on the other hand, was the form taken by adverbs: as, *se sweord scyrð scearp-or* = *the sword cuts sharper*, and *se sweord scyrð scearp-ost* = *the sword cuts sharpest*.

4. In the Anglo-Saxon, the following words exhibit a change of vowel.

Positive.	Comparative.	Superlative.	
Lang,	Lengre,	Lengest.	*Long.*
Strang,	Strengre,	Strengest.	*Strong.*
Geong,	Gyngre,	Gyngest.	*Young.*
Sceort,	Scyrtre,	Scyrtest.	*Short.*
Heáh,	Hyrre,	Hyhst.	*High.*
Eald,	Yldre,	Yldest.	*Old.*

§ 241. Now the fourth of these facts explains the present forms *elder* and *eldest*, the comparatives and superlative of *old*, besides which there are the regular forms *old-er* and *old-est;* between which there is, however, a difference in meaning—*elder* being used as a substantive, and having a plural form, *elders*.

§ 242. The abverbial forms in *-or* and *-ost*, as compared with the adjectival in *-re*, and *-este* explain the form *rather*. This rhymes to *father;* the *a* being full. Nevertheless, the positive form is *rather* meaning *quick*, *easy* = the classical root ῥαδ- in ῥάδιος. What we do *quickly* and *willingly* we do *preferably*. Now if the word *rather* were an adjective, the vowel of the comparative would be sounded as the *a* in *fate*, as it is, however, it is abverbial, and as such is properly sounded as the *a* in *father*.

The difference between the action of the small vowel in *-re*, and of the full in *-or* effects this difference, since *o* being a full vowel, it has the effect of making the *a* full also.

§ 243. The old form in *-s* will be considered, after notice has been taken of what may be called—

§ 244. *Excess of expression.*—Of this two samples have already been given: 1. in words like *songstress;* 2. in words like *children*. This may be called *excess of expression;* the feminine gender, in words like *songstress*, and the plural number, in words like *children*, being expressed twice over. In the vulgarism *betterer* for *better*, and in the antiquated forms *worser* for *worse*, and *lesser* for *less*, we have, in the case of the comparatives, as elsewhere, an excess of expression. In the old High German we have the forms *betseróro, meróro, érëréra* = *better, more, ere.*

§ 245. *Better.*—Although in the superlative form *best*

there is a slight variation from the strict form of that degree, the word *better* is perfectly regular. So far, then, from truth are the current statements that the comparison of the words *good, better*, and *best* is irregular. The inflection is not irregular, but defective. As the statement that applies to *good, better*, and *best* applies to many words besides, it will be well in this place, once for all, to exhibit it in full.

§ 246. *Difference between a sequence in logic and a sequence in etymology.*—The ideas or notions of *thou, thy, thee*, are ideas between which there is a metaphysical or logical connexion. The train of such ideas may be said to form a sequence, and such a sequence may be called a logical one.

The words *thou, thy, thee*, are words between which there is a *formal* or an *etymological* connexion. A train of such words may be called a sequence, and such a sequence may be called an etymological one.

In the case of *thou, thy, thee*, the etymological sequence tallies with the *logical* one.

The ideas of *I, my*, and *me* are also in a logical sequence: but the forms *I, my*, and *me* are not altogether in an etymological one.

In the case of *I, my, me*, the etymological sequence does *not* tally (or tallies imperfectly) with the logical one.

This is only another way of saying that between the words *I* and *me* there is no connexion in etymology.

It is also only another way of saying, that, in the oblique cases, *I*, and, in the nominative case, *me*, are *defective*.

Now the same is the case with *good, better, bad, worse*, &c. *Good* and *bad* are defective in the comparative and superlative degrees; *better* and *worse* are defective in the positive; whilst between *good* and *better*, *bad* and *worse*, there is a sequence in logic, but no sequence in etymology.

§ 247. To return, however, to the word *better;* no absolute positive degree is found in any of the allied languages, and in none of the allied languages is there found any comparative form of *good*. Its root occurs in the following adverbial forms: Mœso-Gothic, *bats;* Old High German, *pats;* Old Saxon and Anglo-Saxon, *bet;* Middle High German, *baz;* Middle Dutch, *bat, bet*.

§ 248. *Worse*.—This word is one of two things.

1. It is a positive form with a comparative sense; in which case *s* is part of the root.

2. It is a comparative degree from the positive form *wor-* (*vair,- wir-, vyr-*), in which case *s* is the *s* of the Old Mœso-Gothic inflexion preserved in this single word.

§ 249. *More*.—In Anglo-Saxon this is *mâ;* in the English of the reign of Elizabeth it is *moe;* and in certain provincial dialects it is *mo*, at the present time.

Notwithstanding this, *i.e.*, the form being positive, the *power* of the word has always been comparative, and meant *more* rather than *much*, or *many*.

§ 250. *Less*.—In Anglo-Saxon *lassa* and *læs*. Here there is no *unequivocal* sign of the comparative degree; what, then, is the nature of the word? Is it a positive form with a comparative power like *moe?* or is it an old comparative in -*s?* This is undecided. What does it come from? Grimm derives it from the Mœso-Gothic root *lasiv = weak*. His doctrine is doubtful. I cannot but believe that it comes from the same root as *litt-le;* where the old Frisian form *litich*, shows that the -*l* is no essential part of the word, and the Danish form *lille* gets rid of the *t*. Still the word is difficult; indeed it is unexplained.

§ 251. *Near, nearer.*—Anglo-Saxon, *neah;* comparative, *nearre, near, nyr;* superlative, *nyhst, nehst.* Observe, in the Anglo-Saxon positive and superlative, the absence of the *r*. This shows that the English positive *near* is the Anglo-Saxon comparative *nearre,* and that in the secondary comparative *nearer,* we have an *excess of expression*. It may be, however, that the *r* in *near* is a mere point of orthography, and that it is not pronounced; since, in the English language the words *father* and *farther* are, for the most part, pronounced alike.

§ 252. *Farther.*—Anglo-Saxon *feor, fyrre, fyrrest.* The *th* seems euphonic, inserted by the same process that gives the δ in ἀνδρὸς, from ἀνὴρ = *man*.

Further.—Confounded with *farther*, although in reality from a different word, *fore*. Old High German, *furdir;* New High German, *der vordere;* Anglo-Saxon, *fyrðre.*

§ 253. *Former.*—A comparative formed from the superlative; *forma* being such. Consequently, an instance of excess of expression, combined with irregularity.

§ 254. In Mœso-Gothic *spêdists* means *last*, and *spêdiza* = *later*. Of the word *spêdists* two views may be taken. According to one it is the positive degree with the addition of *st;* according to the other, it is the comparative degree with the addition only of *t*. Now, Grimm and others lay down as a rule, that the superlative is formed, not directly from the positive, but indirectly through the comparative.

With the exception of *worse* and *less*, all the English comparatives end in *-r:* yet no superlative ends in *-rt*, the form being, not *wise, wiser, wisert*, but *wise, wiser, wisest*. This fact, without invalidating the notion just laid down, gives additional importance to the comparative forms in *s;*

since it is from these, before they have changed to *r*, that we must suppose the superlatives to have been derived. The theory being admitted, we can, by approximation, determine the comparative antiquity of the superlative degree. It was introduced *after* the establishment of the comparative, and *before* the change of -*s* into -*r*.

CHAPTER XI.

THE SUPERLATIVE DEGREE.

§ 255. THE Anglo-Saxon word for *first* was *for-m-a*.

The root was *for* = the Latin *præ*, the Greek πρo, and being the same combination which occurs in *fore*, *fore-m-ost*, &c.

The *m* was the Anglo-Saxon sign of the superlative degree.

It is the *m* in the Latin words *pri-m-us*, *inti-m-us*, *exti-m-us*, *ulti-m-us*, &c.

It occurs even in the Gothic tongues; in other words, besides *for-m-a*.

In short, *m* is an old sign of the superlative degree; probably older than the usual form, *-st*, discussed in § 254. This has some important applications.

§ 256. *Former.*—This is a remarkable word: it is a comparative derived from the Anglo-Saxon superlative, and its analysis is *for-m-er*, with *excess of inflexion*.

§ 257. *Nea-r-est.*—Here the *r* is no part of the original root, as may be seen in § 251. It has grown out of *-ah* pronounced as the *a* in *father*. The true forms are positive, *neah*; comparative, *neah-er*; superlative, *neah-est*. Such, to a certain extent, is really the case.

§ 258. *Next.*—The superlative of *nigh*, contracted from *nigh-est*. The Anglo-Saxon forms were *neah*, *nyh-st*, *neh-st*, *nyh-ste*. In Anglo-Saxon the letter *h* was pronounced strongly, and sounded like *g* or *k*. This fact is still shown in the spelling; as *nigh*. In the word *next* this sound is preserved, slightly changed into that of *k*; *next = nek-st*.

§ 250. *Upmost*, &c.—The common statement concerning words like *upmost* is, that they are compound words, formed by the addition of the word *most:* this, however, is more than doubtful.

The Anglo-Saxon language presents us with the following forms:—

Anglo-Saxon.	English.
Innema (inn-ema),	Inmost (in-m-ost).
Útema (ùt-ma),	Outmost (out-m-ost).
Siðema (sið-ema),	Latest.
Lætema (læt-ema),	Latest.
Niðema (nið-ema),	Nethermost (neth-er-m-ost).
Forma (for-ma),	Foremost (fore-m-ost).
Æftema (aft-ema),	Aftermost (aft-er-m-ost).
Ufema (uf-ema),	Upmost (up-m-ost).
Hindema (hind-ema),	Hindmost (hind-m-ost).
Midema (mid-ema),	Midmost (mid-m-ost).

Now the words in question show at once, that, as far as they are concerned, the *m* that appears in the last syllable of each has nothing to do with the word *most*.

From the words in question there was formed, in Anglo-Saxon, a regular superlative form in the usual manner; *viz*., by the addition of *-st;* as *æfte-m-est, fyr-m-est, læte-m-est, sið-m-est, yfe-m-est, ute-m-est, inne-m-est*.

Hence, in the present English, the different parts of the syllable *most* (in words like *upmost*) come from different quarters. The *m* is the *m* in the Anglo-Saxon words *innema*, &c.; whilst the *-st* is the common sign of the superlative. Hence, in separating such words as *midmost* into its component parts, we should write

THE SUPERLATIVE DEGREE.

Mid-m-ost	*not*	mid-most
Ut-m-ost	—	ut-most.
Up-m-ost	—	up-most.
Fore-m-ost	—	fore-most.
In-m-ost	—	in-most.
Hind-m-ost	—	hind-most.
Out-m-ost	—	out-most.

§ 260. In certain words, however, the syllable *m-ost* is added to a word already ending in *-er*; that is, already marked with the sign of the comparative degree.

Neth-er-m-ost.	Hind-er-m-ost.
Utt-er-m-ost.	Out-er-m-ost.
Upp-er-m-ost.	Inn-er-m-ost.

CHAPTER XII.

THE CARDINAL NUMBERS.

§ 261. GENERALLY speaking, the greater part of the cardinal numbers are undeclined. As far as *number* goes, this is necessary.

One is naturally and exclusively *singular*.

Two is naturally *dual*.

The rest are naturally and exclusively *plural*.

As to the inflection of gender and case, there is no reason why all the numerals should not be as fully inflected as the Latin *unus, una, unum, unius*. It is a mere habit of our language that they are not so in English.

CHAPTER XIII.

THE ORDINAL NUMBERS.

§ 262. By referring to § 259, we see that *-m* was an early sign of the superlative degree. This bears upon the numerals *seven*, *nine*, and *ten*.

These are *cardinal* numbers. Nevertheless, the present chapter is the proper place for noticing them.

There is good reason for believing that the final *-n* is no part of the original root. Thus,—

a. Sev-en = the Latin *sept-em*, where the *-m* is equivalent to the *-n*. But in the Greek ἑπτὰ, and the Scandinavian *syv*, and *sju*, neither *-n* nor *-m* occur.

b. Ni-ne.—This same applies here. The Latin form is *nov-em;* but the Greek and Norse are ἐννέα and *niu*.

c. Ten.—The older form is *ti-h-un*, in Latin *de-c-em*. The English *-n* is the Latin *-m*. Nevertheless, in the Greek and Norse the forms are δέκα and *tuo*.

§ 263. What explains this? The following hypothesis. Some of the best German authorities believe, that the *-m*, expressive of the superlative degree, was also used to denote the *ordinal character (ordinality) of the numerals;* so that the *-m-* in *deci-m-us*, was the *-m-* in *ulti-m-us* and *exti-m-us*. This is the first step in the explanation.

§ 264. The next is, to suppose that certain *cardinal* numerals have taken and retained the *ordinal* form; these being the—

Latin.	English.			Greek.	Norse.
Sept-em,	sev-en, as opposed to the			ἑπτὰ	sjau.
Nov-em,	ni-ne	"	"	ἐννέα,	níu.
Dec-em	te-n	"	"	δέκα	tíu.

I give no opinion as to the accuracy or erroneousness of this view.

§ 265. *Thir-teen*, &c., is *three* with *ten* added, or $3 + 10$.

§ 266. *Thir-ty*, &c., is *three tens* (*three decades*), or 3×10. In Mœso-Gothic we find the *-ty* in the fuller form *tig* = δέκ-ας in Greek.

CHAPTER XIV.

THE ARTICLES.

§ 267. In the generality of grammars the definite article *the*, and the indefinite article *an*, are the very first parts of speech that are considered. This is exceptionable. So far are they from being essential to language, that, in many dialects, they are wholly wanting. In Greek there is no indefinite, in Latin there is neither an indefinite nor a definite article. In the former language they say ἀνήρ τις = *a certain man:* in the latter the words *filius patris* mean equally *the son of the father, a son of a father, a son of the father*, or *the son of a father*. In Mœso-Gothic and in Old Norse, there is an equal absence of the indefinite article; or, at any rate, if there be one at all, it is a different word from what occurs in English. In these the Greek τις is expressed by the Gothic root *sum*.

Now, since it is very evident that, as far as the sense is concerned, the words *some man, a certain man*, and *a man*, are much the same, an exception may be taken to the statement that in Greek and Mœso-Gothic there is no indefinite article. It may, in the present state of the argument, be fairly said that the words *sum* and τις are pronouns with a certain sense, and that *a* and *an* are no more; consequently, that in Greek the indefinite article is τις, in Mœso-Gothic *sum*, and in English *a* or *an*.

A distinction, however, may be made. In the expression ἀνήρ τις (*anar tis*) = *a certain man*, or *a man*, and in the expression *sum mann*, the words *sum* and τις preserve their natural and original meaning; whilst in *a man* and *an ox* the words *a* and *an* are used in a secondary sense. These words, as is currently known, are one and the same, the *n*, in the form *a*, being ejected through a euphonic process. They are, moreover, the same words with the numeral *one;* Anglo-Saxon, *a'n;* Scotch, *ane*. Now, between the words *a man* and *one man*, there is a difference in meaning; the first expression being the most indefinite. Hence comes the difference between the English and Mœso-Gothic expressions. In the one the word *sum* has a natural, in the other, the word *an* has a secondary power.

The same reasoning applies to the word *the*. Compared with *a man*, the words *the man* are very definite. Compared, however, with the words *that man*, they are the contrary. Now, just as *an* and *a* have arisen out of the numeral *one*, so has *the* arisen out of the demonstrative pronoun þæt, or at least from some common root. It will be remembered that in Anglo-Saxon there was a form þe, undeclined, and common to all the cases of all the numbers.

In no language in its oldest stage is there ever a word giving, in its primary sense, the ideas of *a* and *the*. As tongues become modern, some noun with a *similar* sense is used to express them. In the course of time a change of form takes place, corresponding to the change of meaning; e. g., *one* becomes *an*, and afterwards *a*. Then it is that articles become looked upon as separate parts of speech, and are dealt with accordingly. No invalidation of this statement is drawn from the Greek language. Although the first page of the etymology gives us ὀ, ἠ, τὸ (*ho, hæ, to*), as the definite articles, the corresponding page in the syntax informs us, that, in the oldest stage of the language, ὁ (*ho*) = *the*, had the power of οὗτος (*howtos*) = *this*.

The origin of the articles seems uniform. In German *ein*, in Danish *en*, stand to *one* in the same relation that *an* does. The French *un*, Italian and Spanish *uno*, are similarly related to *unus* = *one*.

And as, in English, *the*, in German *der*, in Danish *den*, come from the demonstrative pronouns, so, in the classical languages, are the French *le*, the Italian *il* and *lo*, and the Spanish *el*, derived from the Latin demonstrative *ille*.

In his "Outlines of Logic," the present writer has given reasons for considering the word *no* (as in *no man*) an article.

That *the*, in expressions like *all the more, all the better*, &c., is no article, has already been shown.

CHAPTER XV.

DIMINUTIVES, AUGMENTATIVES, AND PATRONYMICS.

§ 268. COMPARED with the words *lamb, man*, and *hill*, the works *lambkin, mannikin*, and *hillock* convey the idea of comparative smallness or diminution. Now, as the word *hillock = a little hill* differs in *form* from *hill*, we have in English a series of *diminutive* forms, or *diminutives*.

The English diminutives may be arranged according to a variety of principles. Amongst others:

1. *According to their form.*—The word *hillock* is derived from *hill*, by the *addition* of a *syllable*. The word *tip* is derived from *top*, by the *change* of a *vowel*.

2. *According to their meaning.*—In the word *hillock* there is the simple expression of comparative smallness in size. In the word *doggie* for *dog, lassie* for *lass*, the addition of the -*ie* makes the word not so much a diminutive as a term of tenderness or endearment. The idea of smallness, accompanied, perhaps, with that of neatness, generally carries with it the idea of approbation; hence, the word *clean* in English, means, in German, *little = kleine*. The feeling of protection which is extended to small objects engenders the notion of endearment.

§ 269. The Greek word μείωσις (*meiôsis*) means diminution; the Greek word ὑποκόρισμα (*hypokorisma*) means an endearing expression. Hence we get names for the two kinds of diminutives; *viz.*, the term *meiotic* for the true diminutives, and the term *hypocoristic* for the diminutives of endearment.

3. *According to their historical origin.* The syllable -*ock*, as in *hillock*, is of Anglo-Saxon and Gothic origin. The -*et*, as in *lancet*, is of French and classical origin.

4. *According as they affect proper names, or common names.*—*Hawkin, Perkin, Wilkin,* &c. In these words we have the diminutives of *Hal, Peter, Will,* &c.

§ 270. The diminutive forms of Gothic origin are the first to be considered.

1. *Those formed by a change of vowel.*—*Tip*, from *top*. The relation of the feminine to the masculine is allied to the ideas conveyed by many diminutives. Hence in the word *kit*, from *cat*, it is doubtful whether there be meant a female cat or a little cat. *Kid* is a diminutive form of *goat*.

2. *Those formed by the addition of a letter or letters.* —Of the diminutive characteristics thus formed the commonest, beginning from the simpler forms, are

Ie.—Almost peculiar to the Lowland Scotch; as *daddie, lassie, minnie, wifie, mousie, doggie, boatie,* &c.

Ock.—*Bullock, hillock.*

Kin.—*Lambkin, mannikin, ladikin,* &c. As is seen above, common in proper names.

En.—*Chicken, kitten,* from *cock, cat.* The notion of diminution, if indeed that be the notion originally conveyed, lies not in the -*en*, but in the vowel. In the word *chicken*, from *cock*, observe the effect of the small vowel on the *c*.

The consideration of words like *duckling*, and *gosling*, is purposely deferred.

The chief diminutive of classical origin is—

Et, as in *trumpet, lancet, pocket;* the word *pock*, as in *meal-pock = a meal-bag*, being found in the Scottish. From the French *-ette*, as in *caissette, poulette*.

The forms *-rel*, as in *cockerel, pickerel*, and *-let*, as in *streamlet*, require a separate consideration. The first has nothing to do with the Italian forms *acquerella* and *coserella*—themselves, perhaps, of Gothic, rather than of classical origin.

In the Old High-German there are a multitude of diminutive forms in *-el*; as *ouga = an eye, ougili = a little eye; lied = a song, liedel = a little song*. This indicates the nature of words like *cockerel*.

Even in English the diminutive power of *-el* can be traced in the following words:—

Soare = a deer in its third year. *Sor-rel*—a deer in its second year.—See "Love's Labour Lost," with the note.

Tiercel = a small sort of hawk, one-third less (*tierce*) than the common kind.

Kantle = *small corner*, from *cant* = *a corner*.—"Henry IV."

Hurdle; in Dutch *horde;* German, *hurde*. *Hording*, without the *-l*, is used in an allied sense by builders in English.

In the words in point we must assume an earlier form, *cocker* and *piker*, to which the diminutive form *-el* is affixed. If this be true, we have, in English, representatives of the diminutive form *-el* so common in the High Germanic dialects. *Wolfer = a wolf, hunker = a haunch, flitcher = a flitch, teamer = a team, fresher = a frog,*—these are north country forms of the present English.

The termination *-let*, as in *streamlet*, seems to be double, and to consist of the Gothic diminutive *-l*, and the French diminutive *-t*.

§ 271. *Augmentatives.*—Compared with *capello = a hat*, the Italian word *capellone = a great hat*, is an augmentative. The augmentative forms, pre-eminently common in the Italian language, often carry with them a depreciating sense.

The termination *-rd* (in Old High German, *-hart*), as in *drunkard, braggart, laggard, stinkard*, carries with it this idea of depreciation. In *buzzard*, and *reynard*, the name of the fox, it is simply augmentative. In *wizard*, from *witch*, it has the power of a masculine form.

The termination *-rd*, taken from the Gothic, appears in the modern languages of classical origin: French, *vieillard*; Spanish, *codardo*. From these we get, at second-hand, the word *coward*.

The word *sweetheart* is a derived word of this sort, rather than a compound word; since in Old High German and Middle High German, we have the corresponding form *liebhart*. Now the form for *heart* is in German not *hart*, but *herz*.

Words like *braggadocio, trombone, balloon*, being words of foreign origin, prove nothing as to the further existence of augmentative forms in English.

§ 272.—*Patronymics.*—In the Greek language the notion of *lineal descent*, in other words, the relation of the son to the father, is expressed by a particular termination; as Πηλεύς (*Peleus*), Πηλείδης (*Peleidæs*), the son of Peleus. It is very evident that this mode of expression is very different from either the English form *Johnson = the son of John*, or the Gaelic *MacDonald = the son of Donald*. In these last-named words, the words *son* and *Mac* mean the same thing; so that *Johnson* and *MacDonald* are not *derived* but *compound* words. This Greek way of expressing descent is peculiar, and the words wherein it occurs are classed together by the peculiar name *patronymic;* from *patēr = a father,* and *onoma = a name.*

Is there anything in English corresponding to the Greek patronymics?

Not in the *present* English? There was, however, in the Anglo-Saxon.

In the Anglo-Saxon, the terminations *-ing* is as truly patronymic as *-ίδης* in Greek. In the Bible-translation the *son of Elisha* is called *Elising.* In the Anglo-Saxon Chronicle occur such genealogies as the following:—
Ida was Eopping, Eoppa Esing, Esa Inging, Inga Angenviting, Angenvit Alocing, Aloc Beonocing, Beonoc Branding, Brand Bældæging, Bældæg Vódening, Vóden Friðowulfing, Friðowulf Finning, Finn Godwulfing, Godwulf Geating = Ida was the son of Eoppa, Eoppa of Esa, Esa of Inga, Inga of Angenvit, Angenvit of Aloc, Aloc of Beonoc, Beonoc of Brand, Brand of Bældæg, Bældæg of Woden, Woden of Friðowulf, Friðowulf of Finn, Finn of Godwulf, Godwulf of Geat.—In Greek, "Ἴδα ἦν Ἐοππείδης, Ἔοππα Ἡσείδης, Ἦσα Ἰγγείδης, Ἴγγα Ἀγγενφιτείδης, &c. In the plural number these forms denote the *race of;* as *Scyldingas = the Scyldings,* or the race of *Scyld,* &c. Edgar Atheling means Edgar of the race of the nobles.

10*

CHAPTER XVI.

GENTILE FORMS.

§ 273. The only word in the present English that requires explanation is the name of the principality *Wales*.

1. The form is *plural*, however much the meaning may be *singular;* so that the *-s* in *Wale-s* is the *-s* in *fathers*, &c.

2. It has grown out of the Anglo-Saxon from *wealhas* =*foreigners*, from *wealh* = *a foreigner*, the name by which the Welsh are spoken of by the Germans of England, just as the Italians are called Welsh by the Germans of Germany; and just as *wal-nuts* = *foreign nuts*, or *nuces Galliæ*. *Welsh* = *weall-isc* = *foreign*, and is a derived adjective.

3. The transfer of the name of the *people* inhabiting a certain country to the *country* so inhabited, was one of the commonest processes in both Anglo-Saxon and Old English.

CHAPTER XVII.

ON THE CONNEXION BETWEEN THE NOUN AND VERB, AND ON THE INFLECTION OF THE INFINITIVE MOOD.

§ 274. IN order to understand clearly the use of the so-called infinitive mood in English, it is necessary to bear in mind two facts, one a matter of *logic*, the other a matter of *history*.

In the way of *logic*, the difference between a noun and a verb is less marked than it is in the way of *grammar*.

Grammatically, the contrast is considerable. The inflection of nouns expresses the ideas of sex as denoted by gender, and of relation in place as denoted by cases. That of verbs rarely expresses sex, and never relations in place. On the other hand, however, it expresses what no noun ever does or can express; *e. g.*, the relation of the agency to the individual speaking, by means of *person;* the time in which acts take place, by means of *tense;* and the conditions of their occurrence, by means of *mood*.

The idea of *number* is the only one that, on a superficial view, is common to these two important parts of speech.

§ 275. Logically, however, the contrast is inconsiderable. A noun denotes an object of which either the senses or the intellect can take cognizance, and a verb does no more. *To move* = *motion, to rise* = *rising, to err* = *error; to forgive* = *forgiveness*. The only difference between the two parts of speech is this, that, whereas a noun may express any object whatever, verbs can only express those objects which consist in an action. And it is this superadded idea of action that superadds to the verb the phenomena of tense, mood, person, and voice; in other words, the phenomena of conjugation.

§ 276. A noun is a word capable of *declension* only. A verb is a word capable of declension and *conjugation* also. The fact of verbs being declined as well as conjugated must be remembered. *The participle has the declension of a noun adjective, the infinitive mood the declension of a noun substantive. Gerunds and supines, in languages where they occur, are only names for certain cases of the verb.*

§ 277. Although in all languages the verb is equally capable of declension, it is not equally declined. The Greeks, for instance, used forms like

τὸ φθονεῖν = *invidia.*
τοῦ φθονεῖν = *invidiæ.*
ἐν τῷ φθονεῖν = *in invidia.*

§ 278. Returning, however, to the illustration of the substantival character of the so-called infinitive mood, we may easily see—

a. That the name of any action may be used without any mention of the agent. Thus, we may speak of the simple fact of *walking* or *moving*, independently of any specification of the *walker* or *mover*.

β. That, when actions are spoken of thus indefinitely, the idea of either person or number has no place in the conception; from which it follows that the so-called infinitive mood must be at once impersonal, and without the distinction of singular, dual, and plural.

γ. That, nevertheless, the ideas of time and relation in space *have* place in the conception. We can think of a person being *in the act of striking a blow*, of his *having been in the act of striking a blow*, or of his *being about to be in the act of striking a blow*. We can also think of a person being *in the act of doing a good action*, or of his being *from the act of doing a good action*.

§ 279. This has been written to show that verbs of languages in general are as naturally declinable as nouns. What follows will show that the verbs of the Gothic languages in particular were actually declined, and that fragments of this declension remain in the present English.

The inflection of the verb in its impersonal (or infinitive state) consisted, in its fullest form, of three cases, a nominative (or accusative), a dative, and a genitive. The genitive is put last, because its occurrence in the Gothic languages is the least constant.

In Anglo-Saxon the nominative (or accusative) ended in -*an*, with a single *n*.

Lufian	= *to love*	= *amare.*
Bærnan	= *to burn*	= *urere.*
Syllan	= *to give*	= *dare.*

In Anglo-Saxon the dative of the infinitive verb ended in -*nne*, and was preceded by the preposition *to*.

To lufienne	= *ad amandum.*
To bærnenne	= *ad urendum.*
To syllanne	= *ad dandum.*

The genitive, ending in -*es*, occurs only in Old High German and Modern High German, *pläsannes, weinnenes.*

§ 280. With these preliminaries we can take a clear view of the English infinitives. They exist under two forms, and are referable to a double origin.

1. The *independent* form.—This is used after the words *can, may, shall, will,* and some others, as, *I can speak, I may go, I shall come, I will move.* Here there

is no preposition, and the origin of the infinitive is from the form in -*an*.

2. The *prepositional* form.—This is used after the majority of English verbs, as, *I wish to speak*, *I mean to go*, *I intend to come*, *I determine to move*. Here we have the preposition *to* and the origin of the infinitive is from the form *-nne*.

§ 281. Expressions like *to err = error*, *to forgive = forgiveness*, in lines like

"To err is human, to forgive divine,"

are very remarkable. They exhibit the phenomena of a nominative case having grown not only out of a dative but out of a dative *plus* its governing preposition.

CHAPTER XVIII.

ON DERIVED VERBS.

§ 282. Of the divisions of verbs into active and passive, transitive and intransitive, unless there be an accompanying change of *form*, etymology takes no cognisance. The forces of the auxiliary verbs, and the tenses to which they are equivalent, are also points of syntax rather than of etymology.

Four classes, however, of *derived* verbs, as opposed to *simple*, especially deserve notice.

I. Those ending in *-en*; as *soften, whiten, strengthen,* &c. Here the *-en* is a derivational affix; and not a representative of the Anglo-Saxon infinitive form *-an* (as *lufian, barnan = to love, to burn*), and the Old English *-en* (as *tellen, loven*).

II. Transitive verbs derived from intransitives by a change of the vowel of the root.

Primitive Intransitive Form.	Derived Transitive Form.
Rise	Raise.
Lie	Lay.
Sit	Set.
Fall	Fell.
Drink	Drench.

In Anglo-Saxon these words were more numerous than they are at present.

DERIVED VERBS.

Intrans. Infinitive.		Trans. Infinitive.
Yrnan, *to run*		Ærnan, *to make to run.*
Byrnan, *to burn*		Bærnan, *to make to burn.*
Drincan, *to drink*		Drencan, *to drench.*
Sincan, *to sink*		Sencan, *to make to sink.*
Licgan, *to lie*		Lecgan, *to lay.*
Sittan, *to sit*		Settan, *to set.*
Drifan, *to drift*		Dræfan, *to drive.*
Feallan, *to fall*		Fyllan, *to fell.*
Weallan, *to boil*		Wyllan, *to make to boil.*
Flëogan, *to fly*		A-fligan, *to put to flight.*
Büogan, *to bow*		Bígan, *to bend.*
Faran, *to go*		Feran, *to convey.*
Wacan, *to wake*		Weccan, *to waken.*

All these intransitives form their præterite by a change of vowel, as *sink, sank;* all the transitives by the addition of *d* or *t*, as *sell, sell'd.*

III. Verbs derived from nouns by a change of accent; as *to survéy*, from a *súrvey*.

Nouns.	Verbs.	Nouns.	Verbs.
A'bsent	absént.	Cóntrast	contrást.
A'bstract	abstráct.	Cónverse	convérse.
A'ccent	accént.	Cónvert	convért.
A'ffix	affíx.	Déscant	descánt.
Aúgment	augmént.	Désert	desért.
Cólleague	colléague.	Dígest	digést.
Cómpact	compáct.	E'ssay	essáy.
Cómpound	compóund.	E'xtract	extráct.
Cómpress	compréss.	Férment	fermént.
Cóncert	concért.	Fréquent	frequént.
Cóncrete	concréte.	I'mport	impórt.
Cónduct	condúct.	I'ncense	incénse.
Cónfine	confíne.	I'nsult	insúlt.
Cónflict	conflíct.	O'bject	objéct.
Cónserve	consérve.	Pérfume	perfúme.
Cónsort	consórt.	Pérmit	permít.
Cóntract	contráct.	Préfix	prefíx.

DERIVED VERBS.

Nouns.	Verbs.	Nouns.	Verbs.
Prémise	premíse.	Récord	recórd.
Présage	preságe.	Réfuse	refúse.
Présent	presént.	Súbject	subjéct.
Próduce	prodúce.	Súrvey	survéy.
Próject	projéct.	Tórment	tormént.
Prótest	protést.	Tránsfer	transfér.
Rébel	rebél.	Tránsport	transpórt.

Walker attributes the change of accent to the influence of the participial termination -*ing*. All words thus affected are of foreign origin.

IV. Verbs formed from nouns by changing a final *sharp* consonant into its corresponding *flat* one; as,

The use	...	...	*to* use,	*pronounced* uze.
The breath	...	...	*to* breathe	— breadhe.
The cloth	...	...	*to* clothe	— clodhe.

CHAPTER XIX.

ON THE PERSONS.

§ 283. COMPARED with the Latin, the Greek, the Mœso-Gothic, and almost all the ancient languages, there is, in English, in respect to the persons of the verbs, but a very slight amount of inflection. This may be seen by comparing the English word *call* with the Latin *voco*.

Sing.	Plur.	Sing.	Plur.
1. Voc-o	Voc-*amus*.	Call	Call.
2. Voc-as	Voc-*atis*.	Call-est	Call.
3. Voc-at	Voc-*ant*.	* Call-eth	Call.

Here the Latins have different forms for each different person, whilst the English have forms for two only; and even of these one (*callest*) is becoming obsolete. With the forms voc-*o*, voc-*amus*, voc-*atis*, voc-*ant*, there is, in the current English, nothing correspondent.

In the word *am*, as compared with *are* and *art*, we find a sign of the first person singular.

In the old forms *tellen*, *weren*, &c., we have a sign of the plural number.

§ 284. In the Modern English, the Old English, and the Anglo-Saxon, the peculiarities of our personal inflections are very great. This may be seen from the following tables of comparison :—

* Or *call s.*

ON THE PERSONS. 211

Present Tense, Indicative Mood.

Mœso-Gothic.

	1st person.	2nd person.	3rd person.
Singular.	Sŏkja	Sŏkeis	Sŏkeiþ—*seek*.
Plural.	Sŏkjam	Sŏkeiþ	Sokjand.

Old High German.

Singular.	Prennu	Prennis	Prennit—*burn*.
Plural.	Prennames	Prennat	Prennant.

Icelandic.

Singular.	Kalla	Kallar	Kallar—*call*.
Plural.	Köllum	Kalliþ	Kalla.

Old Saxon.

Singular.	Sŏkju	Sŏkis	Sŏkîd—*seek*.
Plural.	Sŏkjad	Sŏkjad	Sŏkjad.

Anglo-Saxon.

Singular.	Lufige	Lufast	Lufað.
Plural.	Lufiað	Lufiað	Lufiað.

Old English.

Singular	Love	Lovest	Loveth.
Plural.	Loven	Loven	Loven.

Modern English.

Singular.	love	Lovest	Loveth (or Loves).
Plural.	Love	Love	Love.

§ 285. Herein remark; 1. the Anglo-Saxon addition of *t* in the second person singular; 2. the identity in form of the three persons of the plural number; 3. the change of -*að* into -*en* in the Old English plural; 4. the total absence of plural forms in the Modern English; 5. the change of the *th* into *s*, in *loveth* and *loves*. These are points bearing especially upon the history of the English persons. The following points indicate a more general question:

1. The full form *prennames* in the newer Old High German, as compared with *sókjam* in the old Mœso-Gothic.

2. The appearance of the *r* in Icelandic.

3. The difference between the Old Saxon and the Anglo-Saxon in the second person singular; the final *t* being absent in Old Saxon.

§ 286. *The person in -t.*—The forms *art, wast, wert, shalt, wilt,* or *ar-t, was-t, wer-t, shal-t, wil-t,* are remarkable. Here the second person singular ends, not in *-st,* but in *t.* The reason for this is to be sought in the Mœso-Gothic and the Icelandic.

In those languages the form of the person changes with the tense, and the second singular of the præterite tense of one conjugation is, not *-s*, but *-t;* as Mœso-Gothic, *svôr = I swore, svôrt = thou swarest, gráip = I griped, gráipt = thou gripedst;* Icelandic, *brannt = thou burnest, gaft = thou gavest.* In the same languages ten verbs are conjugated like præterites. Of these, in each language, *skal* is one.

Mœso-Gothic.

Singular.	Dual.	Plural.
1. Skal	Skulu	Skulum.
2 Skalt	Skuluts	Skuluþ.
3. Skall	Skuluts	Skuluu.

Icelandic.

Singular.	Plural.
1. Skall	Skulum.
2. Skalt	Skuluð.
3. Skal	Skulu.

§ 287. *Thou spakest, thou brakest, thou sungest.**—

---

* *Thou sangest, thou drankest, &c.*—For a reason given in the sequel, these forms are less exceptionable than *sungest, drunkest,* &c.

In these forms there is a slight though natural anomaly. They belong to the class of verbs which form their præterite by changing the vowel of the present; as *sing*, *sang*, &c. Now, all words of this sort in Anglo-Saxon formed their second singular præterite, not in -*st*, but in -*e* ; as þú funde= *thou foundest*, þú sunge= *thou sungest*. The English termination is derived from the present. Observe that this applies only to the præterites formed by changing the vowel. *Thou loved'st* is Anglo-Saxon as well as English, *viz.*, þú lufodest.

§ 288. In the northern dialects of the Anglo-Saxon the -ð of plurals like lufiað = *we love* becomes -*s*. In the Scottish this change was still more prevalent:

> The Scottes come that to this day
> *Havys* and Scotland haldyn ay.
>
> Wintoun, 11, 9, 73.

James I. of England ends nearly all his plurals in -*s*.

CHAPTER XX.

ON THE NUMBERS OF VERBS.

§ 289. As compared with the present plural forms, *we love, ye love, they love,* the Anglo-Saxons had the truly plural forms, *we lufiað, ge lufiað, hi lufiað.* The Old English also had a true plural inflection *we loven, ye loven, they loven.* The present English wants both the form in -*en*, and the form in *að*. In other words, the Anglo-Saxon and the Old English have a plural *personal* characteristic, whilst the Modern English has nothing to correspond with it.

§ 290. In the forms *luf-iað*, and *lov-en*, the change from singular to plural is made by adding a syllable; but there is no reason against the inflection running thus—*I love, thou lovest, he loves; we lave, ye lave, they lave;* in other words, there is no reason against the *vowel* of the root being changed, just as is the case with the form *speak, spoke; fall, fell.*

Now, in Anglo-Saxon, with a great number of verbs such a plural inflection not only actually takes place, but takes place most regularly. It takes place, however, in the past tense only. And this is the case in all the Gothic languages as well as in Anglo-Saxon. Amongst the rest, in—

Mœso-Gothic.

Skáin, *I shone;* skinum, *we shone.*
Smáit, *I smote;* smitum, *we smote.*
Káus, *I chose;* kusum, *we chose.*
Láug, *I lied;* lugum, *we lied.*

Gab, *I gave;* gébum, *we gave.*
At, *I ete;* étum, *we ete.*
Stal, *I stole;* stélum, *we stole.*
Qvam, *I came;* qvémum, *we came.*

Anglo-Saxon.

Arn, *I ran;* urnon, *we run.*
Ongan, *I began;* ongunnon, *we begun.*
Span, *I span;* spunnon, *we spun.*
Sang, *I sang;* sungon, *we sung.*
Swang, *I swang;* swangon, *we swung.*

Dranc, *I drank;* druncon, *we drunk.*
Sanc, *I sank;* suncon, *we sunk.*
Sprang, *I sprang;* sprungon, *we sprung.*
Swam, *I swam;* swummon, *we swum.*
Rang, *I rang;* rungon, *we rung.*

From these examples the reader has himself drawn his inference; *viz.* that words like

Began, begun.
Ran, run.
Span, spun.
Sang, sung.
Swang, swung.
Sprang, sprung.

Sank, sunk.
Swam, swum.
Rang, rung.
Bat, bit.
Smote, smit.
Drank, drunk, &c.,

generally called double forms of the past tense, were originally *different numbers of the same tense*, the forms in *a*, as *swam*, being singular, and the forms in *u*, as *swum*, plural.

CHAPTER XXI.

ON MOODS.

§ 291. THE Anglo-Saxon infinitive has already been considered.

Between the second plural imperative, and the second plural indicative, *speak ye*, and *ye speak*, there is no difference of form.

Between the second singular imperative *speak*, and the second singular indicative, *speakest*, there is a difference in form.

Still, as the imperative form *speak* is distinguished from the indicative form *speakest* by the *negation* of a character rather than by the possession of one, it cannot be said that there is in English any imperative mood.

§ 292. *If he speak*, as opposed to *if he speaks*, is characterized by a negative sign only, and consequently is no true example of a subjunctive. *Be*, as opposed to *am*, in the sentence *if it be so*, is a fresh word used in a limited sense, and consequently no true example of a subjunctive. It is a different word altogether, and is only the subjunctive of *am*, in the way *puss* is the vocative of *cat*.

The only true subjunctive inflection in the English language is that of *were* and *wert*, as opposed to the indicative forms *was* and *wast*.

Indicative.	Subjunctive.	
Singular.	Singular.	Plural.
1. I was.	If I were.	If we were.
2. Thou wast.	If thou wert.	If ye were.
3. He was.	If he were.	If they were.

CHAPTER XXII.

ON TENSES IN GENERAL.

§ 293. The nature of tenses in general is best exhibited by reference to the Greek; since in that language they are more numerous, and more strongly marked than elsewhere.

I strike, I struck.—Of these words, the first implies an action taking place at the time of speaking, the second marks an action that has already taken place.

These two notions of present and of past time, being expressed by a change of form, are true tenses. If there were no change of form, there would be no change of tense. They are the only true tenses in our language. In *I was beating, I have beaten, I had beaten,* and *I shall beat,* a difference of time is expressed; but as it is expressed by *a combination of words,* and not *by a change of form,* no true tenses are constituted.

§ 294. In Greek the case is different. Τύπτω (*typtô*) = *I beat;* ἔτυπτον (*etypton*) = *I was beating;* τύψω (*typsô*) = *I shall beat;* ἔτυψα (*etypsa*) = *I beat;* τέτυφα (*tetyfa*) = *I have beaten;* ἐτετύφειν (*etetyfein*) = *I had beaten.* In these words we have, of the same mood, the same voice, and the same conjugation, six different tenses; whereas, in English, there are but two. The forms τέτυφα and ἔτυψα are so strongly marked, that we recognise them wheresoever they occur. The first is formed by a reduplication of the initial τ, and, consequently, may be called the reduplicate form. As a tense it is called the perfect. In the form ἔτυψα an ε is prefixed, and an σ is added. In the allied language of Italy the ε disappears, whilst the σ (s) remains. Ἔτυψα is said to be an aorist tense. *Scripsi* is to *scribo* as ἔτυπσα is to τύπτω.

§ 295. Now in the Latin language a confusion takes place between these two tenses. Both forms exist. They are used, however, indiscriminately. The aorist form has, besides its own, the sense of the perfect. The perfect has, besides its own, the sense of the aorist. In the following pair of quotations, *vixi*, the aorist form, is translated *I have lived*, while *tetigit*, the perfect form, is translated *he touched*.

> *Vixi*, et quem dederat cursum Fortuna peregi;
> Et nunc magna mei sub terras ibis imago.—*Æn.* iv.

> Ut primum alatis *tetigit* magalia plantis.—*Æn.* iv.

§ 296. When a difference of form has ceased to express a difference of meaning, it has become superfluous. This is the case with the two forms in question. One of them may be dispensed with; and the consequence is, that, although in the Latin language both the perfect and the aorist forms are found, they are, with few exceptions, never found in the same word. Wherever there is the perfect, the aorist is wanting, and *vice versâ*. The two ideas *I have struck* and *I struck* are merged into the notion of past time in general, and are expressed by one of two forms, sometimes by that of the Greek perfect, and sometimes by that of the Greek aorist. On account of this the grammarians have cut down the number of Latin tenses to *five;* forms like *cucurri* and *vixi* being dealt with as one and the same tense. The true view is, that in *curro* the aorist form is replaced by the perfect, and in *vixi* the perfect form is replaced by the aorist.

§ 297. In the *present* English there is no undoubted perfect or reduplicate form. The form *moved* corresponds in meaning not with τέτυφα and *momordi*, but with ἔτυψα and *vixi*. Its sense is that of ἔτυψα, and not that of τέτυφα. The notion given by τέτυφα we express by the circumlocution *I have beaten*. We have no such form as *bebeat* or *memove*. In the Mœso-Gothic, however, there was a true reduplicate form; in other words, a perfect tense as well as an aorist. It is by the possession of this form that the verbs of the first six conjugations are characterized.

	Mœso-Gothic.	English.	Mœso-Gothic.	English.
1st	Falþa,	*I fold*	Fáifalþ,	*I have folded*, or *I folded.*
	Halda,	*I feed*	Háihald,	*I have fed*, or *I fed.*
	Haha,	*I hang*	Háihah,	*I have hanged*, or *I hanged.*
2nd.	Háita,	*I call*	Háiháit,	*I have called*, or *I called.*
	Láika,	*I play*	Láiláik,	*I have played*, or *I played.*
3rd.	Hláupa,	*I run*	Hláiláup,	*I have run*, or *I ran.*
4th.	Slépa,	*I sleep*	Súizlép,	*I have slept*, or *I slept.*
5th.	Láia,	*I laugh*	Láiló,	*I have laughed*, or *I laught.*
	Sáija,	*I sow*	Sáisó,	*I have sown*, or *I sowed.*
6th.	Gréta,	*I weep*	Gáigrót,	*I have wept*, or *I wept.*
	Téka,	*I touch*	Táitók,	*I have touched*, or *I touched.*

In Mœso-Gothic, as in Latin, the perfect forms have, besides their own, an aorist sense, and *vice versâ*.

In Mœso-Gothic, as in Latin, few (if any) words are found in both forms.

In Mœso-Gothic, as in Latin, the two forms are dealt with as a single tense; *láiló* being called the præterite of *láia*, and *svôr* the præterite of *svara*. The true view, however, is that in Mœso-Gothic, as in Latin, there are two past tenses, each having a certain latitude of meaning, and each, in certain words, replacing the other.

The reduplicate form, in other words, the perfect tense, is current in none of the Gothic languages except the

Mœso-Gothic. A trace of it is said to be found in the Anglo-Saxon of the seventh century in the word *heht*, which is considered to be *hê-ht*, the Mœso-Gothic *háiháit, rocavi*. *Did* from *do* is also considered to be a reduplicate form.

§ 298. In the English language the tense corresponding with the Greek aorist and the Latin forms like *vixi*, is formed after two modes; 1, as in *fell, sang*, and *took*, from *fall, sing*, and *take*, by changing the vowel of the present: 2, as in *moved* and *wept*, from *move* and *weep*, by the addition of *-d* or *-t*; the *-d* or *-t* not being found in the original word, but being a fresh element added to it. In forms, on the contrary, like *sang* and *fell*, no addition being made, no new element appears. The vowel, indeed, is changed, but nothing is added. Verbs, then, of the first sort, may be said to form their præterites out of themselves; whilst verbs of the second sort require something from without. To speak in a metaphor, words like *sang* and *fell* are comparatively independent. Be this as it may, the German grammarians call the tenses formed by a change of vowel the *strong* tenses, the *strong* verbs, the *strong* conjugation, or the *strong* order; and those formed by the addition of *d* or *t*, the *weak* tenses, the *weak* verbs, the *weak* conjugation, or the *weak* order. *Bound, spoke, gave, lay*, &c., are *strong*; *moved, favoured, instructed*, &c., are *weak*.

CHAPTER XXIII.

THE STRONG TENSES.

§ 299. THE strong præterites are formed from the present by changing the vowel, as *sing, sang; speak, spoke*

In Anglo-Saxon, several præterites change, in their plural, the vowel of their singular; as

Ic sang, *I sang.*	We sungon, *we sung.*
þu sunge, *thou sungest.*	Ge sungon, *ye sung.*
He sang, *he sang.*	Hi sungon, *they sung.*

The bearing of this fact upon the præterites has already been indicated. In a great number of words we have a double form, as *ran* and *run, sang* and *sung, drank* and *drunk,* &c. One of these forms is derived from the singular, and the other from the plural.

In cases where but one form is preserved, that form is not necessarily the singular; indeed, it is often the plural; —*e. g.,* Ic fand, *I found,* we fundon, *we found,* are the Anglo-Saxon forms. Now the present word *found* comes, not from the singular *fand,* but from the plural *fundon;* although in the Lowland Scotch dialect and in the old writers, the *singular* form occurs;

Donald Caird finds orra things,
Where Allan Gregor *fand* the tings.—SCOTT.

§ 300. The verbs wherein the double form of the present-præterite is thus explained, fall into two classes.

1. In the first class, the Anglo-Saxon forms were *á* in the singular, and *i* in the plural; as—

Sing.	Plur.
Sceán	Scinon (*we shone*).
Arás	Arison (*we arose*).
Smát	Smiton (*we smote*).

This accounts for,—

Present.	Præt. from Sing. form.	Præt. from Plur. form.
Rise	Rose	*Ris.
Smite	Smote	Smit.
Ride	Rode	*Rid.
Stride	Strode	Strid.
Slide	*Slode	Slid.
Chide	*Chode	Chid.
Drive	Drove	*Driv.
Thrive	Throve	Thriv.
Write	Wrote	Writ.
Slit	*Slat	Slit.
Bite	*Bat	Bit.

2. In the second class, the Anglo-Saxon forms were *a* in the singular, and *u* in the plural, as—

Sing.	Plural.
Band	Bundon (*we bound*).
Fand	Fundon (*we found*).
Grand	Grundon (*we ground*).
Wand	Wundon (*we wound*).

* The forms marked thus * are either obsolete or provincial.

This accounts for—

Present.	Præt. from Sing. form.	Præt. from Pl. form.
Swim	Swam	Swum.
Begin	Began	Begun.
Spin	*Span	Spun.
Win	*Wan	†Won.
Sing	Sang	Sung.
Swing	*Swang	Swung.
Spring	Sprang	Sprung.
Sting	*Stang	Stung.
Ring	Rang	Rung.
Wring	*Wrang	Wrung.
Fling	Flang	Flung.
*Hing	Hang	Hung.
String	*Strang	Strung.
Sink	Sank	Sunk.
Drink	Drank	Drunk.
Shrink	Shrank	Shrunk.
Stink	*Stank	Stunk.
Melt	*Molt	—
Help	*Holp	—
Delve	*Dolv	—
Stick	*Stack	Stuck.
Run	Ran	Run.
Burst	Brast	Burst.
Bind	Band	Bound.
Find	*Fand	Found.

§ 301. The following double præterites are differently explained. The primary one *often* (but not *always*) is from the Anglo-Saxon *participle*, the secondary from the Anglo-Saxon *præterite*.

Present.	Primary Præterite.	Secondary Præterite.
Cleave	Clove	*Clave.
Steal	Stole	*Stale.

* Obsolete.   † Sounded *wun*.

Present	Primary Preterite.	Secondary Preterite.
Speak	Spoke	Spake.
Swear	Swore	Sware
Bear	Bore	Bare.
Tear	Tore	*Tare.
Wear	Wore	*Ware.
Break	Broke	Brake.
Get	Got	*Gat.
Tread	Trod	Trad.
Bid	Bade	Bid.
Eat	Ate	Ete.

§ 302. The following verbs have only a single form for the præterite,—

Present.	Preterite.	Present.	Preterite.
Fall	Fell.	Forsake	Forsook.
Befall	Befell.	Eat	Ate.
Hold	Held.	Give	Gave.
Draw	Drew.	Wake	Woke.
Slay	Slew.	Grave	Grove.
Fly	Flew.	Shape	Shope.
Blow	Blew.	Strike	Struck.
Crow	Crew.	Shine	Shone.
Know	Knew.	Abide	Abode.
Grow	Grew.	Strive	Strove.
Throw	Threw.	Climb	Clomb.
Let	Let.	Hide	Hid.
Beat	Beat.	Dig	Dug.
Come	Came.	Cling	Clung.
Heave	Hove.	Swell	Swoll.
Weave	Wove.	Grind	Ground.
Freeze	Froze.	Wind	Wound.
Shear	Shore.	Choose	Chose.
——	Quoth.	Stand	Stood.
Seethe	Sod.	Lie	Lay.
Shake	Shook.	See	Saw.
Take	Took.		

* Obsolete

§ 303. An arrangement of the preceding verbs into classes, according to the change of vowel, is by no means difficult, even in the present stage of the English language. In the Anglo-Saxon, it was easier still. It is also easier in the provincial dialects, than in the literary English. Thus, when

Break is pronounced *Breek*,
Bear — *Beer*,
Tear — *Teer*,
Swear — *Sweer*,
Wear — *Weer*,

as they actually are by many speakers, they come in the same class with,—

Speak pronounced *Speek*,
Cleave — *Cleeve*,

and form their præterite by means of a similar change, *i. e.*, by changing the sound of the *ee* in *feet* (spelt *ea*) into that of the *a* in *fate;* viewed thus, the irregularity is less than it appears to be at first sight.

Again, *tread* is pronounced *tredd*, but many provincial speakers say *treed*, and so said the Anglo-Saxons, whose form was *ic trede = I tread*. Their præterite was *træd*. This again subtracts from the apparent irregularity.

Instances of this kind may be multiplied; the whole question, however, of the conjugation of the *strong verbs* is best considered after the perusal of the next chapter.

CHAPTER XXIV.

THE WEAK TENSES.

§ 304. THE præterite tense of the weak verbs is formed by the addition of -*d* or -*t*.

If necessary, the syllable -*ed* is substituted for -*d*.

The current statement that the syllable -*ed*, rather than the letter -*d* is the sign of the præterite tense, is true only in regard to the written language. In *stabbed, moved, bragged, whizzed, judged, filled, slurred, slummed, shunned, barred, strewed*, the *e* is a point of spelling only. In *language*, except in declamation, there is no second vowel sound. The -*d* comes in immediate contact with the final letter of the original word, and the number of syllables remains the same as it was before. We say *stabd, môvd, bragd*, &c.

§ 305. When, however, the original word ends in -*d* or -*t*, as *slight* or *brand*, then, and then only is there the real addition of the syllable -*ed*; as in *slighted, branded*.

This is necessary, since the combinations *slightt* and *brandd* are unpronounceable.

Whether the addition be -*d* or -*t* depends upon the flatness or sharpness of the preceding letter.

After *b, v, th* (as in *clothe*), *g*, or *z*, the addition is -*d*. This is a matter of necessity. We say *stabd, môvd, clôthd, braggd, whizzd*, because *stabt, môvt, clotht, braggt, whizzt*, are unpronounceable.

After *l, m, n, r, w, y*. or a vowel, the addition is also

-d. This is the *habit* of the English language. *Filt, slurt, strayt,* &c., are as pronounceable as *filld, slurrd, strayd,* &c. It is the habit, however, of the English language to prefer the latter forms.

All this, as the reader has probably observed, is merely the reasoning concerning the *s*, in words like *father's,* &c., applied to another letter and to another part of speech.

§ 306. The verbs of the weak conjugation fall into three classes.

I. In the first there is the simple addition of -d, -t, or -ed.

Serve, served.	Dip, dipped (*dipt*).
Cry, cried.	Slip, slipped (*slipt*).
Betray, betrayed.	Step, stepped (*stept*).
Expell, expelled.	Look, looked (*lookt*).
Accuse, accused.	Pluck, plucked (*pluckt*).
Instruct, instructed.	Toss, tossed (*tost*).
Invite, invited.	Push, pushed (*pusht*).
Waste, wasted.	Confess, confessed (*confest*).

To this class belong the greater part of the weak verbs and all verbs of foreign origin.

§ 307. II. In the second class, besides the addition of -t or -d, the vowel is *shortened,*

Present.	*Præterite.*
Creep	Crept.
Keep	Kept.
Sleep	Slept.
Sweep	Swept.
Weep	Wept.
Lose	Lost.
Mean	*Meant.

* Pronounced *ment*

Here the final consonant is -t.

Present	Preterite
Flee	Fled.
Hear	*Heard.
Shoe	Shod.
Say	†Said.

Here the final consonant is -d.

§ 308. III. In the second class the vowel of the present tense was *shortened* in the præterite. In the third class it is *changed*.

Tell, told.	Sell, sold.
Will, would.	Shall, should.

To this class belong the remarkable præterites of the verbs *seek, beseech, catch, teach, bring, think*, and *buy*, viz., *sought, besought, caught, taught, brought, thought*, and *bought*. In all these, the final consonant is either *g* or *k*, or else a sound allied to those mutes. When the tendency of these sounds to become *h* and *y*, as well as to undergo farther changes, is remembered, the forms in point cease to seem anomalous. In *wrought*, from *work*, there is a transposition. In *laid* and *said* the present forms make a show of regularity which they have not. The true original forms should be *legde* and *sægde*, the infinitives being *lecgan, secgan*. In these words the *i* represents the semivowel *y*, into which the original *g* was changed. The Anglo-Saxon forms of the other words are as follows :—

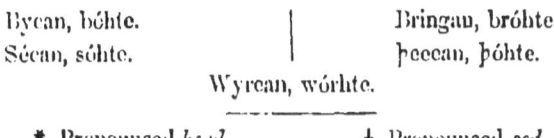

Bycan, bóhte.	Bringan, bróhte.
Sécan, sóhte.	Þeccan, þóhte.
Wyrcan, wórhte.	

---

* Pronounced *herd*. † Pronounced *sed*.

§ 309. Out of the three classes into which the weak verbs in Anglo-Saxon are divided, only one · takes a vowel before the *d* or *t*. The other two add the syllables -*te* or -*de*, to the last letter of the original word. The vowel that, in one out of the three Anglo-Saxon classes, precedes *d* is *o*. Thus we have *lufian, lufode; clypian, clypode*. In the other two classes the forms are respectively *bærnan, bærnde;* and *tellan, tealde*, no vowel being found. The *participle*, however, as stated above, ended, not in -*de* or -*te*, but in -*d* or -*t;* and in two out of the three classes it was preceded by a vowel; the vowel being *e*,—*gelufod, bærned, geteald*. Now in those conjugations where no vowel preceded the *d* of the præterite, and where the original word ended in -*d* or -*t*, a difficulty, which has already been indicated, arose. To add the sign of the præterite to a word like *eard-ian* (*to dwell*) was an easy matter, inasmuch as *eardian* was a word belonging to the first class, and in the first class the præterite was formed in -*ode*. Here the vowel *o* kept the two *d*'s from coming in contact. With words, however, like *métan* and *sendan*, this was not the case. Here no vowel intervened; so that the natural præterite forms were *met-te, send-de*, combinations wherein one of the letters ran every chance of being dropped in the pronunciation. Hence, with the exception of the verbs in the first class, words ending in -*d* or -*t* in the root admitted no additional *d* or *t* in the præterite. This difficulty, existing in the present English as it existed in the Anglo-Saxon, modifies the præterites of most words ending in -*t* or -*d*.

§ 310. In several words there is the actual addition of the syllable -*ed ;* in other words *d* is separated from the last letter of the original word by the addition of a vowel; as *ended, instructed*, &c.

§ 311. In several words the final -*d* is changed into -*t*, as *bend, bent; rend, rent; send, sent; gild, gilt; build, built; spend, spent*, &c.

§ 312. In several words the vowel of the root is changed; as *feed, fed; bleed, bled; breed, bred; meet, met; speed, sped; rēad, rĕad*, &c. Words of this last-named class cause occasional difficulty to the grammarian. No addition is made to the root, and, in this circumstance, they agree with the strong verbs. Moreover, there is a change of the vowel. In this circumstance also they agree with the strong verbs. Hence with forms like *fed* and *led* we are in doubt as to the conjugation. This doubt we have three means of settling, as may be shown by the word *beat*.

a. By the form of the participle.—The -*en* in *beaten* shows that the word *beat* is strong.

b. By the nature of the vowel.—The weak form of *to beat* would be *bet*, or *bĕăt*, after the analogy of *feed* and *read*. By some persons the word is pronounced *bet*, and with those who do so the word is weak.

c. By a knowledge of the older forms.—The Anglo-Saxon form is *beáte, beot*. There is no such a weak form as *beátte, batte*. The præterite of *sendan* is *sende* weak. There is in Anglo-Saxon no such form as *sand*, strong.

In all this we see a series of expedients for distinguishing the præterite form from the present, when the root ends with the same sound with which the affix begins.

The change from a long vowel to a short one, as in *feed, fed*, &c., can only take place where there is a long vowel to be changed.

Where the vowels are short, and, at the same time, the word ends in -*d*, the -*d* of the present may become -*t* in the præterite. Such is the case with *bend, bent*.

When there is no long vowel to shorten, and no ·*d*

to change into -*t*, the two tenses, of necessity, remain alike; such is the case with *cut*, *cost*, &c.

§ 313. The following verbs form their præterite in -*t*:—

Present.	Præterite.		
Leave	† Left	not	‡ Leaved.
Cleave	Cleft	—	Cleaved.
Bereave	Bereft	—	Bereaved.
Deal	* Dealt	—	Dealed.
Feel	Felt	—	Feeled.
Dream	† Dremt	—	Dreamed.
Learn	† Lernt	—	Learned.

§ 314. Certain *so-called* irregularities may now be noticed.—*Made, had.*—In these words there is nothing remarkable but the ejection of a consonant. The Anglo-Saxon forms are *macode* and *hæfde*, respectively. The words, however, in regard to the amount of change, are not upon a *par*. The *f* in *hæfde* was probably sounded as *v*. Now *v* is a letter excessively liable to be ejected, which *k* is not. *K*, before it is ejected, is generally changed into either *g* or *y*.

Would, should, could.—It must not be imagined that *could* is in the same predicament with these words. In *will* and *shall* the -*l* is part of the original word. This is not the case with *can*. For the form *could*, see § 331.

§ 315. *Aught.*—In Anglo-Saxon *áhte*, the præterite of the present form *áh*, plural *ágon*.—As late as the time of Elizabeth we find *owe* used for *own*. The present form *own* seems to have arisen from the plural *ágon*. *Aught* is the præterite of the Anglo-Saxon *áh*; *owed* of the English *owe* = *debeo*; *owned* of the English *own* =

---

* Pronounced *delt*.
† So pronounced.
‡ Pronounced *leevd, cleevd, bereevd, deeld, feeld, dreemd, lernd*.

possideo. The word *own*, in the expression *to own to a thing*, has a totally different origin. It comes from the Anglo-Saxon *an* (plural, *unnon*) = *I give*, or *grant* = *concedo.*

§ 316. *Durst.*—The verb *dare* is both transitive and intransitive. We can say either *I dare do such a thing*, or *I dare (challenge) such a man to do it.* This, in the present tense, is unequivocally correct. In the past the double power of the word *dare* is ambiguous; still it is, to my mind at least, allowable. We can certainly say *I dared him to accept my challenge;* and we can, perhaps, say *I dared venture on the expedition.* In this last sentence, however, *durst* is the preferable expression.

Now, although *dare* is both transitive and intransitive, *durst* is only intransitive. It never agrees with the Latin word *provoco;* only with the Latin word *auedo.* Moreover, the word *durst* has both a present and a past sense. The difficulty which it presents consists in the presence of the *-st*, letters characteristic of the second person singular, but here found in all the persons alike; as *I durst, they durst*, &c.

This has still to be satisfactorily accounted for.

Must.—A form common to all persons, numbers, and tenses. That neither the *-s* nor the *-t* are part of the original root, is indicated by the Scandinavian form *maae* (Danish), pronounced *moh;* præterite *maatt.*

This form has still to be satisfactorily accounted for.

Wist.—In its present form a regular præterite from *wiss* = *know.* The difficulties of this word arise from the parallel forms *wit* (as in *to wit*), and *wot* = *knew.* The following are the forms of this peculiar word:—

In Mœso-Gothic, 1 sing. pres. ind. *váit;* 2. do.,

váist; 1 pl. *vitum;* præterite 1 s. *vissa;* 2 *rissêss;* 1 pl. *rissêdum*. From the form *váist* we see that the second singular is formed after the manner of *must;* that is, *váist* stands instead of *váit-t*. From the form *rissêdum* we see that the præterite is not strong, but weak; therefore that *vissa* is euphonic for *vista*.

In Anglo-Saxon.—*Wát, wást, witon, wiste,* and *wisse, wiston*.—Hence the double forms, *wiste,* and *wisse,* verify the statement concerning the Mœso-Gothic *vissa*.

In Icelandic.—*Veit, veizt, vitum, vissi*. Danish *ved, vide, vidste*. Observe the form *vidste;* since, in it, the *d* of the root (in spelling, at least) is preserved. The *t* of the Anglo-Saxon *wiste* is the *t,* not of the root, but of the inflection.

In respect to the four forms in question, viz., *wit, wot, wiss, wisst,* the first seems to be the root; the second a strong præterite regularly formed, but used (like οἶδα in Greek) with a present sense; the third a weak præterite, of which the *-t* has been ejected by a euphonic process, used also with a present sense; the fourth is a second singular from *wiss* after the manner of *wert* from *were,* a second singular from *wit* after the manner of *must,* a secondary præterite from *wiss,* or finally, the form *wisse,* anterior to the operation of the euphonic process that ejected the *-t*.

§ 317. In the phrase *this will do* = *this will answer the purpose,* the word *do* is wholly different from the word *do,* meaning *to act*. In the first case it is equivalent to the Latin *valere;* in the second to the Latin *facere*. Of the first the Anglo-Saxon inflection is *deáh, dugon, dohte, dohtest,* &c. Of the second it is *dó, doð, dyde,* &c. I doubt whether the præterite *did,* as equivalent to *valebat* = *was good for,* is correct. In the phrase *it did for him* = *it finished him,* either meaning may be allowed.

In the present Danish they write *duger*, but say *duer:* as *duger et noget?* = *Is it worth anything?* pronounced *dooer deh note?* This accounts for the ejection of the *g*. The Anglo-Saxon form *deåh* does the same.

§ 318. *Mind—mind and do so and so.*—In this sentence the word *mind* is wholly different from the noun *mind*. The Anglo-Saxon forms are *geman, gemanst, gemunon*, without the -*d*; this letter occurring only in the præterite tense (*gemunde, gemundon*), of which it is the sign. *Mind* is, then, a præterite form with a present sense; whilst *minded* (as in *he minded his business*) is an instance of excess of inflection; in other words, it is a præterite formed from a præterite.

§ 319. *Yode.*—The obsolete præterite of *go*, now replaced by *went*, the præterite of *wend*. Regular, except that the initial *g* has become *y*.

§ 320. *Did.*—See § 317.

Did, from *do* = *facio*, is a *strong* verb. This we infer from the form of its participle *done*.

If so the final -*d* is not the same as the -*d* in *moved*. What is it? There are good grounds for believing that in the word *did* we have a single instance of the old *reduplicate præterite*. If so, it is the latter *d* which is radical, and the former which is inflectional.

CHAPTER XXV.

ON CONJUGATION.

§ 321. ATTENTION is directed to the following list of verbs. In the present English they all form the præterite in -*d* or -*t* ; in Anglo-Saxon, they all formed it by a change of the vowel. In other words they are *weak verbs that were once strong*.

Præterites.

English.		Anglo-Saxon.	
Present.	*Præterite.*	*Present.*	*Præterite.*
Wreak	Wreaked.	Wrece	Wræ'c.
Fret	Fretted.	Frete	Fræ't.
Mete	Meted.	Mete	Mæ't.
Shear	Sheared.	Scere	Scear.
Braid	Braided.	Brede	Bræ'd.
Knead	Kneaded.	Cnede	Cnæ'd.
Dread	Dreaded.	Dræ'de	Dred.
Sleep	Slept.	Slápe	Slep.
Fold	Folded.	Fealde	Feold.
Wield	Wielded.	Wealde	Weold.
Wax	Waxed.	Weaxe	Weox.
Leap	Leapt.	Hleápe	Hleop.
Sweep	Swept.	Swápe	Sweop.
Weep	Wept.	Wepe	Weop.
Sow	Sowed.	Sáwe	Seow.
Bake	Baked.	Bace	Bók.
Gnaw	Gnawed.	Gnage	Gnóh.
Laugh	Laughed.	Hlihhe	Hlóh.
Wade	Waded.	Wade	Wód.

English.		Anglo-Saxon.	
Present.	Præterite.	Present.	Præterite.
Lade	Laded.	Hlade	Hlód.
Grave	Graved.	Grafe	Gróf.
Shave	Shaved.	Scafe	Scóf.
Step	Stepped.	Steppe	Stóp.
Wash	Washed.	Wacse	Wócs.
Bellow	Bellowed.	Belge	Bealh.
Swallow	Swallowed.	Swelge	Swealh.
Mourn	Mourned.	Murne	Mearn.
Spurn	Spurned.	Spurne	Spearn.
Carve	Carved.	Ceorfe	Cearf.
Starve	Starved.	Steorfe	Stærf.
Thresh	Threshed.	þersce	þærsc.
Hew	Hewed.	Heawe	Heow.
Flow	Flowed.	Flówe	Fleow.
Row	Rowed.	Rówe	Reow.
Creep	Crept.	Creópe	Creáp.
Dive	Dived.	Deófe	Deáf.
Shove	Shoved.	Scéofe	Sceáf.
Chew	Chewed.	Ceúwe	Ceáw.
Brew	Brewed.	Breówe	Breáw.
Lock	Locked.	Lúce	Leác.
Suck	Sucked.	Súce	Seác.
Reek	Reeked.	Reóce	Reác.
Smoke	Smoked.	Smeóce	Smeác.
Bow	Bowed.	Beóge	Beáh.
Lie	Lied.	Leóge	Leáh.
Gripe	Griped.	Grípe	Gráp.
Span	Spanned.	Spanne	Spón.
Eke	Eked.	Eáce	Eóc.
Fare	Fared.	Fare	Fór.

§ 322. Respecting the *strong* verb, the following general statements may be made:

1. Many strong verbs become weak; whilst no weak verb ever becomes strong.

2. All the strong verbs are of Saxon origin. None are classical.

3. The greater number of them are strong throughout the Gothic tongues.

4. No new word is ever, upon its importation, inflected according to the strong conjugation. It is always weak. As nearly as A. D. 1085, the French word *adouber = to dub*, was introduced into English. Its præterite was *dubbade*.

5. All derived words are inflected weak. The intransitive forms *drink* and *lie*, are strong; the transitive forms *drench* and *lay*, are weak.

This shows that the division of verbs into *weak* and *strong* is a truly natural one.

CHAPTER XXVI.

DEFECTIVENESS AND IRREGULARITY.

§ 323. THE distinction between irregularity and defectiveness has been foreshadowed. It is now more urgently insisted on.

The words that have hitherto served as illustrations are the personal pronouns *I* or *me*, the adjectives *good*, *better*, and *best*.

The view of these words was as follows; *viz.*, that none of them were *irregular*, but that they were all *defective*. *Me* wanted the nominative, *I* the oblique cases. *Good* was without a comparative, *better* and *best* had no positive degree.

Now *me* and *better* may be said to make good the defectiveness of *I* and *good*; and *I* and *good* may be said to replace the forms wanting in *me* and *better*. This gives us the principle of *compensation*. To introduce a new term, *I* and *me*, *good* and *better*, may be said to be *complementary* to each other.

What applies to nouns applies to verbs also. *Go* and *went* are not irregularities. *Go* is defective in the past tense. *Went* is without a present. The two words, however, compensate their mutual deficiencies, and are complementary to each other.

The distinction between defectiveness and irregularity, is the first instrument of criticism for coming to true views concerning the proportion of the regular and irregular verbs.

§ 324. The second instrument of criticism in determining the irregular verbs, is the meaning that we attach to the term.

It is very evident that it is in the power of the grammarian to raise the number of etymological irregularities to any amount, by narrowing the definition of the word *irregular;* in other words, by framing an exclusive rule. The current rule of the common grammarians that the præterite is formed *by the addition of -t,* or *-d,* or *-ed ;* a position sufficiently exclusive; since it proscribes not only the whole class of strong verbs, but also words like *bent* and *sent,* where *-t* exists, but where it does not exist as *an addition.* The regular forms, it may be said, should be *bended* and *sended.*

Exclusive, however, as the rule in question is, it is plain that it might be made more so. The regular forms might, by the *fiat* of a rule, be restricted to those in *-d.* In this case words like *wept* and *burnt* would be added to the already numerous list of irregulars.

Finally, a further limitation might be made, by laying down as a rule that no word was regular, unless it ended in *-ed.*

§ 325. Thus much concerning the modes of making rules exclusive, and, consequently, of raising the amount of irregularities. This is the last art that the philosophic grammarian is ambitious of acquiring. True etymology *reduces* irregularity; and that by making the rules of grammar, not exclusive, but general. *The quantum of irregularity is in the inverse proportion to the generality of our rules.* In language itself there is no irregularity. The word itself is only another name for our ignorance of the processes that change words; and, as irregularity is in the direct proportion to the exclusiveness of our rules, the exclusiveness of our rules is in the direct proportion to our ignorance of etymological processes.

§ 326. The explanation of some fresh terms will lead us towards the definition of the word *irregular*.

Vital and obsolete processes.—The word *moved* is formed from *move*, by the addition of *-d*. The addition of *-d* is the process by which the present form is rendered præterite. The word *fell* is formed from *fall*, by changing *a* into *e*. The change of vowel is the process by which the present form is rendered præterite. Of the two processes the result is the same. In what respect do they differ?

For the sake of illustration, let a new word be introduced into the language. Let a præterite tense of it be formed. This præterite would be formed, not by changing the vowel, but by adding *-d*. No *new* verb ever takes a strong præterite. The like takes place with nouns. No *new* substantive would form its plural, like *oxen* or *geese*, by adding *-en*, or by changing the vowel. It would rather, like *fathers* and *horses*, add the lene sibilant.

Now, the processes that change *fall, ox* and *goose* into *fell, oxen,* and *geese,* inasmuch as they cease to operate on the language in its present stage, are *obsolete* processes; whilst those that change *move* into *moved,* and *horse* into *horses,* operating on the language in its present stage, are *vital* processes.

A definition of the word *irregular* might be so framed as to include all words whose forms could not be accounted for by the vital processes. Such a definition would make all the strong verbs irregular.

The very fact of so natural a class as that of the strong

verbs being reduced to the condition of irregulars, invalidates such a definition as this.

§ 327. *Processes of necessity as opposed to processes of habit.*—The combinations *-pd*, *-fd*, *-kd*, *-sd*, and some others, are unpronounceable. Hence words like *step*, *quaff*, *back*, *kiss*, &c., take after them the sound of *-t*: *stept*, *quafft*, &c., being their præterites, instead of *stepd*, *quaffd*. Here the change from *-d* to *-t* is a matter of necessity. It is not so with words like *weep*, and *wept*, &c. Here the change of vowel is not necessary. *Weept* might have been said if the habit of the language had permitted.

A definition of the word *irregular* might be so framed as to include all words whose natural form was modified by any euphonic process whatever. In this case *slept* (modified by a process of necessity), and *wept* (modified by a process of habit), would be equally irregular.

A less limited definition might account words regular as long as the process by which they are deflected from their natural form was a process of necessity. Those, however, which were modified by a process of habit it would class with the irregulars.

Definitions thus limited arise from ignorance of euphonic processes, or rather from an ignorance of the generality of their operation.

§ 328. *Ordinary processes as opposed to extraordinary processes.*—The whole scheme of language is analogical. A new word introduced into a language takes the forms of its cases or tenses, &c., from the forms of the cases or tenses, &c., of the old words. The analogy is extended. Now few forms (if any) are so unique as not to have some others corresponding with them; and few processes of change are so unique as not to affect more words than one. The forms *wept*, and *slept*, correspond with each other. They are brought about by the same process: *viz.*, by the shortening of the vowel in *weep* and *sleep*. The analogy of *weep* is extended to *sleep*, and *vice versâ*. Changing our expression, a common influence affects both words. The alteration itself is the leading fact. The extent of its influence is an instrument of classification. When processes affect a considerable number of words, they may be called *ordinary* processes; as opposed to *extraordinary* processes, which affect one or few words.

When a word stands by itself, with no other corresponding to it, we confess our ignorance, and say that it is affected by an extraordinary process, by a process peculiar to itself, or by a process to which we know nothing similar.

A definition of the word *irregular* might be so framed as to include all words affected by extraordinary processes; the rest being considered regular.

§ 329. *Positive processes as opposed to ambiguous processes.*—The words *wept* and *slept* are similarly affected. Each is changed from *weep* and *sleep* respectively; and we know that the process which affects the one is the process that affects the other also. Here there is a positive process.

Reference is now made to words of a different sort. The nature of the word *worse* has been explained in the Chapter on the Comparative Degree. There the form is accounted for in two ways, of which only one can be the true one. Of the two processes, each might equally have brought about the present form. Which of the two it was, we are unable to say. Here the process is *ambiguous*.

A definition of the word *irregular* might be so framed as to include all words affected by ambiguous processes.

§ 330. *Normal processes as opposed to processes of*

confusion.—Let a certain word come under class A. Let all words under class A be similarly affected. Let a given word come under class A. This word will be affected even as the rest of class A is affected. The process affecting, and the change resulting, will be normal, regular, or analogical.

Let, however, a word, instead of really coming under class A, only *appear* to do so. Let it be dealt with accordingly. The analogy then is a false one. The principle of imitation is a wrong one. The process affecting is a process of confusion.

Examples of this (a few amongst many) are words like *songstress*, *theirs*, *minded*, where the words *songstr-*, *their-*, *mind-*, are dealt with as roots, which they are not.

Ambiguous processes, extraordinary processes, processes of confusion—each, or all of these, are legitimate reasons for calling words irregular. The practice of etymologists will determine what definition is most convenient.

With extraordinary processes we know nothing about the word. With ambiguous processes we are unable to make a choice. With processes of confusion we see the analogy, but, at the same time, see that it is a false one.

§ 331. *Could*.—With all persons who pronounce the *l* this word is truly irregular. The Anglo-Saxon form is *cuðe*. The *l* is inserted by a process of confusion.

Can, cunne, canst, cunnon, cunnan, cuðe, cuðon, cuð —such are the remaining forms in Anglo-Saxon. None of them account for the *l*. The presence of the *l* makes the word *could* irregular. No reference to the allied languages accounts for it.

Notwithstanding this, the presence of the *l* is accounted for. In *would* and *should* the *l* has a proper place. It is part of the original words, *will* and *shall.* A false analogy looked upon *could* in the same light. Hence a true irregularity; *provided that the* l. *be pronounced.*

The l., however, is pronounced by few, and that only in pursuance with the spelling. This reduces the word *could* to an irregularity, not of language, but only of orthography.

That the mere ejection of the *-n* in *can*, and that the mere lengthening of the vowel, are not irregularities, we learn from a knowledge of the processes that convert the Greek ὀδόντος (*odontos*) into ὀδούς (*odous*).

§ 332. The verb *quoth* is truly defective. It is found in only one tense, one number, and one person. It is the third person singular of the præterite tense. It has the further peculiarity of preceding its pronoun. Instead of saying *he quoth*, we say *quoth he*. In Anglo-Saxon, however, it was not defective. It was found in the other tenses, in the other number, and in other moods. *Ic cweðe þú cwyst, he cwyð; ic cwæð, þú cwæðe, he cwæð, we cwædon, ge cwædon, hi cwædon;* imperative, *cweð;* participle, *gecweden*. In the Scandinavian it is current in all its forms. There, however, it means, not *to speak* but to *sing*. As far as its conjugation goes, it is strong. As far as its class goes, it follows the form of *speak, spoke*. Like *speak*, its Anglo-Saxon form is in *æ*, as *cwæð*. Like one of the forms of *speak*, its English form is in *o*, as *quoth, spoke*.

§ 333. The principle that gives us the truest views of the structure of language is that which considers no word irregular unless it be affected by either an *ambiguous* process, or by a *process of confusion*. The words affected by *extraordinary processes* form a provisional class, which a future increase of our etymological knowledge may show to be regular. *Worse* and *could* are the fairest specimens of our irregulars. Yet even *could* is only an irregularity in the written language. The printer makes it, and the printer can take it away. Hence the class, instead of filling pages, is exceedingly limited.

CHAPTER XXVII.

THE IMPERSONAL VERBS.

§ 334. In *me-seems*, and *me-thinks*, the *me* is dative rather than accusative, and = *mihi* and *μοι* rather than *me* and *με*.

§ 335. In *me-listeth*, the *me* is accusative rather than dative, and = *me* and *με* rather than *mihi* and *μοι*.

For the explanation of this difference see *Syntax*, Chapter XXI.

CHAPTER XXVIII.

THE VERB SUBSTANTIVE.

§ 336. THE verb substantive is generally dealt with as an *irregular* verb. This is inaccurate. The true notion is that the idea of *being* or *existing* is expressed by four different verbs, each of which is defective in some of its parts. The parts, however, that are wanting in one verb, are made up by the inflections of one of the others. There is, for example, no præterite of the verb *am*, and no present of the verb *was*. The absence, however, of the present form of *was* is made up by the word *am*, and the absence of the præterite form of *am* is made up by the word *was*.

§ 337. *Was* is defective, except in the præterite tense, where it is found both in the indicative and conjunctive.

Indicative.		Conjunctive.	
Sing.	Plur.	Sing.	Plur.
1. Was	Were.	1. Were	Were.
2. Wast	Were.	2. Wert	Were.
3. Was	Were.	3. Were	Were.

In the older stages of the Gothic languages the word had both a full conjugation and a regular one. In Anglo-Saxon it had an infinitive, a participle present, and a participle past. In Mœso-Gothic it was inflected throughout with *-s;* as *visa, vas, résum, visans*. In that language it has the power of the Latin *maneo = to* *remain*. The *r* first appears in the Old High German, *wisu, was, wârumês, wësaner*. In Norse the *s* entirely disappears, and the word is inflected with *r* throughout; *vera, var, vorum*, &c.

§ 338. *Be* is inflected in Anglo-Saxon throughout the present tense, both indicative and subjunctive. It is found also as an infinitive, *beón*; as a gerund, *to beonne*; and as a participle, *beonde*; in the present English its inflection is as follows:

Presen..

Conjunctive.		Imperative.	
Sing.	*Plur.*	*Sing.*	*Plur.*
Be	Be	—	—
—	—	Be	Be
Be	Be	—	—

Infin. To be.   *Pres. P.* Being.   *Past. Part.* Been.

§ 339. The line in Milton beginning *If thou beest he* —(P. L. b. ii.), leads to the notion that the antiquated form *beest* is not indicative, but conjunctive. Such, however, is not the case: *byst* in Anglo-Saxon is indicative, the conjunctive form being *beó*. *And every thing that pretty bin* (Cymbeline).—Here the word *bin* is the conjunctive plural, in Anglo-Saxon *beón*; so that the words *every thing* are to be considered equivalent to the plural form *all things*. The phrase in Latin would stand thus, *quotquot pulchra sint*; in Greek, thus, *ἃ ἂν κάλα ᾖ*. The *indicative* plural is, in Anglo-Saxon, not *beón*, but *beóð* and *beó*.

§ 340. In the "Deutsche Grammatik" it is stated that the Anglo-Saxon forms *beó, bist, bið, beoð*, or *beó*, have not a present but a *future* sense; that whilst *am* means *I am, beó* means *I shall be*; and that in the older languages it is only where the form *am* is not found that *be* has the power of a present form. The same root occurs in the Slavonic and Lithuanic tongues with the same power; as, *esmi* = *I am*; *busu* = *I shall be*, Lithuanic. *Esmu* = *I am*; *buhshu* = *I shall be*, Livonic.—*Jesm* = *I am*; *budu* = *I shall be*, Slavonic.—*Gsem* = *I am*; *budu* = *I shall be*, Bohemian. This, however, proves, not that there is in Anglo-Saxon a future tense, but that the word *beó* has a future sense. There is no fresh tense where there is no fresh form.

The following is a specimen of the future power of *beón* in Anglo-Saxon:—" *Hi ne beoð na cilde, soðlice, on domesdæge, ac beoð swa micele menn swa swa hi, migton beón gif hi full weoxon on gewunlicre ylde.*"— Ælfric's Homilies. "They *will not be* children, forsooth, on Domesday, but *will be* as much (so muckle) men as they might be if they were full grown (waxen) in customary age."

§ 341. Now, if we consider the word *beón* like the word *weorðan* (see § 343) to mean not so much *to be* as to *become*, we get an element of the idea of futurity. Things which are *becoming anything* have yet something further to either do or suffer. Again, from the idea of futurity we get the idea of contingency, and this explains the subjunctive power of *be*. In English we often say *may* for *shall*, and the same was done in Anglo-Saxon.

§ 342. *Am*.—Of this form it should be stated that the letter -*m* is no part of the original word. It is the sign of the first person, just as it is in *Greek*, and several other languages.

It should also be stated, that although the fact be obscured, and although the changes be insufficiently accounted for, the forms *am, art, are*, and *is*, are not, like *am* and *was*, parts of different words, but forms of one and the same word; in other terms, that, although between *am* and *be* there is no etymological connexion, there is one between *am* and *is*. This we collect from the comparison of the Indo-European languages.

	1.	2.	3.
Sanskrit	*Asmi*	*Asi*	*Asti.*
Zend	*Ahmi*	*Asi*	*Ashti.*
Greek	Εἰμί	Εῖς	Ἐστί.
Latin	*Sum*	*Es*	*Est.*
Lithuanic	*Esmi*	*Essi*	*Esti.*
Old Slavonic	*Yesmy*	*Yesi*	*Yesty.*
Mœso-Gothic	*Im*	*Is*	*Ist.*
Old Saxon	—	*Is	*Ist.*
Anglo-Saxon	*Eom*	*Eart*	*Is.*
Icelandic	*Em*	*Ert*	*Er.*
English	*Am*	*Art*	*Is.*

§ 343. *Worth.*—In the following lines of Scott, the word *worth* = *is*, and is a fragment of the regular Anglo-Saxon verb *weorðan* = *to be*, or *to become;* German *werden*.

> Woe *worth* the chase, woe *worth* the day,
> That cost thy life, my gallant grey.
> *Lady of the Lake.*

---

* Found rarely; *bist* being the current form.—"Deutsche Grammatik," i. 894.

CHAPTER XXIX.

THE PRESENT PARTICIPLE.

§ 344. THE present participle, called also the active participle and the participle in -*ing*, is formed from the original word by adding -*ing*; as, *move, moving*. In the older languages the termination was more marked, being -*nd*. Like the Latin participle in -*ns*, it was originally declined. The Mœso-Gothic and Old High German forms are *habands* and *hapêntér* = *having*, respectively. The -*s* in the one language, and the -*êr* in the other, are the signs of the case and gender. In the Old Saxon and Anglo-Saxon the forms are -*and* and -*ande;* as *bindand, bindande* = *binding*. In all the Norse languages, ancient and modern, the -*d* is preserved. So it is in the Old Lowland Scotch, and in many of the modern provincial dialects of England, where *strikand, goand*, is said for *striking, going*. In Staffordshire, where the -*ing* is pronounced -*ingg*, there is a fuller sound than that of the current English. In Old English the form in -*nd* is predominant, in Middle English the use fluctuates, and in New English the termination -*ing* is universal. In the Scotch of the modern writers we find the form -*in*.

> The rising sun o'er Galston muirs
> Wi' glorious light was glintin';
> The hares were hirplin' down the furs,
> The lav'rocks they were chantin'.
>
> BURNS' *Holy Fair.*

§ 345. It has often been remarked that the participle is used in many languages as a substantive. This is true in Greek,

 Ὁ πράσσων = *the actor,* when a male.
 Ἡ πρασσοῦσα = *the actor,* when a female.
 Τὸ πρᾶττον = *the active principle of a thing.*

But it is also stated, that, in the English language, the participle is used as a substantive in a greater degree than elsewhere, and that it is used in several cases and in both numbers, *e. g.*,

 Rising early is healthy,
 There is health *in rising* early.
 This is the advantage *of rising* early.
 The *risings* in the North, &c.

Some acute remarks of Mr. R. Taylor, in the Introduction to his edition of Tooke's "Diversions of Purley," modify this view. According to these, the *-ing* in words like *rising* is not the *-ing* of the present participle; neither has it originated in the Anglo-Saxon *-end*. It is rather the *-ing* in words like *morning;* which is anything but a participle of the non-existent verb *morn,* and which has originated in the Anglo-Saxon substantival termination *-ung*. Upon this Rask writes as follows:—" *Gitsung, gewilnung* = *desire ; swutelung* = *manifestation ; clænsung* = *a cleansing ; sceawung* = *view, contemplation ; corð-beofung* = *an earthquake ; gesomnung* = *an assembly.* This termination is chiefly used in forming substantives from verbs of the first class in *-ian:* as *hálgung* = *consecration,* from *hálgian* = *to consecrate.* These verbs are all feminine."—" Anglo-Saxon Grammar," p. 107.

Now, whatever may be the theory of the origin of the termination *-ing* in old phrases like *rising early is* *healthy*, it cannot apply to expressions of recent introduction. Here the direct origin in *-ung* is out of the question.

The view, then, that remains to be taken of the forms in question is this:

1. That the older forms in *-ing* are substantival in origin, and = the Anglo-Saxon *-ung*.

2. That the latter ones are *irregularly* participial, and have been formed on a false analogy.

CHAPTER XXX.

THE PAST PARTICIPLE.

§ 346. A. THE *participle in* -EN.—In the Anglo-Saxon this participle was declined like the adjectives. Like the adjectives, it is, in the present English, undeclined.

In Anglo-Saxon it always ended in *-en*, as *sungen, funden, bunden*. In English this *-en* is often wanting, as *found, bound;* the word *bounden* being antiquated.

Words where the *-en* is wanting may be viewed in two lights; 1, they may be looked upon as participles that have lost their termination; 2, they may be considered as præterites with a participial sense.

§ 347. *Drank, drunk, drunken.*—With all words wherein the vowel of the plural differs from that of the singular, the participle takes the plural form. To say *I have drunk*, is to use an ambiguous expression; since *drunk* may be either a participle *minus* its termination, or a præterite with a participial sense. To say *I have drank*, is to use a præterite for a participle. To say *I have drunken*, is to use an unexceptional form.

In all words with a double form, as *spake* and *spoke, brake* and *broke, clave* and *clove,* the participle follows the form in *o*, as *spoken, broken, cloven*. *Spaken, braken, claven* are impossible forms. There are degrees in laxity of language, and to say *the spear is broke* is better than to say *the spear is brake.*

§ 348. As a general rule, we find the participle in *-en* wherever the præterite is strong; indeed, the participle in *-en* may be called the strong participle, or the participle of the strong conjugation. Still the two forms do not always coincide. In *mow, mowed, mown, sow, sowed, sown;* and several other words, we find the participle strong, and the præterite weak. I remember no instances of the converse. This is only another way of saying that the præterite has a greater tendency to pass from strong to weak than the participle.

§ 349. In the Latin language the change from *s* to *r*, and *vice versâ*, is very common. We have the double forms *arbor* and *arbos, honor* and *honos,* &c. Of this change we have a few specimens in English. The words *rear* and *raise*, as compared with each other, are examples. In Anglo-Saxon a few words undergo a similar change in the plural number of the strong præterites.

Ceóse, *I choose;* ceás, *I chose;* curon, *we chose;* gecoren, *chosen.*
Forleóse, *I lose;* forleás, *I lost;* forluron, *we lost;* forloren, *lost.*
Hreose, *I rush;* hreás, *I rushed;* hruron, *we rushed;* gehroren, *rushed.*

This accounts for the participial form *forlorn*, or *lost*, in New High German *verloren*. In Milton's lines,

——————— the piercing air
Burns *frore*, and cold performs the effect of fire,
Paradise Lost, b. ii.,

we have a form from the Anglo-Saxon participle *gefroren* =*frozen.*

§ 350. B. *The participle in* -D, -T, *or* -ED.—In the Anglo-Saxon this participle was declined like the adjective. Like the adjective, it is, in the present English, undeclined.

In Anglo-Saxon it differed in form from the præterite, inasmuch as it ended in -*ed*, or -*t*, whereas the præterite ended in -*ode*, -*de*, or -*te* : as, *lufode, bærnde, dypte*, præterites; *gelufod, barned, dypt*, participles.

As the ejection of the *e* (in one case final in the other not) reduces words like *bærned* and *bærnde* to the same form, it is easy to account for the present identity of form between the weak præterites and the participles in -*d*: *e. g., I moved, I have moved*, &c.

§ 351. *The prefix* Y.—In the older writers, and in works written, like Thomson's "Castle of Indolence," in imitation of them, we find prefixed to the præterite participle the letter *y*-, as, *yclept = called : yclad = clothed : ydrad = dreaded.*

The following are the chief facts and the current opinion concerning this prefix:—

1. It has grown out of the fuller forms *ge-*: Anglo-Saxon, *ge-*: Old Saxon, *gi-*: Mœso-Gothic, *ga-*: Old High German, *ka-, cha-, ga-, ki-, gi-*.

2. It occurs in each and all of the Germanic languages of the Gothic stock.

3. It occurs, with a few fragmentary exceptions, in none of the Scandinavian languages of the Gothic stock.

4. In Anglo-Saxon it occasionally indicates a difference of sense; as, *hâten = called, ge-*hâten *= promised; boren = borne, ge-*boren *= born.*

5. It occurs in nouns as well as verbs.

6. Its power, in the case of nouns, is generally some idea of *association*, or *collection*.—Mœso-Gothic, *sinþs = a journey, ga-sinþa = a companion;* Old High German, *perc = hill; ki-perki (gebirge) = a range of hills.*

7. But it has also a *frequentative* power; a frequentative power, which is, in all probability, secondary to its collective power; since things which recur frequently recur

with a tendency to collection or association; Middle High German, *ge-rassel* = *rustling* ; *ge-rumpel*—*c-rumple*.

8. And it has also the power of expressing the possession of a quality.

Anglo-Saxon.	English.	Anglo-Saxon.	Latin.
Feax	Hair	Ge-feax	Comatus.
Heorte	Heart	Ge-heort	Cordatus.
Stence	Odour	Ge-stence	Odorus.

This power is also a collective, since every quality is associated with the object that possesses it; *a sea with waves* = *a wavy sea*.

9. Hence it is probable that the *ga-*, *ki-*, or *gi-*, Gothic, is the *cum* of Latin languages. Such, at least, is Grimm's view, as given in the "Deutsche Grammatik," i. 1016.

Concerning this, it may be said that it is deficient in an essential point. It does not show how the participle past is collective. Undoubtedly it may be said that every such participle is in the condition of words like *ge-feax* and *ge-heort* ; *i. e.*, that they imply an association between the object and the action or state. But this does not seem to be Grimm's view; he rather suggests that the *ge* may have been a prefix to verbs in general, originally attached to all their forms, but finally abandoned everywhere, except in the case of the participle.

The theory of this prefix has yet to assume a satisfactory form.

CHAPTER XXXI.

COMPOSITION.

§ 352. In the following words, amongst many others, we have palpable and indubitable specimens of composition—*day-star, vine-yard, sun-beam, apple-tree, ship-load, silver-smith,* &c. The words *palpable* and *indubitable* have been used, because in many cases, as will be seen hereafter, it is difficult to determine whether a word be a true compound or not.

§ 353. Now, in each of the compounds quoted above, it may be seen that it is the second word which is qualified, or defined, by the first, and that it is not the first which is qualified, or defined, by the second. Of *yards, beams, trees, loads, smiths,* there may be many sorts, and, in order to determine what *particular* sort of *yard, beam, tree, load,* or *smith,* may be meant, the words *vine, sun, apple, ship,* and *silver,* are prefixed. In compound words it is the *first* term that defines or particularises the *second*.

§ 354. That the idea given by the word *apple-tree* is not referable to the words *apple* and *tree,* irrespective of the order in which they occur, may be seen by reversing the position of them. The word *tree-apple,* although not existing in the language, is as correct a word as *thorn-apple.* In *tree-apple,* the particular sort of *apple* meant is denoted by the word *tree,* and if there were in our gardens various sorts of plants called *apples*, of which some grew along the ground and others upon trees, such a word as *tree-apple* would be required in order to be opposed to *earth-apple*, or *ground-apple*, or some word of the kind.

In the compound words *tree-apple* and *apple-tree*, we have the same elements differently arranged. However, as the word *tree-apple* is not current in the language, the class of compounds indicated by it may seem to be merely imaginary. Nothing is farther from being the case. A *tree-rose* is a *rose* of a particular sort. The generality of *roses* being on *shrubs*, this grows on a *tree*. Its peculiarity consists in this fact, and this particular character is expressed by the word *tree* prefixed. A *rose-tree* is a *tree* of a particular sort, distinguished from *apple-trees*, and *trees* in general (in other words, particularised or defined), by the word *tree* prefixed.

A *ground-nut* is a *nut* particularised by growing in the ground. A *nut-ground* is a *ground* particularised by producing nuts.

A *finger-ring*, as distinguished from an *ear-ring*, and from *rings* in general (and so particularised), is a *ring* for the *finger*. A *ring-finger*, as distinguished from *fore-fingers*, and from *fingers* in general (and so particularised), is a *finger* whereon *rings* are worn.

§ 355. At times this rule seems to be violated. The words *spit-fire* and *dare-devil* seem exceptions to it. At the first glance it seems, in the case of a *spit-fire*, that what he (or she) *spits* is *fire ;* and that, in the case of a *dare-devil*, what he (or she) *dares* is the *devil*. In this case the initial words *spit* and *dare* are particularised by the final ones *fire* and *devil*. The true idea, however, confirms the original rule. A *spit-fire* voids his fire by spitting. A *dare-devil*, in meeting the fiend, would not shrink from him, but would defy him. A *spit-fire* is not one who spits fire, but one whose fire is *spit*. A *dare-devil* is not one who dares even the devil, but one by whom the devil is even dared.

§ 356. Of the two elements of a compound word, which is the most important? In one sense the latter, in another sense the former. The latter word is the most *essential*; since the general idea of *trees* must exist before it can be defined or particularised; so becoming the idea which we have in *apple-tree*, *rose-tree*, &c. The former word, however, is the most *influential*. It is by this that the original idea is qualified. The latter word is the staple original element: the former is the superadded influencing element. Compared with each other, the former element is active, the latter passive. Etymologically speaking, the former element, in English compounds, is the most important.

§ 357. Most numerous are the observations that bear upon the detail of the composition of words; *e.g.*, how nouns combine with nouns, as in *sun-beam*; nouns with verbs, as in *dare-devil*, &c. It is thought however, sufficient in the present work to be content with, 1. defining the meaning of the term composition; 2. explaining the nature of some obscure compounds.

Composition is the joining together, *in language*, of *two different words*, and *treating the combination as a single term*. Observe the words in italics.

In language.—A great number of our compounds, like the word *merry-making*, are divided by the sign -, or the hyphen. It is very plain that if all words *spell* with a hyphen were to be considered as compounds, the formation of them would be not a matter of speech, or language, but one of writing or spelling. This distinguishes compounds in language from mere printers' compounds.

Two.—For this, see § 369.

Different.—In Old High German we find the form *sëlp-sëlpo*. Here there is the junction of two words, but not the junction of two *different* ones. This distinguishes composition from gemination.

Words.—In *father-s, clear-er, four-th,* &c., there is the addition of a letter or a syllable, and it may be even of the part of a word. There is no addition, however, of a whole word. This distinguishes composition from derivation.

Treating the combination as a single term.—In determining between derived words and compound words, there is an occasional perplexity; the perplexity, however, is far greater in determining between a *compound word* and *two words*. In the eyes of one grammarian the term *mountain height* may be as truly a compound word as *sun-beam*. In the eyes of another grammarian it may be no compound word, but two words, just as *Alpine height* is two words; *mountain* being dealt with as an adjective. It is in the determination of this that the accent plays an important part.

§ 358. As a preliminary to a somewhat subtle distinction, the attention of the reader is drawn to the following line, slightly altered, from Churchill:—

" Then rést, my friénd, *and spáre* thy précious breath."

On each of the syllables *rést, friénd, spáre, préc-, breáth,* there is an accent. Each of these syllables must be compared with the one that precedes it; *rest* with *then*, *friend* with *my*, and so on throughout the line. Compared with the word *and*, the word *spare* is not only accented, but the accent is conspicuous and prominent. There is so little on *and*, so much on *spare*, that the disparity of accent is very manifest.

Now, if in the place of *and*, there were some other word, a word not so much accented as *spare*, but still more accented than *and*, this disparity would be diminished, and the accents of the two words might be said to be at *par*, or nearly so. As said before, the line was slightly altered from Churchill, the real reading being

" Thén rést, my friénd, *spare*, *spare* thy précious bréath."

In the true reading we actually find what had previously only been supposed. In the words *spare*, *spare*, the accents are nearly at *par*. Such the difference between accent at *par* and disparity of accent.

Good illustrations of the parity and disparity of accent may be drawn from certain names of places. Let there be such a sentence as the following: *the lime house near the bridge north of the new port*. Compare the parity of accent on the pairs of words *lime* and *house*, *bridge* and *north*, *new* and *port*, with the disparity of accent in the compound words *Limehouse*, *Bridgenorth*, and *Newport*. The separate words *beef steak*, where the accent is nearly at *par*, compared with the compound word *sweepstakes*, where there is a great disparity of accent, are further illustrations of the same difference.

The difference between a compound word and a pair of words is further illustrated by comparing such terms as the following:—*black bird*, meaning a *bird that is black*, with *bláckbird* = the Latin *merula; blúe bèll*, meaning a *bell that is blue*, with *blúebell*, the flower. Expressions like a *shárp edgéd instrument*, meaning *an instrument that is sharp and has edges*, as opposed to *a shárp-edgcd instrument*, meaning *an instrument with sharp edges*, further exemplify this difference.

Subject to a few exceptions, it may be laid down, that, in the English language, *there is no composition unless there is either a change of form or a change of accent.*

§ 359. The reader is now informed, that unless he has taken an exception to either a statement or an inference, he has either seen beyond what has been already laid down by the author, or else has read him with insufficient attention. This may be shown by drawing a distinction between a compound form and a compound idea.

In the words *a red house*, each word preserves its natural and original meaning, and the statement suggested by the term is *that a house is red*. By a parity of reasoning *a mad house* should mean a *house that is mad;* and provided that each word retain its *natural meaning* and its *natural accent*, such is the fact. Let a *house* mean, as it often does, a *family*. Then the phrase, *a mad house*, means that the *house, or family, is mad*, just as a *red house* means that the *house is red*. Such, however, is not the current meaning of the word. Every one knows that *a mad house* means *a house for mad men;* in which case it is treated as a compound word, and has a marked accent on the first syllable; just as *Límehouse* has. Now, compared with the word *red house*, meaning a house of a *red colour*, and compared with the words *mad house*, meaning a *deranged family*, the word *madhouse*, in its common sense, expressed a compound idea; as opposed to two ideas, or a double idea. The word *beef steak* is evidently a compound idea; but as there is no disparity of accent, it is not a compound word. Its sense is compound. Its form is not compound but double. This indicates the objection anticipated, which is this: *viz.*, that a definition, which would exclude such a word as *beef steak* from the list of compounds, is, for that very reason, exceptionable. I answer to this, that the term in question is a compound idea, and not a compound form; in other words, that it is a compound in logic, but not a compound in etymology. Now etymology, taking cognisance of forms only, has nothing to do with ideas, except so far as they influence forms.

Such is the commentary upon the words, *treating the combination as a single term;* in other words, such the difference between a compound word and two words. The rule, being repeated, stands (subject to exceptions indicated above) thus:—*there is no true composition without either a change of form or a change of accent.*

§ 360. As I wish to be clear upon this point, I shall illustrate the statement by its application.

The term *trée-róse* is often pronounced *trée róse;* that is, with the accent at *par*. It is compound in the one case; it is a pair of words in the other.

The terms *mountain ash* and *mountain height* are generally (perhaps always) pronounced with an equal accent on the syllables *mount-* and *ash, mount-* and *height*, respectively. In this case the word *mountain* must be dealt with as an adjective, and the words considered as two. The word *moúntain wave* is often pronounced with a visible diminution of accent on the last syllable. In this case there is a disparity of accent, and the word is compound.

§ 361. The following quotation indicates a further cause of perplexity in determining between compound words and two words:—

1.
A wet sheet and a blowing gale,
  A breeze that follows fast;
That fills the white and swelling sail,
  And bends the *gallant mast.*
                    ALLAN CUNNINGHAM.

2.
Britannia needs no bulwarks,
  No towers along the steep;
Her march is o'er the *mountain-wave,*
  Her home is on the deep.
                    THOMAS CAMPBELL.

To speak first of the term *gallant mast*. If *gallant* mean *brave*, there are *two words*. If the words be two, there is a stronger accent on *mast*. If the accent on *mast* be stronger, the rhyme with *fast* is more complete; in other words, the metre favours the notion of the words being considered as *two*. *Gallant-mast*, however, is a compound word, with an especial nautical meaning. In this case the accent is stronger on *gal-* and weaker on *-mast*. This, however, is not the state of things that the metre favours. The same applies to *mountain wave*. The same person who in prose would throw a stronger accent on *mount-* and a weaker one on *wave* (so dealing with the word as a compound), might, in poetry, make the words *two*, by giving to the last syllable a parity of accent.

The following quotation from Ben Jonson may be

read in two ways; and the accent may vary with the reading:

1.
Lay thy bow of pearl apart,
And thy *silver shining* quiver.

2.
Lay thy bow of pearl apart,
And thy *silver-shining* quiver.

Cynthia's Revels.

§ 362. *On certain words wherein the fact of their being compound is obscured.*—Composition is the addition of a word to a word, derivation is the addition of certain letters or syllables to a word. In a compound form each element has a separate and independent existence; in a derived form, only one of the elements has such. Now it is very possible that in an older stage of a language two words may exist, may be put together, and may so form a compound, each word having, then, a separate and independent existence. In a later stage of language, however, only one of these words may have a separate and independent existence, the other having become obsolete. In this case a compound word would take the appearance of a derived one, since but one of its elements could be exhibited as a separate and independent word. Such is the case with, amongst others, the word *bishop-ric*. In the present language the word *ric* has no separate and independent existence. For all this, the word is a true compound, since, in Anglo-Saxon, we have the noun *rice* as a separate, independent word, signifying *kingdom* or *domain*.

Again, without becoming obsolete, a word may alter its form. This is the case with most of our adjectives in -*ly*. At present they appear derivative; their termination -*ly* having no separate and independent existence. The older language, however, shows that they are compounds; since -*ly* is nothing else than -*lic*, Anglo-Saxon; -*lih*, Old High German; -*leiks*, Mœso-Gothic; = *like*, or *similis*, and equally with it an independent separate word.

§ 363. "Subject to a few exceptions, it may be laid down, that *there is no true composition unless there is either a change of form or a change of accent.*"—Such is the statement made in § 358. The first class of exceptions consists of those words where the natural tendency to disparity of accent is traversed by some rule of euphony. For example, let two words be put together, which at their point of contact form a combination of sounds foreign to our habits of pronunciation. The rarity of the combination will cause an effort in utterance. The effort in utterance will cause an accent to be laid on the latter half of the compound. This will equalize the accent, and abolish the disparity. The word *monkshood*, the name of a flower (*aconitum napellus*), where, to my ear at least, there is quite as much accent on the -*hood* as on the *monks*-, may serve in the way of illustration. *Monks* is one word, *hood* another. When joined together, the *h*- of the -*hood* is put in immediate apposition with the *s* of the *monks*-. Hence the combination *monkshood*. At the letters *s* and *h* is the point of contact. Now the sound of *s* followed immediately by the sound of *h* is a true aspirate. But true aspirates are rare in the English language. Being of rare occurrence, the pronunciation of them is a matter of attention and effort; and this attention and effort create an accent which otherwise would be absent.

Hence words like *mónks-hóod, wéll-héad,* and some others.

Real reduplications of consonants, as in *hóp-póle,* may have the same parity of accent with the true aspirates: and for the same reasons. They are rare combinations that require effort and attention.

§ 364. The second class of exceptions contains those words wherein between the first element and the second there is so great a disparity, either in the length of the vowel, or the length of the syllable *en masse,* as to counteract the natural tendency of the first element to become accented. One of the few specimens of this class (which after all may consist of double words) is the term *upstánding.* Here it should be remembered, that words like *hapházard, foolhárdy, uphólder,* and *withhóld* come under the first class of the exceptions.

§ 365. The third class of exceptions contains words like *perchánce* and *perháps.* In all respects but one these are double words, just as *by chance* is a double word. *Per,* however, differs from *by* in having no separate existence. This sort of words we owe to the multiplicity of elements (classical and Gothic) in the English language.

§ 366. *Peacock, peahen.*—If these words be rendered masculine or feminine by the addition of the elements *-cock* and *-hen,* the statements made in the beginning of the present chapter are invalidated. Since, if the word *pea-* be particularized, qualified, or defined by the words *-cock* and *-hen,* the *second* term defines or particularises the *first,* which is contrary to the rule of § 356. The truth, however, is, that the words *-cock* and *-hen* are defined by the prefix *pea-.* Preparatory to the exhibition of this, let us remember that the word *pea* (although now found in composition only) is a true and independent substantive, the name of a species of fowl, like *pheasant, partridge,* or any other appellation. It is the Latin *pavo,* German *pfau.* Now if the word *peacock* mean a *pea* (*pfau* or *pavo*) that is a male, then do *woodcock, black-cock,* and *bantam-cock,* mean *woods, blacks,* and *bantams* that are male. Or if the word *peahen* mean a *pea* (*pfau* or *pavo*) that is female, then do *moorhen* and *guineahen* mean *moors* and *guineas* that are female. Again, if a *peahen* mean a *pea* (*pfau* or *pavo*) that is female, then does the compound *pheasant-hen* mean the same as *hen-pheasant;* which is not the case. The fact is that *peacock* means a *cock that is a pea* (*pfau* or *pavo*); *peahen* means a *hen that is a pea* (*pfau* or *pavo*); and, finally, *peafowl* means a *fowl that is a pea* (*pfau* or *pavo*). In the same way *moorfowl* means, not a *moor that is connected with a fowl,* but a *fowl that is connected with a moor.*

§ 367. It must be clear that in every compound word there are, at least, two parts; *i. e.,* the whole or part of the original, and the whole or part of the superadded word. In the most perfect forms of inflection, however, there is a *third* element, *viz.,* a vowel, consonant, or syllable that joins the first word with the second.

In the older forms of all the Gothic languages the presence of this third element was the rule rather than the exception. In the present English it exists in but few words.

a. The -*a*- in *black-a-moor* is possibly such a connecting element.

b. The -*in*- in *night-in-gale* is most probably such a connecting element. Compare the German form *nacht-*

i-gale, and remember the tendency of vowels to take the sound of *-ng* before *g*.

§ 368. *Improper compounds.*—The *-s-* in words like *Thur-s-day*, *hunt-s-man*, may be one of two things.

a. It may be the sign of the genitive case, so that *Thursday* = *Thoris dies*. In this case the word is an *improper compound*, since it is like the word *pater-familias* in Latin, in a common state of syntactical construction.

b. It may be a connecting sound, like the *-i-* in *nacht-i-gale*. Reasons for this view occur in the following fact:—

In the modern German languages the genitive case of feminine nouns ends otherwise than in *-s*. Nevertheless, the sound of *-s-* occurs in composition equally, whether the noun it follows be masculine or feminine. This fact, as far as it goes, makes it convenient to consider the sound in question as a connective rather than a case. Probably, it is neither one nor the other exactly, but the effect of a false analogy.

§ 369. *Decomposites.*—" Composition is the joining together of *two* words."—See § 357.

Words like *mid-ship-man*, *gentle-man-like*, &c., where the number of verbal elements seems to amount to *three*, are no exception to this rule; since *compound radicals* like *midship* and *gentleman*, are, for the purposes of composition, single words. Compounds wherein one element is compound are called *decomposites*.

§ 370. There are a number of words which are never found by themselves; or, if so found, have never the same sense that they have in *combination*. Mark the word *combination*. The terms in question are points of *combination*, not of composition: since they form not the parts of words, but the parts of phrases. Such are the expressions *time and tide—might and main—rede me my riddle—pay your shot—rhyme and reason*, &c. These words are evidently of the same class, though not of the same species with *bishopric, colewort, spillikin, gossip, mainswearer*, &c.

These last-mentioned terms give us obsolete words preserved in composition. The former give us obsolete words preserved in combination.

CHAPTER XXXII.

ON DERIVATION AND INFLECTION.

§ 371. DERIVATION, like *etymology*, is a word used in a wide and in a limited sense. In the wide sense of the term, every word, except it be in the simple form of a root, is a derived word. In this sense the cases, numbers, and genders of nouns, the persons, moods, and tenses of verbs, the ordinal numbers, the diminutives, and even the compound words, are alike matters of derivation. In the wide sense of the term the word *fathers*, from *father*, is equally in a state of derivation with the word *strength* from *strong*.

In the use of the word, even in its limited sense, there is considerable laxity and uncertainty.

Gender, number, case.—These have been called the *accidents* of the noun, and these it has been agreed to separate from derivation in its stricter sense, or from derivation properly so called, and to class together under the name of declension. Nouns are *declined*.

Person, number, tense, voice.—These have been called the *accidents* of a verb, and these it has been agreed to separate from derivation properly so called, and to class together under the name of conjugation. Verbs are *conjugated*.

Conjugation and declension constitute inflection. Nouns and verbs, speaking generally, are inflected.

Inflection, a part of derivation in its wider sense, is separated from derivation properly so called, or from derivation in its limited sense.

The degrees of comparison, or certain derived forms of adjectives; the ordinals, or certain derived forms of the numerals; the diminutives, &c., or certain derived forms of the substantive, have been separated from derivation properly so called, and considered as parts of inflection. I am not certain, however, that for so doing there is any better reason than mere convenience.

Derivation proper, the subject of the present chapter, comprises all the changes that words undergo, which are not referable to some of the preceding heads. As such, it is, in its details, a wider field than even composition. The details, however, are not entered into.

§ 372. Derivation proper may be divided according to a variety of principles. Amongst others—

1. *According to the evidence.*—In the evidence that a word is not simple, but derived, there are at least two degrees.

a. That the word *strength* is a derived word I collect to a certainty from the word *strong*, an independent form, which I can separate from it. Of the nature of the word *strength* there is the clearest evidence, or evidence of the first degree.

b. Fowl, hail, nail, sail, tail, soul; in Anglo-Saxon, *fugel, hægel, nægel, segel, tægel, sawel.*—These words are by the best grammarians considered as derivatives. Now, with these words I cannot do what was done with the word *strength*, I cannot take from them the part which I look upon as the derivational addition, and after that leave an independent word. *Strength -th* is a true word; *fowl* or *fugel -l* is no true word. If I believe these latter words to be derivations at all, I do it because I find in words like *harelle*, &c., the *-l* as a derivational addition. Yet, as the fact of a word being sometimes used as a derivational addition does not preclude it from being at other times a part of the root, the evidence that the words in question are not simple, but derived, is not cogent. In other words, it is evidence of the second degree.

II. *According to the effect.*—The syllable *-en* in the word *whiten* changes the noun *white* into a verb. This is its effect. We may so classify derivational forms as to arrange combinations like *-en* (whose effect is to give the idea of the verb) in one order; whilst combinations like *-th* (whose effect is, as in the word *strength*, to give the idea of abstraction) form another order.

III. *According to the form.*—Sometimes the derivational element is a vowel (as the *-ie* in *doggie*), sometimes a consonant (as the *-th* in *strength*), sometimes a vowel and consonant combined; in other words a syllable (as the *-en*, in *whiten*), sometimes a change of vowel without any addition (as the *-i* in *tip*, compared with *top*), sometimes a change of consonant without any addition (as the *z* in *prize*, compared with *price*). Sometimes it is a change of accent, like a súrvey, compared with *to survéy*. To classify derivations in this manner, is to classify them according to their form.

IV. *According to the historical origin of the derivational elements.*

V. *According to the number of the derivational elements.*—In *fisher*, as compared with *fish*, there is but one derivational affix. In *fishery*, as compared with *fish*, the number of derivational elements is two.

§ 373. In words like *bishopric*, and many others mentioned in the last Chapter, we had compound words under the appearance of derived ones; in words like *upmost*, and many others, we have derivation under the appearance of composition.

CHAPTER XXXIII.

ADVERBS.

§ 374. *Adverbs.*—The adverbs are capable of being classified after a variety of principles.

Firstly, they may be divided according to their meaning. In this case we speak of the adverbs of *time, place, number, manner.*

§ 375. *Well, better, ill, worse.*—Here we have a class of adverbs expressive of degree, or intensity. Adverbs of this kind are capable of taking an inflection, viz., that of the comparative and superlative degrees.

Now, then, here, there.—In the idea expressed by these words there are no degrees of intensity. Adverbs of this kind are incapable of taking any inflection.

Adverbs differ from nouns and verbs in being susceptible of one sort of inflection only, viz., that of degree.

§ 376. Secondly, adverbs may be divided according to their form and origin.

Better, worse.—Here the words are sometimes adverbs; sometimes adjectives.—*This book is better than that*—here *better* agrees with *book*, and is, therefore, adjectival. *This looks better than that*—here *better* qualifies *looks*, and is therefore adverbial. Again; *to do a thing with violence* is equivalent *to do a thing violently*. This shows how adverbs may arise out of cases. In words like the English *better*, the Latin *vi* = *violenter*, the Greek καλὸν = καλῶς, we have adjectives in their degrees, and substantives in their cases, with adverbial powers. In other words, nouns are deflected from their natural sense to an adverbial one. Adverbs of this kind are adverbs of *deflection*.

Brightly, bravely.—Here an adjective is rendered adverbial by the addition of the derivative syllable *-ly*. Adverbs like *brightly*, &c., may be called adverbs of *derivation*.

Now.—This word has not satisfactorily been shown to have originated as any other part of speech but as an adverb. Words of this sort are adverbs *absolute*.

§ 377. *When, now, well, worse, better*—here the adverbial expression consists in a single word, and is *simple*. *To-day, yesterday, not at all, somewhat*—here the adverbial expression consists of a compound word, or a phrase. This indicates the division of adverbs into *simple* and *complex*.

§ 378. Adverbs of deflection may originally have been—

a. Substantive; as *needs* in such expressions as *I needs must go.*

b. Adjectives; as the *sun shines bright.*

c. Prepositions; as *I go in, we go out;* though, it should be added, that in this case we may as reasonably derive the preposition from the adverb as the adverb from the preposition.

§ 379. Adjectives of deflection derived from substantives may originally have been—

a. Substantives in the genitive *case;* as *needs.*

b. Substantives in the dative *case;* as *whil-om*, an antiquated word meaning *at times*, and often improperly spelt *whilome*. In such an expression as *wait a while*, the word still exists; and *while = time*, or rather *pause;* since, in Danish, *hvile = rest*.

El-se (for *ell-es*); *unawar-es*; *eftsoon-s* are *adjectives* in the genitive case. *By rights* is a word of the same sort; the *-s* being the sign of the genitive singular like the *-s* in *father's*, and not of the accusative plural like the *-s* in *fathers*.

Once (*on-es*); *twice* (*twi-es*); *thrice* (*thri-es*) are *numerals* in the genitive case.

§ 380. *Darkling.*—This is no participle of a verb *darkle*, but an adverb of derivation, like *unwaringûn = unawares*, Old High German; *stillinge = secretly*, Middle High German; *blindlings = blindly*, New High German; *darnungo = secretly*, Old Saxon; *nichtinge = by night*, Middle Dutch; *blindeling = blindly*, New Dutch; *bæclinga = backwards*, *handlunga = hand to hand*, Anglo-Saxon; and, finally, *blindlins, backlins, darklins, middlins, scantlins, stridelins, stowlins*, in Lowland Scotch.

CHAPTER XXXIV.

ON CERTAIN ADVERBS OF PLACE.

§ 381. It is a common practice for languages to express by different modifications of the same root the three following ideas:—
1. The idea of rest *in* a place.
2. The idea of motion *towards* a place.
3. The idea of motion *from* a place.

This habit gives us three correlative adverbs—one of *position*, and two of *direction*.

§ 382. It is also a common practice of language to depart from the original expression of each particular idea, and to interchange the signs by which they are expressed; so that a word originally expressive of simple position or *rest in a place* may be used instead of the word expressive of direction, *or motion between two places*. Hence we say, *come here*, when *come hither* would be the more correct expression.

§ 383. The full amount of change in this repect may be seen from the following table, illustrative of the forms *here, hither, hence*.

Mœso-Gothic.	þar, þaþ, þaþro,	*there, thither, thence.*
	hér, hiþ, hidrô,	*here, hither, hence.*
Old High German . . .	huâr, huara, huanana,	*where, whither, whence.*
	dâr, dara, danana,	*there, thither, thence.*
	hear, héra, hinana,	*here, hither, hence.*

Old Saxon	huar, huar, huanan,	where, whither, whence.
	thar, thar, thanan,	there, thither, thence.
	hër, hër, hënan,	here, hither, hence.
Anglo-Saxon	þar, þider, þonan,	there, thither, thence.
	hvar, hrider, hvonan,	where, whither, whence.
	hër, hider, hënan,	here, hither, hence.
Old Norse	þar, þaðra, þaðan,	there, thither, thence,
	hvar, hvert, hvaðan,	where, whither, whence.
	hër, höðra, hëðan,	here, hither, hence.
Middle High German .	dâ, dan, dannen,	there, thither, thence.
	wâ, war, wannen,	where, whither, whence.
	hie, hër, hennen,	here, hither, hence.
Modern High German .	da, dar, dannen,	there, thither, thence.
	wo, wohin, wannen,	where, whither, whence.
	hier, her, hinnen,	here, hither, hence.

§ 384. Local terminations of this kind, in general, were commoner in the earlier stages of language than at present. The following are from the Mœso Gothic:—

Innaþrô = *from within.*
Utaþrô = *from without.*
Inþaþrô = *from above.*
Fáirraþrô = *from afar.*
Allaþrô = *from all quarters.*

§ 385. The -*ce* (= *es*) in *hen-ce, when-ce, then-ce,* has yet to be satisfactorily explained. The Old English is *whenn-es, thenn-es.* As far, therefore, as the spelling is concerned, they are in the same predicament with the word *once,* which is properly *on-es,* the genitive of *one.* This origin is probable, but not certain.

§ 386. Yonder.—In the Mœso-Gothic we have the following forms: *jáinar, jáina, jánþrô* = *illic, illuc, illinc.* They do not, however, quite explain the form *yon-d-er.* It is not clear whether the *d* = the -*d* in *jáind,* or the *þ* in *jainþro.*

§ 387. *Anon*, is used by Shakspeare, in the sense of *presently*.—The probable history of this word is as follows: the first syllable contains a root akin to the root *yon*, signifying *distance in place*. The second is a shortened form of the Old High German and Middle High German, -*nt*, a termination expressive, 1, of removal in *space*; 2, of removal in *time*; Old High German, *ënont, ënnont;* Middle High German, *ënentlig, jenunt = beyond*.

CHAPTER XXXV.

ON WHEN, THEN, AND THAN.

§ 388. The Anglo-Saxon adverbs are *whenne* and *þenne* = *when, then*.

The masculine accusative cases of the relative and demonstrative pronoun are *hwæne* (*hwone*) and *þæne* (*þone*).

Notwithstanding the difference, the first form is a variety of the second; so that the adverbs *when* and *then* are really pronominal in origin.

§ 389. As to the word *than*, the conjunction of comparison, it is another form of *then;* the notions of *order*, *sequence*, and *comparison* being allied.

This is good; then (or *next in order*) *that is good*, is an expression sufficiently similar to *this is better than that* to have given rise to it; and in Scotch and certain provincial dialects we actually find *than* instead of *then*.

CHAPTER XXXVI.

PREPOSITIONS AND CONJUNCTIONS.

§ 390. *Prepositions.*—Prepositions are wholly unsusceptible of inflection.

§ 391. *Conjunctions.*—Conjunctions, like prepositions, are wholly unsusceptible of inflection.

§ 392. *Yes, no.*—Although *not* may be considered to be an adverb, *nor* a conjunction, and *none* a noun, these two words, the direct categorical affirmative, and the direct categorical negative, are referable to none of the current parts of speech. Accurate grammar places them in a class by themselves.

§ 393. *Particles.*—The word particle is a collective term for all those parts of speech that are *naturally* unsusceptible of inflection; comprising, 1, interjections; 2, direct categorical affirmatives; 3, direct categorical negatives; 4, absolute conjunctions; 5, absolute prepositions; 6, adverbs unsusceptible of degrees of comparison; 7, inseparable prefixes.

CHAPTER XXXVII.

ON THE GRAMMATICAL POSITION OF THE WORDS MINE AND THINE.

§ 394. THE inflection of pronouns has its natural peculiarities in language. It has also its natural difficulties in philology. These occur not in one language in particular, but in all generally.

The most common peculiarity in the grammar of pronouns is the fact of what may be called their *convertibility*. Of this *convertibility* the following statements serve as illustration :—

1. *Of case.*—In our own language the words *my* and *thy* although at present possessives, were previously datives, and, earlier still, accusatives. Again, the accusative *you* replaces the nominative *ye*, and *vice versâ*.

2. *Of number.*—The words *thou* and *thee* are, except in the mouths of Quakers, obsolete. The plural forms, *ye* and *you*, have replaced them.

3. *Of person.*—The Greek language gives us examples of this in the promiscuous use of νιν, μιν, σφε, and ἑαυτοῦ; whilst *sich* and *sik* are used with a similar latitude in the Middle High German and Scandinavian.

4. *Of class.*—The demonstrative pronouns become—

    a. Personal pronouns.
    b. Relative pronouns.
    c. Articles.

The reflective pronoun often becomes reciprocal.

§ 395. These statements are made for the sake of illustrating, not of exhausting, the subject. It follows, however, as an inference from them, that the classification of pronouns is complicated. Even if we knew the original power and derivation of every form of every pronoun in a language, it would be far from an easy matter to determine therefrom the paradigm that they should take in grammar. To place a word according to its power in a late stage of language might confuse the study of an early stage. To say that because a word was once in a given class, it should always be so, would be to deny that in the present English *they, these,* and *she* are personal pronouns at all

The two tests, then, of the grammatical place of a pronoun, its *present power* and its *original power*, are often conflicting.

§ 396. In the English language the point of most importance in this department of grammar is the place of forms like *mine* and *thine;* in other words, of the forms in *-n.*

Now, if we take up the common grammars of the English language *as it is*, we find, that, whilst *my* and *thy* are dealt with as genitive cases, *mine* and *thine* are considered adjectives. In the *Anglo-Saxon* grammars, however, *min* and *þin*, the older forms of *mine* and *thine*, are treated as genitives or possessives.

§ 397. This gives us two views of the words *my* and *thy.*

a. They may be genitives or possessives, which were originally datives or accusatives; in which case they are deduced from the Anglo-Saxon *mee* and *þee.*

b. They may be the Anglo-Saxon *min* and *þin*, *minus* the final *-n.*

Each of these views has respectable supporters. The former is decidedly preferred by the present writer.

§ 398. What, however, are *thine* and *mine?* Are they adjectives like *meus, tuus,* and *suus,* or cases like *mei, tui, sui,* in Latin, and *hi-s* in English?

It is no answer to say that sometimes they are one and sometimes the other. They were not so originally. They did not begin with meaning two things at once; on the contrary, they were either possessive cases, of which the power became subsequently adjectival, or adjectives, of which the power became subsequently possessive.

§ 399. In Anglo-Saxon and in Old Saxon there is but one form to express the Latin *mei* (or *tui*), on the one side, and *meus, mea, meum* (or *tuus,* &c.), on the other. In several other Gothic tongues, however, there was the following difference of form:

Mœso-Gothic	meina	= *mei* as opposed to meins	= *meus.*
	þeina	= *tui*	þeins	= *tuus.*
Old High German . .	min	= *mei*	miner	= *meus.*
	din	= *tui*	diner	= *tuus.*
Old Norse	min	= *mei*	minn	= *meus.*
	þin	= *tui*	þinn	= *tuus.*
Middle Dutch	mins	= *mei*	min	= *meus.*
	dins	= *tui*	din	= *tuus.*
Modern High German . .	mein	= *mei*	meiner	= *meus.*
	dein	= *tui*	deiner	= *tuus.*

In these differences of form lie the best reasons for the assumption of a genitive case, as the origin of an adjectival form; and, undoubtedly, in those languages where both forms occur, it is convenient to consider one as a case and one as an adjective.

§ 400. But this is not the present question. In Anglo-Saxon there is but one form, *min* and *þin* = *mei* and *meus*, *tui* and *tuus*, indifferently. Is this form an oblique case or an adjective?

This involves two sorts of evidence.

§ 401. *Etymological evidence.*—Assuming two powers for the words *min* and *þin*, one genitive, and one adjectival, which is the original one? Or, going beyond the Anglo-Saxon, assuming that of two *forms* like *meina* and *meins*, the one has been derived from the other, which is the primitive, radical, primary, or original one?

Men, from whom it is generally unsafe to differ, consider that the adjectival form is the derived one; and, as far as forms like *miner*, as opposed to *min*, are concerned, the evidence of the foregoing list is in their favour. But what is the case with the Middle Dutch? The genitive *mins* is evidently the derivative of *min*.

The reason why the forms like *miner* seem derived is because they are longer and more complex than the others. Nevertheless, it is by no means an absolute rule in philology that the least compound form is the oldest. A word may be adapted to a secondary meaning by a change in its parts in the way of omission, as well as by a change in the way of addition.

§ 402. As to the question whether it is most likely for an adjective to be derived from a case, or a case from an adjective, it may be said, that philology furnishes instances both ways. *Ours* is a case derived, in syntax at least, from an adjective. *Cujum* (as in *cujum pecus*) and *sestertium* are Latin instances of a nominative case being evolved from an oblique one.

§ 403. *Syntactic evidence.*—If in Anglo-Saxon we found such expressions as *dæl min* = *pars mei*, *half þin*

= *dimidium tui*, we should have a reason, as far as it went, for believing in the existence of a true genitive. Such instances, however, have yet to be quoted.

§ 404. Again—as *min* and *þin* are declined like adjectives, even as *meus* and *tuus* are so declined, we have means of ascertaining their nature from the form they take in certain constructions; thus, *minra* = *meorum*, and *minre* = *meæ*, are the genitive plural and the dative singular respectively. Thus, too, the Anglo-Saxon for *of thy eyes* should be *eagena þinra*, and the Anglo-Saxon for *to my widow*, should be *wuduwan minre*; just as in Latin, they would be *oculorum tuorum*, and *viduæ meæ*.

If, however, instead of this we find such expressions as *eagena þin*, or *wuduwan min*, we find evidence in favour of a genitive case; for then the construction is not one of concord, but one of government, and the words *þin* and *min* must be construed as the Latin forms *tui* and *mei* would be in *oculorum mei*, and *viduæ mei*; viz.: as genitive cases. Now, whether a sufficient proportion of such constructions exist or not, they have not yet been brought forward.

Such instances, even if quoted, would not be conclusive.

§ 405. Why would they not be conclusive? Because *even of the adjective there are uninflected forms.*

As early as the Mœso-Gothic stage of our language, we find rudiments of this omission of the inflection. The possessive pronouns in the *neuter singular* sometimes take the inflection, sometimes appear as crude forms, *nim thata badi theinata* = ἆρόν σου τὸν κράββατον (Mark ii. 9), opposed to *nim thata badi thein*, two verses afterwards. So also with *mein* and *meinata*. It is remarkable that this omission should begin with forms so marked as those of the neuter (-*ata*). It has, perhaps, its origin in the adverbial character of that gender.

Old High German.—Here the nominatives, both masculine and feminine, lose the inflection, whilst the neuter retains it—*thin dohter, sîn quenâ, min dohter, sinaz lib.* In a few cases, when the pronoun comes after, even the *oblique* cases drop the inflection.

Middle High German.—*Preceding* the noun, the nominative of all genders is destitute of inflection; *sîn lib, min ere, din lib,* &c. *Following* the nouns, the oblique cases do the same; *ine herse sin.* The influence of position should here be noticed. Undoubtedly a place *after* the substantive influences the omission of the inflection. This appears in its *maximum* in the Middle High German. In Mœso-Gothic we have *mein leik* and *leik meinata.*

§ 406. Now by assuming the extension of the Middle High German omission of the inflection to the Anglo-Saxon; and by supposing it to affect the words in question in *all* positions (*i. e.*, both before and after their nouns), we may explain the constructions in question, in case they occur. But, as already stated, no instances of them have been quoted.

To suppose *two* adjectival forms, one inflected (*min, minre,* &c.), and one uninflected, or common to all genders and both numbers (*min*), is to suppose no more than is the case with the uninflected þe, as compared with the inflected þæt.

§ 407. Hence, the evidence required in order to make a single instance of *min* or þin, the *necessary* equivalents to *mei* and *tui*, rather than to *meus* and *tuus*, must consist in the quotation from the Anglo-Saxon of some text, wherein *min* or *þin* occurs with a feminine substantive, in an *oblique* case, the pronoun *preceding* the noun. When this has been done, it will be time enough to treat *mine* and *thine* as the equivalents to *mei* and *tui*, rather than as those to *meus* and *tuus*.

CHAPTER XXXVIII.

ON THE CONSTITUTION OF THE WEAK PRÆTERITE.

§ 408. THE remote origin of the weak præterite in *-d* or *-t*, has been considered by Grimm. He maintains that it is the *d* in *d-d*, the reduplicate præterite of *do*. In all the Gothic languages the termination of the past tense is either *-da*, *-ta*, *-de*, *-ði*, *-d*, *-t*, or *-ed*, for the singular, and *-don*, *-ton*, *-tûmés*, or *-ðum*, for the plural; in other words, *d*, or an allied sound, appears once, if not oftener. In the *plural* præterite of the *Mœso-Gothic*, however, we have something more, *viz.*, the termination *-dédum*; as *nas-idêdum, nas-idêduþ, nas-idedun*, from *nas-ja*; *sôk-idêdum, sôk-idêduþ, sôk-iddûn*, from *sôk-ja*; *salb-ódedum, salb-ódêduþ, salb-ôdêdun*, from *salbó*. Here there is a second *d*. The same takes place with the dual form *salb-ôdêduts*, and with the subjunctive forms, *salb-ódédjan, salb-ôdêduts, salb-ôdedi, salb-ôdêdeits, salb-ôdédeima, salb-ôdedeiþ, salb-ódedina*. The English phrase, *we did salve*, as compared with *salb-ódedum*, is confirmatory of this.

§ 409. Some remarks of Dr. Trithen's on the Slavonic præterite, in the "Transactions of the Philological Society," induce me to prefer a different doctrine, and to identify the *-d* in words like *moved*, &c., with the *-t* of the passive participles of the Latin language; as found in mon-*it*-us, voc-*at*-us, rap-*t*-us, and probably in Greek forms like τυφ-θ-είς.

CONSTITUTION OF WEAK PRÆTERITE.

1. The Slavonic præterite is commonly said to possess genders: in other words, there is one form for speaking of a past action when done by a male, and another for speaking of a past action when done by a female.

2. These forms are identical with those of the participles, masculine or feminine, as the case may be. Indeed the præterite is a participle. If, instead of saying *ille amavit*, the Latins said *ille amatus*, whilst, instead of saying *illa amavit*, they said *illa amata*, they would exactly use the grammar of the Slavonians.

3. Hence, as one class of languages, at least, gives us the undoubted fact of an active præterite being identical with a passive participle, and as the participle and præterite in question are nearly identical, we have a fair reason for believing that the *d*, in the English active præterite, is the *d* of the participle, which in its turn, is the *t* of the Latin passive participle.

§ 410. The following extract gives Dr. Trithen's remarks on the Slavonic verb in his own words:—

"A peculiarity which distinguishes the grammar of all the Slavish languages, consists in the use of the past participle, taken in an active sense, for the purpose of expressing the præterite. This participle generally ends in *l*; and much uncertainty prevails both as to its origin and its relations, though the termination has been compared by various philologists with similar affixes in the Sanscrit, and the classical languages.

"In the Old Slavish, or the language of the church, there are three methods of expressing the past tense: one of them consists in the union of the verb substantive with the participle; as,

Rek esm'	*chital esmi'*
Rek esi'	*chital esi'*
Rek est'	*chital est'.*

"In the corresponding tense of the Slavonic dialect we have the verb substantive placed before the participle:

Ya sam imao	mi' smo imali
Ti si imao	vi' ste imali
On ye imao	omi su imali.

" In the Polish it appears as a suffix:

Czytalem	czytalismy
Czytales	czytaliscie
Czytal	czytalie.

" And in the Servian it follows the participle:

Igrao sam	igrali smo
Igrao si	igrali ste
Igrao ye	igrali su.

"The ending -ao, of *igrao* and *imao*, stands for the Russian *al*, as in some English dialects *a'* is used for *all*."

PART V.

SYNTAX.

CHAPTER I.

ON SYNTAX IN GENERAL.

§ 411. The word *syntax* is derived from the Greek *syn* (*with* or *together*) and *taxis* (*arrangement*). It relates to the arrangement, or putting together, of words. Two or more words must be used before there can be any application of syntax.

There is to me a father.—Here we have a circumlocution equivalent to *I have a father*. In the English language the circumlocution is unnatural. In the Latin it is common. To determine this, is a matter of idiom rather than of syntax.

§ 412. In the English, as in all other languages, it is convenient to notice certain so-called figures of speech. They always furnish convenient modes of expression, and sometimes, as in the case of the one immediately about to be noticed, *account* for facts.

§ 413. *Personification.*—The ideas of apposition and collectiveness account for the apparent violations of the concord of number. The idea of personification applies to the concord of gender. A masculine or feminine gender, characteristic of persons, may be substituted for the neuter gender, characteristic of things. In this case the term is said to be personified.

The cities who aspired to liberty.—A personification of the idea expressed by *cities* is here necessary to justify the expression.

It, the sign of the neuter gender, as applied to a male or female *child*, is the reverse of the process.

§ 414. *Ellipsis* (from the Greek *elleipein* = *to fall short*), or a *falling short*, occurs in sentences like *I sent to the bookseller's.* Here the word *shop* or *house* is understood. Expressions like *to go on all fours*, and *to eat of the fruit of the tree*, are reducible to ellipses.

§ 415. *Pleonasm* (from the Greek *pleonazein* = *to be in excess*) occurs in sentences like *the king, he reigns.* Here the word *he* is superabundant.

My banks, they are furnished,—the most straitest sect,—these are pleonastic expressions. In *the king, he reigns*, the word *king* is in the same predicament as in *the king, God bless him*.

The double negative, allowed in Greek and Anglo-Saxon, but not admissible in English, is pleonastic.

The verb *do*, in *I do speak*, is *not* pleonastic. In respect to the sense it adds intensity. In respect to the construction it is not in apposition, but in the same predicament with verbs like *must* and *should*, as in *I must go*, &c.; *i. e.*, it is a verb followed by an infinitive. This we know from its power in those languages where the infinitive has a characteristic sign; as, in German,

<blockquote>Die Augen *thaten* ihm winken.—GOETHE.</blockquote>

Besides this, *make* is similarly used in Old English, —*But men make draw the branch thereof, and beren him to be graffed at Babyloyne.*—Sir J. Mandeville.

§ 416. *The figure zeugma.*—*They wear a garment*

like that of the Scythians, but a language peculiar to themselves.—The verb, naturally applying to *garment* only, is here used to govern *language*. This is called in Greek, *zeugma* (junction).

§ 417. *My paternal home was made desolate, and he himself was sacrificed.*—The sense of this is plain; *he* means *my father*. Yet no such substantive as *father* has gone before. It is supplied, however, from the word *paternal*. The sense indicated by *paternal* gives us a subject to which he can refer. In other words, the word *he* is understood, according to what is indicated, rather than according to what is expressed. This figure in Greek is called *pros to semainomenon* (*according to the thing indicated*).

§ 418.—*Apposition,—Cæsar, the Roman emperor, invades Britain.*—Here the words *Roman emperor* explain, or define, the word *Cæsar;* and the sentence, filled up, might stand, *Cæsar, that is, the Roman emperor*, &c. Again, the word *Roman emperor* might be wholly ejected; or, if not ejected, they might be thrown into a parenthesis. The practical bearing of this fact is exhibited by changing the form of the sentence, and inserting the conjunction *and*. In this case, instead of one person, two are spoken of, and the verb *invades* must be changed from the singular to the plural.

Now the words *Roman emperor* are said to be in apposition to *Cæsar*. They constitute, not an additional idea, but an explanation of the original one. They are, as it were, *laid alongside* (*appositi*) *of* the word *Cæsar*. Cases of doubtful number, wherein two substantives precede a verb, and wherein it is uncertain whether the verb should be singular or plural, are decided by determining whether the substantives be in apposition or the contrary. No matter how many nouns there may be, as long as it can be shown that they are in apposition, the verb is in the singular number.

§ 419. *Collectiveness as opposed to plurality.*—In sentences like *the meeting* was *large, the multitude* pursue *pleasure, meeting* and *multitude* are each collective nouns; that is, although they present the idea of a single object, that object consists of a plurality of individuals. Hence, *pursue* is put in the plural number. To say, however, *the meeting were large* would sound improper. The number of the verb that shall accompany a collective noun depends upon whether the idea of the multiplicity of individuals, or that of the unity of the aggregate, shall predominate.

Sand and salt and a mass of iron is *easier to bear than a man without understanding.*—Let *sand and salt and a mass of iron* be dealt with as a series of things the aggregate of which forms a mixture, and the expression is allowable.

The king and the lords and commons forms *an excellent frame of government.*—Here the expression is doubtful. Substitute *with* for the first *and*, and there is no doubt as to the propriety of the singular form *is.*

§ 420. *The reduction of complex forms to simple ones.*—Take, for instance, the current illustration, viz., *the-king-of-Saxony's army.*—Here the assertion is, not that the army belongs to *Saxony*, but that it belongs to the *king of Saxony;* which words must, for the sake of taking a true view of the construction, be dealt with as a single word in the possessive case. Here two cases are dealt with as one; and a complex term is treated as a single word.

The same reason applies to phrases like *the two king Williams.* If we say *the two kings William,* we must account for the phrase by apposition.

14*

§ 421. *True notion of the part of speech in use.*—In *he is gone*, the word *gone* must be considered as equivalent to *absent;* that is, as an adjective. Otherwise the expression is as incorrect as the expression *she is eloped*. Strong participles are adjectival oftener than weak ones: their form being common to many adjectives.

True notion of the original form.—In the phrase *I must speak*, the word *speak* in an infinitive. In the phrase *I am forced to speak*, the word *speak* is (in the present English) an infinitive also. In one case, however, it is preceded by *to;* whilst in the other, the particle *to* is absent. The reason for this lies in the original difference of form. *Speak—to* = the Anglo-Saxon *sprécan*, a simple infinitive; *to speak*, or *speak + to* = the Anglo-Saxon *to sprécanne*, an infinitive in the dative case.

§ 422. *Convertibility.*—In the English language, the greater part of the words may, as far as their form is concerned, be one part of speech as well as another. Thus the combinations *s-a-n-th*, or *f-r-e-n-k*, if they existed at all, might exist as either nouns or verbs, as either substantives or adjectives, as conjunctions, adverbs, or prepositions. This is not the case in the Greek languages. There, if a word be a substantive, it will probably end in *-s;* if an infinitive verb, in *-ein*, &c. The bearings of this difference between languages like the English and languages like the Greek will soon appear.

At present, it is sufficient to say that a word, originally one part of speech (*e. g.*, a noun), may become another (*e. g.*, a verb). This may be called the convertibility of words.

There is an etymological convertibility, and a syntactic convertibility; and although, in some cases, the line of demarcation is not easily drawn between them, the distinction is intelligible and convenient.

§ 423. *Etymological convertibility.*—The words *then* and *than*, now adverbs or conjunctions, were once cases: in other words, they have been converted from one part of speech to another. Or, they may even be said to be cases, at the present moment; although only in an historical point of view. For the practice of language, they are not only adverbs or conjunctions, but they are adverbs or conjunctions exclusively.

§ 424. *Syntactic convertibility.*—The combination *to err*, is at this moment an infinitive verb. Nevertheless it can be used as the equivalent to the substantive *error*.

To err is human = *error is human*. Now this is an instance of syntactic conversion. Of the two meanings, there is no doubt as to which is the primary one; which primary meaning is part and parcel of the language at this moment.

The infinitive, when used as a substantive, can be used in a singular form only.

To err = *error*; but we have no such form as *to errs* = *errors*. Nor is it wanted. The infinitive, in a substantival sense, always conveys a general statement, so that even when singular, it has a plural power; just as *man is mortal* = *men are mortal*.

§ 425. *The adjective used as a substantive.*—Of these, we have examples in expressions like the *blacks of Africa*—*the bitters and sweets of life*—*all fours were put to the ground.* These are true instances of conversion, and are proved to be so by the fact of their taking a plural form.

Let the blind lead the blind is not an instance of conversion. The word *blind* in both instances remains an adjective, and is shown to remain so by its being uninflected.

§ 426. *Uninflected parts of speech, used as substantive.*—When King Richard III. says, *none of your ifs*, he uses the word *if* as a substantive = *expressions of doubt.*

So in the expression *one long now*, the word *now* = *present time.*

§ 427. The convertibility of words in English is very great; and it is so because the structure of the language favours it. As few words have any peculiar signs expressive of their being particular parts of speech, interchange is easy, and conversion follows the logical association of ideas unimpeded.

The convertibility of words is in the inverse ratio to the amount of their inflection.

CHAPTER II.

SYNTAX OF SUBSTANTIVES.

§ 428. THE phenomena of convertibility have been already explained.

The remaining points connected with the syntax of substantives, are chiefly points of ellipsis.

Ellipsis of substantives.—The historical view of phrases, like *Rundell and Bridge's, St. Paul's,* &c., shows that this ellipsis is common to the English and the other Gothic languages. Furthermore, it shows that it is met with in languages not of the Gothic stock; and, finally, that the class of words to which it applies, is, there or thereabouts, the same generally.

§ 429. The following phrases are referable to a different class of relations—

1. *Right and left*—supply *hand.* This is, probably, a real ellipsis. The words *right* and *left*, have not yet become true substantives; inasmuch as they have no plural forms. In this respect they stand in contrast with *bitter* and *sweet;* inasmuch as we can say *he has tasted both the bitters and sweets of life.* Nevertheless, the expression can be refined on.

2. *All fours. To go on all fours.* No ellipsis. The word *fours* is a true substantive, as proved by its existence as a plural.

CHAPTER III.

SYNTAX OF ADJECTIVES.

§ 430. *Pleonasm.*—Pleonasm can take place with adjectives only in the expression of the degrees of comparison. Over and above the etymological signs of the comparative and superlative degrees, there may be used the superlative words *more* and *most*.

And this pleonasm really occurs—

> *The* more serener *spirit.*
> *The* most straitest *sect.*

These are instances of pleonasm in the strictest sense of the term.

§ 431. Collocation.—As a general rule, the adjective precedes the substantive—*a good man,* not *a man good.*

When, however, the adjective is qualified by either the expression of its degree, or accompanied by another adjective, it may follow the substantive—

> A man *just and good.*
> A woman *wise and fair.*
> A hero *devoted to his country.*
> A patriot *disinterested to a great degree.*

Single simple adjectives thus placed after their substantive, belong to the poetry of England, and especially to the ballad poetry—*sighs profound—the leaves green.*

§ 432. *Government.*—The only adjective that governs a case, is the word *like.* In the expression, *this is like him*, &c., the original power of the dative remains. This we infer—

1. From the fact that in most languages which have inflections to a sufficient extent, the word meaning *like* governs a dative case.

2. That if ever we use in English any preposition at all to express similitude, it is the preposition *to*—*like to me*, *like to death*, &c.

Expressions like *full of meat, good for John*, are by no means instances of the government of adjectives; the really governing words being the prepositions *to* and *for* respectively.

§ 433. The positive degree preceded by the adjective *more*, is equivalent to the comparative form—*e. g.*, *more wise* = *wiser*.

The reasons for employing one expression in preference to the other, depend upon the nature of the particular word used.

When the word is at one and the same time of Anglo-Saxon origin and monosyllabic, there is no doubt about the preference to be given to the form in -*er*. Thus, *wis-er* is preferable to *more wise*.

When, however, the word is compound, or trisyllabic, the combination with the word *more*, is preferable.

> *more fruitful* . . . . . *fruitfuller.*
> *more villainous* . . . . *villanouser.*

Between these two extremes there are several intermediate forms, wherein the use of one rather than another will depend upon the taste of the writer. The question, however, is a question of euphony, rather than of aught else. It is also illustrated by the principle of not multiplying secondary elements. In such a word as *fruit-full-er*, there are two additions to the root. The same is the case with the superlative, *fruit-full-est*.

§ 434. In the Chapter on the Comparative Degree is indicated a refinement upon the current notions as to the power of the comparative degree, and reasons are given for believing that the fundamental notion expressed by the comparative inflexion is the idea of comparison or contrast between *two* objects.

In this case, it is better in speaking of only two objects to use the comparative degree rather than the superlative—even when we use the definite article *the*. Thus—

> This is *the better* of the two

is preferable to

> This is *the best* of the two.

This principle is capable of an application more extensive than our habits of speaking and writing will verify. Thus to go to other parts of speech, we should logically say—

> Whether of the two,

rather than

> Which of the two.
> Either the father or the son,

but not

> Either the father, the son, or the daughter.

This statement may be refined on. It is chiefly made for the sake of giving fresh prominence to the idea of duality, expressed by the terminations *-er* and *-ter*.

§ 435. The absence of inflection simplifies the syntax of adjectives. Violations of concord are impossible. We could not make an adjective disagree with its substantive if we wished.

CHAPTER IV.

SYNTAX OF PRONOUNS.

§ 436. *Pleonasm in the syntax of pronouns.*—In the following sentences the words in italics are pleonastic:

1. The king *he* is just.
2. I saw *her*, the queen.
3. The men, *they* were there.
4. The king, *his* crown.

Of these forms, the first is more common than the second and third, and the fourth more common than the first.

§ 437. The fourth has another element of importance. It has given rise to the absurd notion that the genitive case in *-'s* (*father-'s*) is a contraction from *his* (*father his*).

To say nothing about the inapplicability of this rule to feminine genders, and plural numbers, the whole history of the Indo-Germanic languages is against it.

1. We cannot reduce *the queen's majesty* to *the queen his majesty*.
2. We cannot reduce *the children's bread* to *the children his bread*..
3. The Anglo-Saxon forms are in *-es*, not in *his*.
4. The word *his* itself must be accounted for; and that cannot be done by assuming it to be *he* + *his*.
5. The *-s* in *father's* is the *-is* in *patris*, and the *-ος* in πατέρος

§ 438. The preceding examples illustrate an apparent paradox, *viz.*, the fact of pleonasm and ellipsis being closely allied. *The king he is just*, dealt with as a *single* sentence, is undoubtedly pleonastic. But it is not necessary to be considered as a mere simple sentence. *The king*—may represent a first sentence incomplete, whilst *he is just* represents a second sentence in full. What is pleonasm in a single sentence is ellipsis in a double one.

CHAPTER V.

THE TRUE PERSONAL PRONOUNS.

§ 439. *Personal pronouns.*—The use of the second person plural instead of the second singular has been noticed already. This use of one number for another is current throughout the Gothic languages. A pronoun so used is conveniently called the *pronomen reverentiæ*.

§ 440. *Dativus ethicus.*—In the phrase

Rob me the exchequer,—Henry IV.,

the *me* is expletive, and is equivalent to *for me*. This expletive use of the dative is conveniently called the *dativus ethicus*.

§ 441. *The reflected personal pronoun.*—In the English language there is no equivalent to the Latin *se*, the German *sich*, and the Scandinavian *sik*, and *sig*.

It follows from this that the word *self* is used to a greater extent than would otherwise be the case.

I strike me is awkward, but not ambiguous.

Thou strikest thee is awkward, but not ambiguous.

He strikes him is ambiguous; inasmuch as *him* may mean either the *person who strikes* or some one else. In order to be clear we add the word *self* when the idea is reflective. *He strikes himself* is, at once idiomatic and unequivocal.

So it is with the plural persons.

We strike us is awkward, but not ambiguous.

Ye strike you is the same.

They strike them is ambiguous.

This shows the value of a reflective pronoun for the third person.

As a general rule, therefore, whenever we use a verb reflectively we use the word *self* in combination with the personal pronoun.

Yet this was not always the case. The use of the simple personal pronoun was current in Anglo-Saxon, and that, not only for the first two persons, but for the third as well.

The exceptions to this rule are either poetical expressions, or imperative moods.

> He sat *him* down at a pillar's base.—BYRON.
> Sit thee down.

§ 442. *Reflective neuters.*—In the phrase *I strike me*, the verb *strike* is transitive; in other words, the word *me* expresses the object of an action, and the meaning is different from the meaning of the simple expression *I strike*.

In the phrase *I fear me* (used by Lord Campbell in his lives of the Chancellors), the verb *fear* is intransitive or neuter; in other words, the word *me* (unless, indeed, *fear* mean *terrify*), expresses no object of any action at all; whilst the meaning is the same as in the simple expression *I fear*.

Here the reflective pronoun appears out of place, *i. e.*, after a neuter or intransitive verb.

Such a use, however, is but the fragment of an extensive system of reflective verbs thus formed, developed in different degrees in the different Gothic languages; but in all more than in the English.

§ 443. *Equivocal reflectives.*—The proper place of the reflective is *after* the verb.

The proper place of the governing pronoun is, in the indicative and subjunctive moods, *before* the verb.

Hence in expressions like the preceding there is no doubt as to the power of the pronoun.

The imperative mood, however, sometimes presents a complication. Here the governing person may follow the verb.

Mount ye = either *be mounted*, or *mount yourselves*. In phrases like this, and in phrases

> *Busk ye, busk ye,* my bonny, bonny bride,
> *Busk ye, busk ye,* my winsome marrow,

the construction is ambiguous. *Ye* may either be a nominative case governing the verb *busk*, or an accusative case governed by it.

This is an instance of what may be called the *equivocal reflective*.

CHAPTER VI.

ON THE SYNTAX OF THE DEMONSTRATIVE PRONOUNS, AND THE PRONOUNS OF THE THIRD PERSON.

§ 444. As *his* and *her* are genitive cases (and not adjectives), there is no need of explaining such combinations as *his mother*, *her father*, inasmuch as no concord of gender is expected. The expressions are respectively equivalent to

mater ejus, not *mater sua*;
pater ejus, — *pater suus*.

§ 445. It has been stated that *its* is a secondary genitive, and it may be added, that it is of late origin in the language. The Anglo-Saxon form was *his*, the genitive of *he* for the neuter and masculine equally. Hence, when, in the old writers, we meet *his*, where we expect *its*, we must not suppose that any personification takes place, but simply that the old genitive common to the two genders is used in preference to the modern one limited to the neuter, and irregularly formed.

The following instances are the latest specimens of its use:

"The apoplexy is, as I take it, a kind of lethargy. I have read the cause of *his* effects in Galen; *it* is a kind of deafness."—2 *Henry IV* i. 2.

"If the salt have lost *his* savour, wherewith shall it be seasoned? *It* is neither fit for the land, nor yet for the dunghill; but men cast *it* out."—*Luke* xiv. 35.

"Some affirm that every plant has *his* particular fly or caterpillar, which it breeds and feeds."—WALTON's *Angler*.

"This rule is not so general, but that *it* admitteth of *his* exceptions."—CAREW.

CHAPTER VII.

ON THE CONSTRUCTION OF THE WORD SELF.

§ 446. The undoubted constructions of the word *self*, in the present state of the cultivated English, are threefold.

1. *Government.*—In *my-self*, *thy-self*, *our-selves*, and *your-selves*, the construction is that of a common substantive with an adjective or genitive case. *My-self* = *my individuality*, and is similarly construed — *mea individualitas* (or *persona*), or *mei individualitas* (or *persona*).

2. *Apposition.*—In *him-self* and *them-selves*, when accusative, the construction is that of a substantive in apposition with a pronoun. *Himself* = *him, the individual.*

3. *Composition.*—It is only, however, when *himself* and *themselves*, are in the *accusative* case, that the construction is appositional. When they are used as *nominatives*, it must be explained on another principle. In phrases like

>*He himself* was present.
>*They themselves* were present,

there is neither apposition nor government; *him* and *them*, being neither related to *my* and *thy*, so as to be governed, nor yet to *he* and *they*, so as to form an apposition. In order to come under one of these conditions, the phrases should be either *he his self* (*they their selves*), or else *he he self* (*they they selves*). In this difficulty, the only logical view that can be taken of the matter, is to consider the words *himself* and *themselves*, not as two words, but as a single word compounded; and even then, the compound will be of an irregular kind; inasmuch as the inflectional element -*m*, is dealt with as part and parcel of the root.

§ 447. *Her-self.*—The construction here is ambiguous. It is one of the preceding constructions. Which, however it is, is uncertain; since *her* may be either a so-called genitive, like *my*, or an accusative like *him*.

Itself—is also ambiguous. The *s* may represent the -*s* in *its*, as well as the *s*- in *self*.

This inconsistency is as old as the Anglo-Saxon stage of the English language.

CHAPTER VIII.

ON THE POSSESSIVE PRONOUNS.

§ 448. THE possessive pronouns fall into two classes. The first contains the forms like *my* and *thy*, &c.; the second, those like *mine* and *thine*, &c.

My, thy, his (as in *his book*), *her, its* (as in *its book*), *our, your, their,* are conveniently considered as the equivalents to the Latin forms *mei, tui, ejus, nostrum, vestrum, eorum.*

Mine, thine, his (as in *the book is his*), *hers, ours, yours, theirs* are conveniently considered as the equivalents to the Latin forms *meus, mea, meum; tuus, tua, tuum; suus, sua, suum; noster, nostra, nostrum; vester, vestra, vestrum.*

§ 449. There is a difference between the construction of *my* and *mine*. We cannot say *this is mine hat*, and we cannot say *this hat is my*. Nevertheless, this difference is not explained by any change of construction from that of adjectives to that of cases. As far as the syntax is concerned the construction of *my* and *mine* is equally that of an adjective *agreeing* with a substantive, and of a genitive (or possessive) case *governed* by a substantive.

Now a common genitive case can be used in two ways; either as part of a term, or as a whole term (*i. e.*, absolutely). —1. As part of a term—*this is John's hat.* 2. As a whole term—*this hat is John's.*

And a common adjective can be used in two ways; either as part of a term, or as a whole term (*i. e.* absolutely).—1. As part of a term—*these are good hats.* 2. As a whole term—*these hats are good.*

Now whether we consider *my*, and the words like it, as adjectives or cases, they possess only *one* of the properties just illustrated, *i. e.*, they can only be used as part of a term—*this is my hat;* not *this hat is my.*

And whether we consider *mine*, and the words like it, as adjectives or cases, they possess only *one* of the properties just illustrated, *i. e.*, they can only be used as whole terms, or absolutely—*this hat is mine;* not *this is mine hat.*

For a full and perfect construction whether of an adjective or a genitive case, the possessive pronouns present the phenomenon of being, singly, incomplete, but, nevertheless, complementary to each other when taken in their two forms.

§ 450. In the absolute construction of a genitive case, the term is formed by the single word, only so far as the *expression* is concerned. A substantive is always *understood* from what has preceded.—*This discovery is Newton's* = *this discovery is Newton's discovery.*

The same with adjectives.—*This weather is fine* = *this weather is fine weather.*

And the same with absolute pronouns.—*This hat is mine* = *this hat is my hat;* and *this is a hat of mine* = *this is a hat of my hats.*

§ 451. In respect to all matters of syntax considered exclusively, it is so thoroughly a matter of indifference whether a word be an adjective or a genitive case that Wallis considers the forms in -'s, like *father's*, not as genitive cases but as adjectives. Looking to the logic of the question alone he is right, and looking to the practical syntax of the question he is right also. He is only wrong on the etymological side of the question.

"Nomina substantiva apud nos nullum vel generum vel casuum discrimen sortiuntur."—p. 76.

"Duo sunt adjectivorum genera, a substantivis immediate descendentia, quæ semper substantivis suis præponuntur. Primum quidem adjectivum possessivum libet appellare. Fit autem a quovis substantivo, sive singulari sive plurali, addito -s.—Ut *man's nature, the nature of man*, natura humana vel hominis; *men's nature*, natura humana vel hominum; *Virgil's poems, the poems of Virgil*, poemata Virgilii vel Virgiliana."—p. 89.

CHAPTER IX.

THE RELATIVE PRONOUNS.

§ 452. It is necessary that the relative be in the same *gender* as the antecedent—*the man who—the woman who —the thing which*.

§. 453. It is necessary that the relative be in the same *number* with the antecedent.

§ 454. It is *not* necessary for the relative to be in the same *case* with its antecedent.

    1. John, *who* trusts me, comes here.
    2. John, *whom* I trust, comes here.
    3. John, *whose* confidence I possess, comes here.
    4. I trust John *who* trusts me.

§ 455. The reason why the relative must agree with its antecedent in both number and gender, whilst it need not agree with it in case, is found in the following observations.

    1. All sentences containing a relative contain two verbs—*John who* (1) *trusts me* (2) *comes here*.

    2. Two verbs express two actions—(1) *trust* (2) *come*.

    3. Whilst, however, the actions are two in number, the person or thing which does or suffers them is single —*John*.

    3. *He* (*she* or *it*) is single *ex vi termini*. The relative expresses the *identity* between the subjects (or objects)

of the two actions. Thus *who* = *John*, or is another name for John.

5. Things and persons that are one and the same, are of one and the same gender. The *John* who *trusts* is necessarily of the same gender with the *John* who *comes*.

6. Things and persons that are one and the same, are of one and the same number. The number of *Johns* who *trust*, is the same as the number of *Johns* who *come*. Both these elements of concord are immutable.

7. But a third element of concord is not immutable. The person or thing that is an agent in the one part of the sentence, may be the object of an action in the other. The *John* whom I *trust* may *trust* me also. Hence

a. I trust John—*John* the object.
b. John trusts me—*John* the agent.

§ 456. As the relative is only the antecedent in another form, it may change its case according to the construction.

1. I trust John—(2) *John* trusts me.
2. I trust John—(2) *He* trusts me.
3. I trust John—(2) *Who* trusts me.
4. John trusts me—(2) I trust *John*.
5. John trusts me—(2) I trust *him*.
6. John trusts me—(2) I trust *whom*.
7. John trusts me—(2) *Whom* I trust.
8. John—(2) *Whom* I trust trusts me.

§ 457. *The books I want are here.*—This is a specimen of a true ellipsis. In all such phrases in *full*, there are *three* essential elements.

1. The first proposition; as *the books are here*.
2. The second proposition; as *I want*.
3. The word which connects the two propositions, and without which, they naturally make separate, independent, unconnected statements.

Now, although true and unequivocal ellipses are scarce, the preceding is one of the most unequivocal kind—the word which connects the two propositions being wanting.

§ 458. *When there are two words in a clause, each capable of being an antecedent, the relative refers to the latter.*

1. *Solomon the son of David that slew Goliah.*— This is unexceptionable.

2. *Solomon the son of David who built the temple.*— This is exceptionable.

Nevertheless, it is defensible, on the supposition that *Solomon-the-son-of-David* is a single many-worded name.

CHAPTER X.

ON THE INTERROGATIVE PRONOUN.

§ 459. QUESTIONS are of two sorts, direct and oblique.
Direct.—Who is he?
Oblique.—Who do you say that he is?
All difficulties about the cases of the interrogative pronoun may be determined by framing an answer, and observing the case of the word with which the interrogative coincides. Whatever be the case of this word will also be the case of the interrogative.

DIRECT.

Qu. Who is this?—*Ans. I.*
Qu. Whose is this?—*Ans. His.*
Qu. Whom do you seek?—*Ans. Him.*

OBLIQUE.

Qu. Who do you say that it is?—*Ans. He.*
Qu. Whose do you say that it is?—*Ans. His.*
Qu. Whom do you say that they seek?—*Ans. Him.*

Note.—The answer should always be made by means of a pronoun, as by so doing we distinguish the accusative case from the nominative.

Note.—And, if necessary, it should be made in full. Thus the full answer to *whom do you say that they seek?* is, *I say that they seek him.*

§ 460. Nevertheless, such expressions as *whom do*

they say that it is? are common, especially in oblique questions.

"And he axed him and seide, *whom* seien the people that I am?—Thei answereden and seiden, Jon Baptist—and he seide to hem, But *whom* seien ye that I am?"—WICLIF, *Luke* ix.

"Tell me in sadness *whom* she is you love."
Romeo and Juliet, i. 1.

"And as John fulfilled his course, he said, *whom* think ye that I am?"—*Acts* xiii. 25.

This confusion, however, is exceptionable.

CHAPTER XI.

THE RECIPROCAL CONSTRUCTION.

§ 461. IN all sentences containing the statement of a reciprocal or mutual action there are in reality two assertions, *viz.*, the assertion that A. *strikes* (or *loves*) B., and the assertion that B. *strikes* (or *loves*) A.; the action forming one, the reaction another. Hence, if the expressions exactly coincided with the fact signified, there would always be two propositions. This, however, is not the habit of language. Hence arises a more compendious form of expression, giving origin to an ellipsis of a peculiar kind. Phrases like *Eteocles and Polynices killed each other* are elliptical, for *Eteocles and Polynices killed—each the other*. Here the second proposition expands and explains the first, whilst the first supplies the verb to the second. Each, however, is elliptic.

§ 462. This is the syntax. As to the power of the words *each* and *one* in the expression (*each other* and *one another*), I am not prepared to say that in the common practice of the English language there is any distinction between them. A distinction, however, if it existed, would give strength to our language. Where two persons performed a reciprocal action on another, the expression might be *one another*; as *Eteocles and Polynices killed one another*. Where more than two persons were engaged on each side of a reciprocal action, the expression might be *each other;* as, *the ten champions praised each other.*

This amount of perspicuity is attained, by different processes, in the French, Spanish, and Scandinavian languages.

1. French.—*Ils* (*i. e.*, A. and B.) *se battaient—l'un l'autre. Ils* (A. B. C.) *se battaient—les uns les autres.* In Spanish, *uno otro* = *l'un l'autre*, and *unos otros* = *les uns les autres.*

2. Danish.—*Hinander* = the French *l'un l'autre;* whilst *hverandre* = *les uns les autres.*

CHAPTER XII.

THE INDETERMINATE PRONOUNS.

§ 463. DIFFERENT nations have different methods of expressing indeterminate propositions.

Sometimes it is by the use of the passive voice. This is the common method in Latin and Greek, and is also current in English—*dicitur*, λέγεται, *it is said*.

Sometimes the verb is reflective—*si dice* = *it says itself*, Italian.

Sometimes the plural pronoun of the third person is used. This also is an English locution—*they say* = *the world at large says*.

Finally, the use of some word = *man* is a common indeterminate expression.

The word *man* has an indeterminate sense in the Modern German; as *man, sagt* = *they say*.

The word *man* was also used indeterminately in the Old English, although it is not so used in the Modern.

In the Old English, the form *man* often lost the -*n*, and became *me*.—" Deutsche Grammatik." This form is also extinct.

§ 464. The present indeterminate pronoun is *one*; as *one says* = *they say* = *it is said* = *man sagt*, German = *on dit*, French = *si dice*, Italian.

It has been stated, that the indeterminate pronoun *one* has no etymological connection with the numeral *one*; but that it is derived from the French *on* = *homme*

= *homo* = *man*; and that it has replaced the Old English *man* or *me*.

§ 465. Two other pronouns, or, to speak more in accordance with the present habit of the English language, one pronoun, and one adverb of pronominal origin, are also used indeterminately, *viz.*, *it* and *there*.

§ 466. *It* can be either the subject or the predicate of a sentence,—*it is this, this is it, I am it, it is I*. When *it* is the subject of a proposition, the verb necessarily agrees with it, and can be of the singular number only; no matter what be the number of the predicate—*it is this, it is these*.

When *it* is the predicate of a proposition, the number of the verb depends upon the number of the subject. These points of universal syntax are mentioned here for the sake of illustrating some anomalous forms.

§ 467. *There* can only be the predicate of a subject. It differs from *it* in this respect. It follows also that it must differ from *it* in never affecting the number of the verb. This is determined by the nature of the subject—*there is this, there are these*.

When we say *there is these*, the analogy between the words *these* and *it* misleads us; the expression being illogical.

Furthermore, although a predicate, *there* always stands in the beginning of propositions, *i. e.*, in the place of the subject. This also misleads.

§ 468. Although *it*, when the subject, being itself singular, absolutely requires that its verb should be singular also, there is a tendency to use it incorrectly, and to treat it as a plural. Thus, in German, when the predicate is plural, the verb joined to the singular form *es* (= *it*) is plural—*es sind menschen*, literally translated = *it are men*; which, though bad English, is good German.

CHAPTER XIII.

THE ARTICLES.

§ 469. THE rule of most practical importance about the articles is the rule that determines when the article shall be repeated as often as there is a fresh substantive, and when it shall not.

When two or more substantives following each other denote the same object, the article precedes the first only. We say, *the secretary and treasurer* (or, *a secretary and treasurer*), when the two offices are held by one person.

When two or more substantives following each other denote different objects, the article is repeated, and precedes each. We say, *the* (or *a*) *secretary and the* (or *a*) *treasurer*, when the two offices are held by different persons.

This rule is much neglected.

CHAPTER XIV.

THE NUMERALS.

§ 470. THE numeral *one* is naturally single. All the rest are naturally plural.

Nevertheless such expressions—*one two* (= *one collection of two*), *two threes* (= *two collections of three*) are legitimate. These are so, because the sense of the word is changed. We may talk of several *ones* just as we may talk of several *aces ;* and of *one two* just as of *one pair*.

Expressions like *the thousandth-and-first* are incorrect. They mean neither one thing nor another: 1001st being expressed by *the thousand-and-first*, and 1000th + 1st being expressed by *the thousandth and the first*.

Here it may be noticed that, although I never found it to do so, the word *odd* is capable of taking an ordinal form. The *thousand-and-odd-th* is as good an expression as the *thousand-and-eight-th*.

The construction of phrases like the *thousand-and first* is the same construction as we find in the *king of Saxony's army*.

§ 471. It is by no means a matter of indifference whether we say the *two first* or the *first two*.

The captains of two different classes at school should be called the *two first boys*. The first and second boys of the same class should be called the *first two boys*. I believe that when this rule is attended to, more is due to the printer than to the author: such, at least, is the case with myself.

CHAPTER XV.

ON VERBS IN GENERAL.

§ 472. For the purposes of syntax it is necessary to divide verbs into the five following divisions: transitive, intransitive, auxiliary, substantive, and impersonal.

Transitive verbs.—In transitive verbs the action is never a simple action. It always affects some object or other,—*I move my limbs; I strike my enemy.* The presence of a transitive verb implies also the presence of a noun; which noun is the name of the object affected. A transitive verb, unaccompanied by a noun, either expressed or understood, is a contradiction in terms. The absence of the nouns, in and of itself, makes it intransitive. *I move* means, simply, *I am in a state of moving.* *I strike* means, simply, *I am in the act of striking.* Verbs like *move* and *strike* are naturally transitive.

Intransitive verbs.—An act may take place, and yet no object be affected by it. *To hunger, to thirst, to sleep, to wake,* are verbs that indicate states of being, rather than actions affecting objects. Verbs like *hunger* and *sleep* are naturally intransitive.

Many verbs, naturally transitive, may be used as intransitive,—*e. g., I move, I strike,* &c.

Many verbs, naturally intransitive, may be used as transitives,—*e. g., I walked the horse = I made the horse walk.*

This variation in the use of one and the same verb

is of much importance in the question of the government of verbs.

A. Transitive verbs are naturally followed by some noun or other; and that noun is *always* the name of something affected by them *as an object*.

B. Intransitive verbs are not naturally followed by any noun at all; and when they are so followed, the noun is *never* the name of anything affected by them *as an object*.

Nevertheless, intransitive verbs may be followed by nouns denoting the manner, degree, or instrumentality of their action,—*I walk with my feet = incedo pedibus*.

§ 473. *The auxiliary verbs* will be noticed fully in Chapter XXIII.

§ 474. The verb *substantive* has this peculiarity, *viz.*, that for all purposes of syntax it is no verb at all. *I speak* may, logically, be reduced to *I am speaking;* in which case it is only the *part* of a verb. Etymologically, indeed, the verb substantive is a verb; inasmuch as it is inflected as such: but for the purposes of construction, it is a copula only, *i. e.*, it merely denotes the agreement or disagreement between the subject and the predicate.

For the *impersonal* verbs see Chapter XXI.

CHAPTER XVI.

THE CONCORD OF VERBS.

§ 475. THE verb must agree with its subject in person, *I walk*, not *I walks : he walks*, not *he walk*.

It must also agree with it in number,—*we walk*, not *we walks : he walks*, not *he walk*.

Clear as these rules are, they require some expansion before they become sufficient to solve all the doubtful points of English syntax connected with the concord of the verb.

A. *It is I, your master, who command you.* Query? would *it is I, your master, who commands you*, be correct? This is an example of a disputed point of concord in respect to the person of the verb.

B. *The wages of sin is death.* Query? would *the wages of sin* are *death* be correct? This is an example of a disputed point of concord in respect to the number of the verb.

§ 476. In respect to the concord of person the following rules will carry us through a portion of the difficulties.

Rule.—In sentences where there is but one proposition, when a noun and a pronoun of different persons are in apposition, the verb agrees with the first of them,—*I, your master, command you* (not *commands*) *: your master, I, commands you* (not *command*).

To understand the nature of the difficulty, it is necessary to remember that subjects may be extremely complex as well as perfectly simple; and that a complex subject may contain, at one and the same time, a noun substantive and a pronoun,—*I, the keeper; he, the merchant*, &c.

Now all noun-substantives are naturally of the third person—*John speaks, the men run, the commander gives orders.* Consequently the verb is of the third person also.

But the pronoun with which such a noun-substantive may be placed in apposition, may be a pronoun of either person, the first or second: *I* or *thou*—*I the commander—thou the commander.*—In this case the construction requires consideration. With which does the verb agree? with the substantive which requires a third person? or with the pronoun which requires a first or second?

Undoubtedly the idea which comes first is the leading idea; and, undoubtedly, the idea which explains, qualifies, or defines it, is the subordinate idea: and, undoubtedly, it is the leading idea which determines the construction of the verb. We may illustrate this from the analogy of a similar construction in respect to number—*a man with a horse and a gig meets me on the road.* Here the ideas are three; nevertheless the verb is singular. No addition of subordinate elements interferes with the construction that is determined by the leading idea. In the expression *I, your master*, the ideas are two; *viz.*, the idea expressed by *I*, and the idea expressed by *master*. Nevertheless, as the one only explains or defines the other, the construction is the same as if the idea were single. *Your master, I*, is in the same condition. The general statement is made concerning the *master*, and it is intended to say what *he* does. The word *I* merely defines the expression by stating who the master is. Of the two expressions the latter is the awkwardest. The construction, however, is the same for both.

From the analysis of the structure of complex subjects of the kind in question, combined with a rule concerning the position of the subject, which will soon be laid down, I believe that, for all single propositions, the foregoing rule is absolute.

Rule.—In all single propositions the verb agrees in person with the noun (whether substantive or pronoun) which comes first.

§ 477. But the expression *it is I your master, who command* (or *commands*) *you*, is not a single proposition. It is a sentence containing two propositions.

1. *It is I.*
2. *Who commands you.*

Here the word *master* is, so to say, undistributed. It may belong to either clause of the sentence, *i. e.*, the whole sentence may be divided into

Either—*it is I your master*—
Or—*your master who commands you.*

This is the first point to observe. The next is that the verb in the second clause (*command* or *commands*) is governed, not by either the personal pronoun or the substantive, but by the relative, *i.e.*, in the particular case before us, not by either *I* or *master*, but by *who*.

And this brings us to the following question—with which of the two antecedents does the *relative* agree? with *I* or with *master* ?

This may be answered by the two following rules;—

Rule 1.—When the two antecedents are in the

same proposition, the relative agrees with the first Thus—

    1. It is *I* your *master*—
    2. Who *command* you.

Rule 2.—When the two antecedents are in different propositions, the relative agrees with the second. Thus—

    1. It is *I*—
    2. Your *master* who *commands* you.

This, however, is not all. What determines whether the two antecedents shall be in the same or in different propositions? I believe that the following rules for what may be called *the distribution of the substantive antecedent* will bear criticism.

Rule 1. That when there is any natural connection between the substantive antecedent and the verb governed by the relative, the antecedent belongs to the second clause. Thus, in the expression just quoted, the word *master* is logically connected with the word *command;* and this fact makes the expression, *It is I your master who commands you* the better of the two.

Rule 2. That when there is no natural connection between the substantive antecedent and the verb governed by the relative, the antecedent belongs to the first clause. *It is I, John, who command* (not *commands*) *you.*

To recapitulate, the train of reasoning has been as follows:—

1. The person of the second verb is the person of the relative.

2. The person of the relative is that of one of two antecedents.

3. Of such two antecedents the relative agrees with the one which stands in the same proposition with itself.

4. Which position is determined by the connection or want of connection between the substantive antecedent and the verb governed by the relative.

Respecting the person of the verb in the *first* proposition of a complex sentence there is no doubt. *I, your master, who commands you to make haste, am* (not *is*) *in a hurry.* Here, *I am in a hurry* is the first proposition; *who commands you to make haste*, the second.

It is not difficult to see why the construction of sentences consisting of two propositions is open to an amount of latitude which is not admissible in the construction of single propositions. As long as the different parts of a complex idea are contained within the limits of a single proposition, their subordinate character is easily discerned. When, however, they amount to whole propositions, they take the appearance of being independent members of the sentence.

§ 478. *The concord of number.*—It is believed that the following three rules will carry us through all difficulties of the kind just exhibited.

Rule 1. That the verb agrees with the subject, and with nothing but the subject. The only way to justify such an expression as *the wages of sin is death,* is to consider *death* not as the subject, but as the predicate; in other words, to consider the construction to be, *death is the wages of sin.*

Rule 2. That, except in the case of the word *there*, the word which comes first is generally the subject.

Rule 3. That no number of connected singular nouns can govern a plural verb, unless they be connected by a copulative conjunction. *The sun* and *moon shine,*—*the sun* in conjunction with *the moon shines.*

§ 479. *Plural subjects with singular predicates.*—

The wages of sin *are* death.—Honest men *are* the salt of the earth.

Singular subjects with plural predicates.—These constructions are rarer than the preceding: inasmuch as two or more persons (or things) are oftener spoken of as being equivalent to one, than one person (or thing) is spoken of as being equivalent to two or more.

> Sixpence *is* twelve halfpennies.
> He *is* all head and shoulders.
> Vulnera totus *erat.*
> Tu *es* deliciæ meæ.

> Ἔκτορ, ἀτὰρ σύ μοι ἐσσὶ πατὴρ καὶ πότνια μήτηρ,
> Ἠδὲ κασίγνητος, σὺ δέ μοι θαλερὸς παρακοίτης.

CHAPTER XVII.

ON THE GOVERNMENT OF VERBS.

§ 480. The government of verbs is of two sorts, (1.) *objective*, and (2.) *modal*.

It is objective where the noun which follows the verb is the name of some object affected by the action of the verb,—as *he strikes me ; he wounds the enemy.*

It is modal when the noun which follows the verb is not the name of any object affected by the verb, but the name of some object explaining the manner in which the action of the verb takes place, the instrument with which it is done, the end for which it is done, &c.

The government of all transitive verbs is necessarily objective. It may also be modal,—*I strike the enemy with the sword =ferio hostem gladio.*

The government of all intransitive verbs can only be modal,—*I walk with the stick.* When we say, *I walk the horse*, the word *walk* has changed its meaning, and signifies *make to walk*, and is, by the very fact of its being followed by the name of an object, converted from an intransitive into a transitive verb.

The modal construction may also be called the *adverbial construction ;* because the effect of the noun is akin to that of an adverb,—*I fight with bravery = I fight bravely : he walks a king = he-walks regally.* The modal (or adverbial) construction, sometimes takes the appearance of the objective : inasmuch as intransitive verbs are frequently followed by a substantive, *e. g.*, *to sleep the sleep of the righteous.* Here, nevertheless, this is no proof of government. For a verb to be capable of governing an objective case, it must be a verb signifying an action affecting an object; which is not the case here. The sentence means, to *sleep as the righteous sleep,* or *according to the sleep of the righteous.*

CHAPTER XVIII.

ON THE PARTICIPLES.

§ 481. The present participle, or the participle in *-ing*, must be considered in respect to its relations with the substantive in *-ing*. *Dying-day* is, probably, no more a participle than *morning-walk*. In respect to the syntax of such expressions as the forthcoming, I consider that they are *either* participles or substantives.

1. When substantives, they are in regimen, and govern a genitive case— *What is the meaning of the lady's holding up her train?* Here the word *holding* = *the act of holding*.—*Quid est significatio elevationis pallæ de parte fœminæ*.

2. When participles, they are in apposition or concord, and would, if inflected, appear in the same case with the substantive, or pronoun, preceding them— *What is the meaning of the lady holding up her train?* Here the word *holding* = *in the act of holding*, and answers to the Latin *fœminæ elevantis*.—*Quid est significatio fœminæ elevantis pallam?*

§ 482. The past participle corresponds not with the Greek form τυπτόμενος, but with the form τετυμμένος. *I am beaten* is essentially a combination, expressive not of present but of past time, just like the Latin *sum verberatus*. Its Greek equivalent is not εἰμὶ τυπτόμενος = *I am a man in the act of being beaten*, but εἰμὶ τετυμμένος = *I am a man who has been beaten.* It is past in respect to the action, though present in respect to the state brought about by the action. This essentially past element in the so-called present expression, *I am beaten*, will be again referred to.

CHAPTER XIX.

ON THE MOODS.

§ 483. THE infinitive mood is a noun. The current rule that *when two verbs come together the latter is placed in the infinitive mood*, means that one verb can govern another only by converting it into a noun—*I begin to move* = *I begin the act of moving.* Verbs, *as verbs*, can only come together in the way of apposition—*I irritate, I beat, I talk at him, I call him names,* &c.

§ 484. The construction, however, of English infinitives is two fold. (1.) Objective. (2.) Gerundial.

When one verb is followed by another without the preposition *to*, the construction must be considered to have grown out of the objective case, or from the form in *-an*.

Such is the case with the following words, and, probably, with others:

I may go,	*not* I may *to* go.
I might go,	— I might *to* go.
I can move,	— I can *to* move.
I could move,	— I could *to* move.
I will speak,	— I will *to* speak.
I would speak,	— I would *to* speak.
I shall wait,	— I shall *to* wait.
I should wait,	— I should *to* wait.
Let me go,	— Let me *to* go.
He let me go,	— He let me *to* go.
I do speak,	— I do *to* speak.

I did speak, *not* I did *to* speak.
I dare go, — I dare *to* go.
I durst go, — I durst *to* go.

This, in the present English, is the rarer of the two constructions.

When a verb is followed by another, preceded by the preposition *to*, the construction must be considered to have grown out of the so-called gerund, *i. e.*, the form in *-nne*, *i. e.*, the dative case—*I begin to move.* This is the case with the great majority of English verbs.

§ 485. *Imperatives* have three peculiarities. (1.) They can only, in English, be used in the second person—*go thou on, get you gone,* &c.: (2.) They take pronouns after, instead of before them: (3.) They often omit the pronoun altogether.

CHAPTER XX.

ON THE TENSES

§ 486. Notwithstanding its name, the present tense in English does not express a strictly *present* action. It rather expresses an habitual one. *He speaks well = he is a good speaker.* If a man means to say that he is in the act of speaking, he says *I am speaking.*

It has also, especially when combined with a subjunctive mood, a future power—*I beat you* (= *I will beat you*) *if you don't leave off.*

§ 487. The English præterite is the equivalent, not to the Greek perfect but the Greek aorist. *I beat* = ἔτυψα not τέτυφα. The true perfect is expressed, in English, by the auxiliary *have* + the past participle.

CHAPTER XXI.

SYNTAX OF THE PERSONS OF VERBS.

§ 488. *The concord of persons.*—A difficulty that occurs frequently in the Latin language is rare in English. In expressions like *ego et ille* followed by a verb, there arises a question as to the person in which that verb should be used. Is it to be in the first person in order to agree with *ego*, or in the *third* in order to agree with *ille?* For the sake of laying down a rule upon these and similar points, the classical grammarians arrange the persons (as they do the genders) according to their *dignity*, making the verb (or adjective if it be a question of gender) agree with the most *worthy*. In respect to persons, the first is more worthy than the second, and the second more worthy than the third. Hence, the Latins said—

> *Ego et Balbus sustulimus* manus.
> *Tu et Balbus sustulistis* manus.

Now, in English, the plural form is the same for all three persons. Hence we say *I and you are friends, you and I are friends, I and he are friends*, &c., so that for the practice of language, the question as to the relative dignity of the three persons is a matter of indifference.

Nevertheless, it *may* occur even in English. Whenever two or more pronouns of different persons, and of the *singular* number, follow each other *disjunctively*, the question of concord arises. *I or you,—you or he,*

—*he* or *I*. I believe that, in these cases, the rule is as follows :—

1. Whenever the words *either* or *neither* precede the pronouns, the verb is in the third person. *Either you or I is in the wrong;* *neither you nor I is in the wrong*.

2. Whenever the disjunctive is simple (*i. e.* unaccompanied with the word *either* or *neither*) the verb agrees with the *first* of the two pronouns.

> *I* (or *he*) *am* in the wrong.
> *He* (or *I*) *is* in the wrong.
> *Thou* (or *he*) *art* in the wrong.
> *He* (or *thou*) *is* in the wrong.

Now, provided that they are correct, it is clear that the English language knows nothing about the relative degrees of dignity between these three pronouns; since its habit is to make the verb agree with the one which is placed first—whatever may be the person. I am strongly inclined to believe that the same is the case in Latin; in which case (in the sentence *ego et Balbus sustulimus manus*) *sustulimus* agrees, in person, with *ego*, not because the first person is the worthiest, but because it comes first in the proposition.

§ 489. In the Chapter on the Impersonal Verbs, it is stated that the construction of *me-thinks* is peculiar.

This is because in Anglo-Saxon the word þincan = *seem*. Hence *me-thinks* is φαίνεταί μοι, or *mihi videtur*, and *me* is a *dative* case, not an *accusative*.

The þencan = *think*, was, in Anglo-Saxon, a different word.

CHAPTER XXII.

ON THE VOICES OF VERBS.

§ 490. IN English there is neither a passive nor a middle voice.

The following couplet from Dryden's "Mac Flecnoe" exhibits a construction which requires explanation:—

> An ancient fabric, raised to 'inform the sight,
> There stood of yore, and Barbican *it hight*.

Here the word *hight* = *was called*, and seems to present an instance of the participle being used in a passive sense without the so-called verb substantive. Yet it does no such thing. The word is no participle at all; but a simple preterite. Certain verbs are *naturally* either passive or active, as one of two allied meanings may predominate. *To be called* is passive; so is, *to be beaten*. But, *to bear as a name* is active; so is, *to take a beating*. The word, *hight*, is of the same class of verbs with the Latin *vapulo;* and it is the same as the Latin word, *cluo*. —*Barbican cluit* = *Barbican audivit* = *Barbican it hight*.

CHAPTER XXIII.

ON THE AUXILIARY VERBS.

§ 491. THE auxiliary verbs, in English, play a most important part in the syntax of the language. They may be classified upon a variety of principles. The following, however, are all that need here be applied.

A. *Classification of auxiliaries according to their inflection or non-inflectional powers.*—Inflectional auxiliaries are those that may either replace or be replaced by an inflection. Thus—*I am struck* = the Latin *ferior*, and the Greek τύπτομαι. These auxiliaries are in the same relation to verbs that prepositions are to nouns. The inflectional auxiliaries are,—

1. *Have;* equivalent to an inflection in the way of tense—*I have bitten* = *mo-mordi.*
2. *Shall;* ditto. *I shall call* = *voc-abo.*
3. *Will;* ditto. *I will call* = *voc-abo.*
4. *May;* equivalent to an inflection in the way of mood. *I am come that I may see* = *venio ut vid-eam.*
5. *Be;* equivalent to an inflection in the way of voice. *To be beaten* = *verberari*, τύπτεσθαι.
6. *Am, art, is, are;* ditto. Also equivalent to an inflection in the way of tense. *I am moving* = *move-o.*
7. *Was, were;* ditto, ditto. *I was beaten* = ἐ-τύφθην. *I was moving* = *move-bam.*

Do, can, must, and *let,* are non-inflectional auxiliaries.

B. *Classification of auxiliaries according to their*

non-auxiliary significations.—The power of the word *have* in the combination of *I have a horse* is clear enough. It means possession. The power of the same word in the combination *I have been* is not so clear; nevertheless it is a power which has grown out of the idea of possession. This shows that the power of a verb as an auxiliary may be a modification of its original power; *i. e.*, of the power it has in non-auxiliary constructions. Sometimes the difference is very little: the word *let*, in *let us go*, has its natural sense of permission unimpaired. Sometimes it is lost altogether. *Can* and *may* exist only as auxiliaries.

1. Auxiliary derived from the idea of possession—*have.*

2. Auxiliaries derived from the idea of existence—*be, is, was.*

3. Auxiliary derived from the idea of future destination, dependent upon circumstances external to the agent—*shall.* There are etymological reasons for believing that *shall* is no present tense, but a perfect.

4. Auxiliary derived from the idea of future destination, dependent upon the volition of the agent—*will. Shall* is simply predictive; *will* is predictive and promissive as well.

5. Auxiliary derived from the idea of power, dependent upon circumstances external to the agent—*may.*

6. Auxiliary derived from the idea of power, dependent upon circumstances internal to the agent—*can. May* is simply permissive; *can* is potential. In respect to the idea of power residing in the agent being the cause which determines a contingent action, *can* is in the same relation to *may* as *will* is to *shall.*

" *May* et *can*, cum eorum præteritis imperfectis, *might* et *could*, potentiam innuunt: cum hoc tamen discrimine: *may* et *might* vel de jure rel saltem de rei possibilitate, dicuntur, at *can* et *could* de viribus agentis."—WALLIS, p. 107.

7. Auxiliary derived from the idea of sufferance—*let*.

8. Auxiliary derived from the idea of necessity—*must*.

" *Must* necessitatem innuit. Debeo, oportet, necesse est urere, *I must burn*. Aliquando sed rarius in præterito dicitur *must* (quasi ex *must'd* seu *must't* contractum). Sic, si de præterito dicatur, *he must* (seu *must't*) *be burnt*, oportebat uri seu necesse habuit ut ureretur."—WALLIS, 107.

9. Auxiliary derived from the idea of action—*do*.

C. *Classification of auxiliary verbs in respect to their mode of construction.*—Auxiliary verbs combine with others in three ways.

1. *With participles.*—*a*) With the present, or active, participle—*I am speaking:* *b*) With the past, or passive, participle—*I am beaten, I have beaten.*

2. *With infinitives.*—*a*) With the objective infinitive—*I can speak:* *b*) With the gerundial infinitive—*I have to speak.*

3. *With both infinitives and participles.*—*I shall have done, I mean to have done.*

D. *Auxiliary verbs may be classified according to their effect.*—Thus—*have* makes the combination in which it appears equivalent to a tense; *be* to a passive form; *may* to a sign of mood, &c.

This sketch of the different lights under which auxiliary verbs may be viewed, has been written for the sake of illustrating, rather than exhausting, the subject.

§ 492. The combination of the auxiliary, *have*, with the past participle requires notice. It is, here, advisable to make the following classifications.

1. The combination with the participle of a *transitive*

AUXILIARY VERBS.

verb.—*I have ridden the horse; thou hast broken the sword; he has smitten the enemy.*

2. The combination with the participle of an *intransitive* verb,—*I have waited; thou hast hungered; he has slept.*

3. The combination with the participle of the verb substantive, *I have been; thou hast been; he has been.*

It is by examples of the first of these three divisions that the true construction is to be shown.

For an object of any sort to be in the possession of a person, it must previously have existed. If I possess a horse, that horse must have had a previous existence.

Hence, in all expressions like *I have ridden a horse,* there are two ideas, a past idea in the participle, and a present idea in the word denoting possession.

For an object of any sort, affected in a particular manner, to be in the possession of a person, it must previously have been affected in the manner required. If I possess a horse that has been ridden, the riding must have taken place before I mention the fact of the ridden horse being in my possession; inasmuch as I speak of it as a thing already done,—the participle, *ridden,* being in the past tense.

I have ridden a horse = *I have a horse ridden* = *I have a horse as a ridden horse,* or (changing the gender and dealing with the word *horse* as a thing) *I have a horse as a ridden thing.*

In this case the syntax is of the usual sort. (1) *Have—own* = *habeo* = *teneo;* (2) *horse* is the accusative case *equum;* (3) *ridden* is a past participle agreeing either with *horse,* or *with a word in apposition with it understood.*

Mark the words in italics. The word *ridden* does not agree with *horse,* since it is of the neuter gender.

Neither if we said *I have ridden the horses*, would it agree with *horses;* since it is of the singular number.

The true construction is arrived at by supplying the word *thing*. *I have a horse as a ridden thing* = *habeo equum equitatum* (neuter). Here the construction is the same as *triste lupus stabulis.*

I have horses as a ridden thing = *habeo equos equitatum* (singular, neuter). Here the construction is—

> "Triste ..... maturis frugibus imbres,
> Arboribus venti, nobis Amaryllidos iræ."

or in Greek—

> Δεινὸν γυναιξὶν αἱ δὲ ὠδίνων γοναί.

The classical writers supply instances of this use of *have*. *Compertum habeo*, milites, verba viris virtutem non addere = *I have discovered* = *I am in possession of the discovery.* Quæ cum ita sint, satis de Cæsare hoc dictum habeo.

The combination of *have* with an intransitive verb is irreducible to the idea of possession: indeed, it is illogical. In *I have waited*, we cannot make the idea expressed by the word *waited* the object of the verb *have* or *possess*. The expression has become a part of language by means of the extension of a false analogy. It is an instance of an illegitimate imitation.

The combination of *have* with *been* is more illogical still, and is a stronger instance of the influence of an illegitimate imitation. In German and Italian, where even *intransitive* verbs are combined with the equivalents to the English *have* (*haben*, and *avere*), the verb substantive is not so combined; on the contrary, the combinations are

> Italian; *io sono stato* = *I am been.*
> German; *ich bin gewesen* = ditto.

which is logical.

§ 493. *I am to speak.*—Three facts explain this idiom.

1. The idea of *direction towards an object* conveyed by the dative case, and by combinations equivalent to it.

2. The extent to which the ideas of necessity, obligation, or intention are connected with the idea of *something that has to be done,* or *something towards which some action has a tendency.*

3. The fact that expressions like the one in question historically represent an original dative case, or its equivalent; since *to speak* grows out of the Anglo-Saxon form *to sprecanne,* which, although called a gerund, is really a dative case of the infinitive mood.

When Johnson thought that, in the phrase *he is to blame,* the word *blame* was a noun, if he meant a noun in the way that *culpa* is a noun, his view was wrong. But if he meant a noun in the way that *culpare, ad culpandum,* are nouns, it was right.

§ 494. *I am to blame.*—This idiom is one degree more complex than the previous one; since *I am to blame = I am to be blamed.* As early, however, as the Anglo-Saxon period the gerunds were liable to be used in a passive sense: *he is to lufigenne* = not *he is to love,* but *he is to be loved.*

The principle of this confusion may be discovered by considering that *an object to be blamed,* is *an object for some one to blame, an object to be loved* is *an object for some one to love.*

§ 495. *I am beaten.*—This is a present combination, and it is present on the strength of the verb *am,* not on the strength of the participle *beaten,* which is præterite.

The following table exhibits the *expedients* on the part of the different languages of the Gothic stock, since the loss of the proper passive form of the Mœso-Gothic.

Language	Latin *datur,*	Latin *datus est.*
Mœso-Gothic	gibada,	ist, vas, varth gibans.
Old High German	ist, wirdit kepan,	was, warth kepan.
Notker	wirt keben,	ist keben.
Middle High German	wirt geben,	ist geben.
New High German	wird gegeben,	ist gegeben worden.
Old Saxon	is, wirtheth gebhan,	was, warth gebhan.
Middle Dutch	es, blift ghegheven,	waert, bléf ghegeven.
New Dutch	wordt gegeven,	es gegeven worden.
Old Frisian	werth ejeven,	is ejeven.
Anglo-Saxon	weorded gifen,	is gifen.
English	is given,	has been given.
Old Norse	er gefinn,	hefr verit gefinn.
Swedish	gifves,	har varit gifven.
Danish	bliver, vorder given,	har varet given.

"Deutsche Grammatik, iv. 19."

CHAPTER XXIV.

THE SYNTAX OF ADVERBS.

§ 496. THE syntax of the adverb is simpler than that of any other part of speech, excepting, perhaps, that of the adjective.

Adverbs have no concord.

Neither have they any government. They *seem*, indeed, to have it, when they are in the comparative or superlative degree; but it is merely apparent. In *this is better than that*, the word *that* is governed neither by *better* nor by *than*. It is not governed at all. It is a nominative case; the subject of a separate proposition. *This is better* (*i. e.*, *more good*) *than that is good*. Even if we admit such an expression as *he is stronger than me* to be good English, there is no adverbial government. *Than*, if it govern *me* at all, governs it as a preposition.

The position of an adverb is, in respect to matters of syntax, pre-eminently parenthetic; *i. e.*, it may be omitted without injuring the construction. *He is fighting—now; he was fighting—then; he fights—bravely; I am almost —tired*, &c.

§ 497. By referring to the Chapter on the Adverbs, we shall find that the neuter adjective is frequently converted into an adverb by deflection. As any neuter adjective may be so deflected, we may justify such expressions as *full* (for *fully*) as *conspicuous* (for *con-*

spicuously), and *peculiar* (for *peculiarly*) *bad grace*, &c. We are not, however, bound to imitate everything that we can justify.

§ 498. The termination *-ly* was originally adjectival. At present it is a derivational syllable by which we can convert an adjective into an adverb: *brave, brave-ly*. When, however, the adjective ends in *-ly* already, the formation is awkward. *I eat my daily bread* is unexceptionable English; *I eat my bread daily* is exceptionable. One of two things must here take place: the two syllables *ly* are packed into one (the full expression being *dai-li-ly*), or else the construction is that of a neuter adjective deflected.

Adverbs are convertible. *The then men* = οἱ νῦν βρότοι, &c. This will be seen more clearly in the Chapter on Conjunctions.

§ 499. It has been remarked that in expressions like *he sleeps the sleep of the righteous*, the construction is adverbial. So it is in expressions like *he walked a mile, it weighs a pound*. The ideas expressed by *mile* and *pound* are not the names of anything that serves as either object or instrument to the verb. They only denote the *manner* of the action, and define the meaning of the verb.

§ 500. *From whence, from thence.*—This is an expression which, if it have not taken root in our language, is likely to do so. It is an instance of excess of expression in the way of syntax; the *-ce* denoting direction *from* a place, and the preposition doing the same. It is not so important to determine what this construction *is*, as to suggest what it is *not*. It is *not* an instance of an adverb governed by a preposition. If the two words be dealt with as logically separate, *whence* (or *thence*) must be a noun = *which place* (or *that* *place*); just as *from then till now* = *from that time to this*. But if (which is the better view) the two words be dealt with as one (*i. e.*, as an improper compound) the preposition *from* has lost its natural power, and become the element of an adverb.

CHAPTER XXV.

ON PREPOSITIONS.

§ 501. ALL prepositions govern an oblique case. If a word ceases to do this, it ceases to be a preposition. In the first of the two following sentences the word *up* is a preposition, in the second an adverb.

1. *I climbed up the tree.*
2. *I climbed up.*

All prepositions in English, precede the noun which they govern. *I climbed up the tree,* never *I climbed the tree up.* This is a matter not of government, but of collocation. It is the case in most languages; and, from the frequency of its occurrence, the term *pre-position* (or *prefix*) has originated. Nevertheless, it is by no means a philological necessity. In many languages the prepositions are *post-positive*, following their noun.

§ 502. No preposition, in the present English, governs a genitive case. This remark is made, because expressions like the *part of the body* = *pars corporis,*—*a piece of the bread* = *portio panis,* make it appear as if the preposition *of* did so. The true expression is, that the preposition *of,* followed by an objective case is equivalent in many instances, to the genitive case of the classical languages.

CHAPTER XXVI.

ON CONJUNCTIONS.

§ 503. A CONJUNCTION is a part of speech which connects *propositions,—the day is bright*, is one proposition. *The sun shines*, is another. *The day is bright* because *the sun shines* is a pair of propositions connected by the conjunction, *because*.

From this it follows, that whenever there is a conjunction, there are two subjects, two copulas, and two predicates: *i. e.*, two propositions in all their parts.

But this may be expressed compendiously. *The sun shines, and the moon shines* may be expressed by the *sun and moon shine*.

Nevertheless, however compendious may be the expression, there are always two propositions wherever there is one conjunction. A part of speech that merely combines two words is a preposition,—*the sun along with the moon shines*.

It is highly important to remember that conjunctions connect propositions.

It is also highly important to remember that many double propositions may be expressed so compendiously as to look like one. When this takes place, and any question arises as to the construction, they must be exhibited in their fully expanded form, *i. e.*, the second subject, the second predicate, and the second copula must be supplied. This can always be done from the first proposition,—

he likes you better than me = *he likes you better than he likes me.* The compendious expression of the second proposition is the first point of note in the syntax of conjunctions.

§ 504. The second point in the syntax of conjunctions is the fact of their great convertibility. Most conjunctions have been developed out of some other part of speech.

The conjunction of comparison, *than*, is derived from the adverb of time, *then:* which is derived from the accusative singular of the demonstrative pronoun.

The conjunction, *that*, is derived also from a demonstrative pronoun.

The conjunction, *therefore*, is a demonstrative pronoun + a preposition.

The conjunction, *because*, is a substantive governed by a preposition.

One and the same word, in one and the same sentence, may be a conjunction or preposition, as the case may be.

All fled but John.—If this mean *all fled except John*, the word *but* is a preposition, the word *John* is an accusative case, and the proposition is single. If instead of *John*, we had a personal pronoun, we should say *all fled but him.*

All fled but John.—If this mean *all fled but John did not fly*, the word *but* is a conjunction, the word *John* is a nominative case, and the propositions are two in number. If, instead of *John*, we had a personal pronoun, we should say, *all fled but he.*

From the fact of the great convertibility of conjunctions it is often necessary to determine whether a word be a conjunction or not. *If it be a conjunction, it cannot govern a case. If it govern a case it is no conjunction but a preposition.* A conjunction cannot govern a case, for the following reasons,—the word that follows it *must* be the subject of the second proposition, and as such, a nominative case.

§ 505. The third point to determine in the syntax of conjunctions is the certainty or uncertainty in the mind of the speaker as to the facts expressed by the propositions which they serve to connect.

1. Each proposition may contain a certain, definite, absolute fact—*the day is clear* because *the sun shines.* Here there is neither doubt nor contingency of either the *day being clear,* or of the *sun shining.*

Of two propositions one may be the condition of the other—*the day will be clear* if *the sun shine.* Here, although it is certain that *if the sun shine the day will be clear,* there is no certainty of *the sun shining.* Of the two propositions one only embodies a certain fact, and that is certain only conditionally.

Now an action, wherein there enters any notion of uncertainty, or indefinitude, and is at the same time connected with another action, is expressed, not by the indicative mood, but by the subjunctive. *If the sun* shine (not *shines*) *the day will be clear.*

Simple uncertainty will not constitute a subjunctive construction,—*I am,* perhaps, *in the wrong.*

Neither will simple connection.—*I am wrong,* because *you are right.*

But, the two combined constitute the construction in question,—*if I be wrong, you are right.*

Now, a conjunction that connects two certain propositions may be said to govern an indicative mood.

And a conjunction that connects an uncertain proposition with a certain one, may be said to govern a subjunctive mood.

The government of mood is the only form of government of which conjunctions are capable.

§ 506. Previous to the question of the government of conjunctions in the way of mood, it is necessary to notice certain points of agreement between them and the relative pronouns; inasmuch as, in many cases, the relative pronoun exerts the same government, in the way of determining the mood of the verb, as the conjunction.

Between the relative pronouns and conjunctions in general there is this point of connection,—both join propositions. Wherever there is a relative, there is a second proposition. So there is wherever there is a conjunction.

Between certain relative pronouns and those particular conjunctions that govern a subjunctive mood there is also a point of connection. Both suggest an element of uncertainty or indefinitude. This the relative pronouns do, through the logical elements common to them and to the interrogatives: these latter essentially suggesting the idea of doubt. Wherever the person, or thing, connected with an action, and expressed by a relative is indefinite, there is room for the use of a subjunctive mood. Thus— "he that troubled you shall bear his judgment, *whosoever he be.*"

§ 507. By considering the nature of such words as *when*, their origin as relatives on the one hand, and their conjunctional character on the other hand, we are prepared for finding a relative element in words like *till, until, before, as long as,* &c. These can all be expanded into expressions like *until the time when, during the time when,* &c. Hence, in an expression like *seek out his wickedness till thou* find (not *findest*) *none*, the principle of the construction is nearly the same as in *he that troubled you*, &c., or *vice versâ*.*

§ 508. In most conditional expressions the subjunctive mood should follow the conjunction. All the following expressions are conditional.

  1. *Except* I *be* by Silvia in the night,
   There is no music in the nightingale.
           SHAKSPEARE.
  2. Let us go and sacrifice to the Lord our God, *lest* he *fall* upon with pestilence.—*Old Testament*.
  3. —— Revenge back on itself recoils.
   Let it. I reck not, *so* it *light* well aimed.
           J. MILTON.
  4. *If* this *be* the case.
  5. *Although* my house *be* not so with God.—*Old Testament*.
  6. He shall not eat of the holy thing *unless* he *wash* his flesh with water.—*Old Testament*.

Expressions like *except* and *unless* are equally conditional with words like *if* and *provided that*, since they are equivalent to *if—not*.

Expressions like *though* and *although* are peculiar. They join propositions, of which the one is a *primâ facie* reason against the existence of the other: and this is the conditional element. In the sentence, *if the children be so badly brought-up, they are not to be trusted*, the bad bringing-up is the reason for their *being unfit to be trusted;* and, as far as the expression is concerned, *is admitted to be so*. The only uncertainty lies in the question as to the degree of the badness of the education. The inference from it is unequivocal.

* Notwithstanding the extent to which a relative may take the appearance of a conjunction, there is always one unequivocal method of deciding its true nature. The relative is always a *part* of the second proposition. A conjunction is *no part* of either.

But if, instead of saying *if*, we say *although*, and omit the word *not*, so that the sentence run *although the children be so badly brought-up they are to be trusted*, we do two things: we indicate the general relation of cause and effect that exists between *bad bringing-up* and *unfitness for being trusted*, but we also, at the same time, take an exception to it in the particular instance before us. These remarks have been made for the sake of showing the extent to which words like *though*, &c., are conditional.

It must be remembered, however, that conjunctions, like the ones lately quoted, do not govern subjunctive moods because they are conditional, but because, in the particular condition which they accompany, there is an element of uncertainty.

§ 509. This introduces a fresh question. Conditional conjunctions are of two sorts:—

1. Those which express a condition as an actual fact, and one admitted as such by the speaker.

2. Those which express a condition as a possible fact, and one which the speaker either does not admit, or admits only in a qualified manner.

Since *the children are so badly brought-up*, &c.—This is an instance of the first construction. The speaker admits as an actual fact the *bad bringing-up of the children*.

If *the children be so badly brought-up*, &c.—This is an instance of the second construction. The speaker admits as a possible (perhaps, as a probable) fact the *bad bringing-up of the children:* but he does not adopt it as an indubitable one.

§ 510. Now, if every conjunction had a fixed unvariable meaning, there would be no difficulty in determining whether a condition was absolute, and beyond doubt, or possible, and liable to doubt. But such is not the case.

Although may precede a proposition which is admitted as well as one which is doubted.

> *a.* Although *the children* are, &c.
> *b.* Although *the children* be, &c.

If, too, may precede propositions wherein there is no doubt whatever implied: in other words it may be used instead of *since*.

In some languages this interchange goes farther than in others; in the Greek, for instance, such is the case with εἰ, to a very great extent indeed.

Hence we must look to the meaning of the sentence in general, rather than to the particular conjunction used.

It is a philological fact that *if* may stand instead of *since*.

It is also a philological fact that when it does so it should be followed by the indicative mood.

This is written in the way of illustration. What applies to *if* applies to other conjunctions as well.

§ 511. As a point of practice, the following method of determining the amount of doubt expressed in a conditional proposition is useful:—

Insert, immediately after the conjunction, one of the two following phrases,—(1.) *as is the case;* (2.) *as may or may not be the case.* By ascertaining which of these two supplements expresses the meaning of the speaker, we ascertain the mood of the verb which follows.

When the first formula is the one required, there is no element of doubt, and the verb should be in the indicative mood. *If (as is the case), he is gone, I must follow him.*

When the second formula is the one required, there *is* an element of doubt, and the verb should be in the subjunctive mood. *If (as may or may not be the case) he be gone, I must follow him.*

§ 512. The use of the word *that* in expressions like *I eat that I may live*, &c., is a modification of the subjunctive construction, that is conveniently called *potential*. It denotes that one act is done for the sake of supplying the *power* or opportunity for the performance of another.

The most important point connected with the powers of *that* is the so-called *succession of tenses*.

§ 513. *The succession of tenses.*—Whenever the conjunction *that* expresses intention, and consequently connects two verbs, the second of which takes place *after* the first, the verbs in question must be in the same tense.

> I *do* this *that* I *may* gain by it.
> I *did* this *that* I *might* gain by it.

In the Greek language this is expressed by a difference of mood; the subjunctive being the construction equivalent to *may* the optative to *might*. The Latin idiom coincides with the English.

A little consideration will show that this rule is absolute. For a man *to be doing* one action (in present time) in order that some other action may *follow* it (in past time) is to reverse the order of cause and effect. To do anything in A. D. 1851, that something may result from it in 1850 is a contradiction; and so it is to say *I* do *this* that *I* might *gain by it*.

The reasons against the converse construction are nearly, if not equally cogent. To have done anything at any *previous* time in order that a *present* effect may follow, is, *ipso facto*, to convert a past act into a present one, or, to speak in the language of the grammarian, to convert an aorist into a perfect. To say *I* did *this* that *I may gain by it*, is to make, by the very effect of the expression, either *may* equivalent to *might*, or *did* equivalent to *have done*.

I did *this* that *I* might *gain*.
I have done *this* that *I* may *gain*.

§ 514. *Disjunctives.*—Disjunctives (*or, nor*) are of two sorts, real and nominal.

A king or queen always rules in England. Here the disjunction is real; *king* or *queen* being different names for different objects. In all *real* disjunctions the inference is, that if one out of two (or more) individuals (or classes) do not perform a certain action, the other does.

A sovereign or supreme ruler always rules in England. Here the disjunction is nominal; *sovereign* and *supreme governor* being different names for the same object. In all nominal disjunctives the inference is, that if an agent (or agents) do not perform a certain action under one name, he does (or they do) it under another.

Nominal disjunctives are called by Harris *sub*disjunctives.

In the English language there is no separate word to distinguish the nominal from the real disjunctive. In Latin, *vel* is considered by Harris to be disjunctive, *sive* subdisjunctive. As a periphrasis, the combination *in other words* is subdisjunctive.

Both nominal and real disjunctives agree in this,—whatever may be the number of nouns which they connect, the construction of the verb is the same as if there were but one—Henry, *or* John, *or* Thomas, *walks* (not *walk*); the sun, *or* solar luminary, *shines* (not *shine*). The disjunctive *isolates* the subject, however much it may be placed in juxtaposition with other nouns.

CHAPTER XXVII.

THE SYNTAX OF THE NEGATIVE.

§ 515. WHEN the verb is in the infinitive mood, the negative precedes it.—*Not to advance is to retreat.*

When the verb is not in the infinitive mood, the negative follows it.—*He advanced not. I cannot.*

This rule is absolute. It only *seems* to precede the verb in such expressions as *I do not advance, I cannot advance, I have not advanced,* &c. However, the words *do, can,* and *have,* are no infinitives; and it consequently follows them. The word *advance* is an infinitive, and it consequently precedes it. Wallis's rule makes an equivalent statement, although differently. " Adverbium negandi *not* (non) verbo postponitur (nempe auxiliari primo si adsit; aut si non adsit auxiliare, verbo principali): aliis tamen orationis partibus præfigi solet."—P. 113.

That the negative is rarely used, except with an auxiliary, in other words, that the presence of a negative converts a simple form like *it burneth not* into the circumlocution it *does not burn,* is a fact in the practice of the English language. The syntax is the same in either expression.

§ 516. What may be called the *distribution* of the negative is pretty regular in English. Thus, when the word *not* comes between an indicative, imperative, or subjunctive mood and an infinitive verb, it almost always is taken with the word which it *follows*—*I can not eat* may mean either *I can*—*not eat* (*i. e.*, *I can abstain*), or *I can not*—*eat* (*i. e.*, *I am unable to eat*); but, as stated above, it *almost* always has the latter signification.

But not *always*. In Byron's "Deformed Transformed" we find the following lines:—

> Clay! not dead but soulless,
>   Though no mortal man would choose thee,
> An immortal no less
>   Deigns *not to refuse* thee.

Here *not to refuse* = *to accept;* and is probably a Grecism. *To not refuse* would, perhaps, be better.

The next expression is still more foreign to the English idiom:—

> For *not* to have been dipped in Lethe's lake
> Could save the son of Thetis from to die.

Here *not* is to be taken with *could*.

§ 517. In the present English, two negatives make an affirmative. *I have not not seen him* = *I have seen him*. In Greek this was not the case. *Duæ aut plures negativæ apud Græcos vehementius negant* is a well known rule. The Anglo-Saxon idiom differed from the English and coincided with the Greek. The French negative is only apparently double; words like *point*, *pas*, mean not *not*, but *at all*. *Je ne parle pas* = *I not speak at all*, not *I not speak no*.

§ 518. *Questions of appeal.*—All questions imply want of information; want of information may then imply doubt; doubt, perplexity; and perplexity the absence of an alternative. In this way, what are called, by Mr. Arnold,[*] *questions of appeal*, are, practically speaking, neg-

---

[*] "Latin Prose Composition," p. 123.

atives. *What should I do?* when asked in extreme perplexity, means that nothing can well be done. In the following passage we have the presence of a question instead of a negative :—

> Or hear'st thou (*cluis*, Lat.) rather pure ethereal stream,
> Whose fountain who (*no one*) shall tell?
> *Paradise Lost.*

CHAPTER XXVIII.

ON THE CASE ABSOLUTE.

§ 519. BROADLY speaking, all adverbial constructions are absolute. The term, however, is conveniently limited to a particular combination of the noun, verb, and participle. When two actions are connected with each other, either by the fact of their simultaneous occurrence, or as cause and effect, they may be expressed within the limits of a single proposition, by expressing the one by means of a verb, and the other by means of a noun and participle agreeing with each other. *The door being open, the horse was stolen.*

Considering the nature of the connection between the two actions, we find good grounds for expecting *à priori* that the participle will be in the instrumental case, when such exists in the language: and when not, in some case allied to it, *i. e.*, the ablative or dative.

In Latin the ablative is the case that is used absolutely. *Sole orto, claruit dies.*

In Anglo-Saxon the absolute case was the dative. This is logical.

In the present English, however, the nominative is the absolute case. *He made the best proverbs, him alone excepted*, is an expression of Tillotson's. We should now write *he alone excepted.* The present mode of expression is only to be justified by considering the nominative form to be a dative one, just as in the expression *you are here*, the word *you*, although an accusative, is considered as a nominative. A real nominative absolute is as illogical as a real accusative case governing a verb.

PART VI.

PROSODY.

§ 520. The word *Prosody* is derived from a Greek word (*prosodia*) signifying *accent*. It is used by Latin and English grammarians in a wider sense, and includes not only the doctrines of accent and quantity, but also the laws of metre and versification.

§ 521. Observe the accents in the following lines:—

> Then fáre thee wéll, mine ówn dear lóve,
> The wórld hath nów for ús
> No greáter grief, no paín abóve
> The paín of párting thús.
>
> MOORE.

Here the syllables accented are the 2nd, 4th, 6th, 8th, 10th, 12th, 14th, 16th, 18th, 20th, 22nd, 24th, 26th, 28th; that is, every other syllable.—Again,

> At the clóse of the dáy, when the hámlet is stíll,
> And the mórtals the swéets of forgétfulness próve,
> And when nóught but the tórrent is heárd on the híll,
> And there's noúght but the níghtingale's sóng in the gróve.
>
> BEATTIE.

Here the syllables accented are the 3rd, 6th, 9th, 12th, 15th, 18th, 21st, 24th, 27th, 30th, 33rd, 36th, 39th, 42nd, 45th, 48th; that is, every third syllable.

§ 522. *Metre is a general term for the recurrence*

within certain intervals of syllables similarly affected. The syllables that have just been numbered are similarly affected, being similarly accented. Accent is not the only quality of a syllable, which by returning at regular intervals can constitute metre. It is the one, however, upon which English metre depends. English metre essentially consists in the regular recurrence of syllables similarly *accented.*

> *Abbot.*—And why' not líve and áct with óther mén?
> *Manfred.*—Becaúse my náture wás avérse from lífe;
> And yét not crúel, fór I woúld not máke,
> But fínd a désolátion :—líke the wínd,
> The réd-hot breáth of thé most lóne simoóm,
> Which dwélls but ín the désert, ánd sweeps o'ér
> The bárren sánds which beár no shrúbs to blást,
> And révels ó'er their wíld and árid wáves,
> And seéketh nót so thát it ís not soúght,
> But béing mét is deádly: súch hath beén
> The páth of my' existence.   BYRON.

§ 523. *Measures.*—For every accented syllable in the following line, write the letter *a*, and for every unaccented one, the letter *x*, so that *a* may stand for an accent, *x* for the absence of one—

> The wáy was lóng, the wínd was cóld.
>   SCOTT.

or expressed symbolically

$$x\ a\ x\ a\ x\ a\ x\ a,$$

where *x* coincides with *the*, *a* with *way*, &c.

§ 524. Determine the length of the line in question.—It is plain that this may be done in two ways. We may either measure by the syllables, and say that the line consists of eight syllables; or by the accents, and say that it consists of four accents. In this latter case we take the accented syllable with its corresponding unaccented one, and, grouping the two together, deal with the pair at once. Now, a group of syllables thus taken together is called a *measure*. In the line in question *the way* ($x\ a$) is one measure, *was long* ($x\ a$) another, and so on throughout; the line itself consisting of four measures.

§ 525. *Trisyllabic measures.*—The number of measures consisting of two syllables, or dissyllabic measures, is necessarily limited to two, expressed $a\ x$ and $x\ a$ respectively. But beyond these there are in the English language measures of three syllables, or trisyllabic measures. The number of these is necessarily limited to three.

The first of these is exhibited in the word *mérrily* ($a\ x\ x$).

> Mérrily, mérrily shall I live nów,
> Únder the blóssom that hángs on the boúgh.
> SHAKSPEARE.

The second is exhibited by the word *disáble* ($x\ a\ x$).

> But vaínly thou wárrest,
> For this is alóne in
> Thy pówer to decláre,
> That in the dim fórest
> Thou heárd'st a low moáning,
> And sáw'st a bright lády surpássingly fair.
> COLERIDGE.

§ 526. The third is exhibited by the word *cavaliér* ($x\ x\ a$).

> There's a beaúty for éver unfádingly bríght,
> Like the lóng ruddy lápse of a súmmer-day's night.
> MOORE.

When grouped together according to certain rules, measures form lines and verses; and lines and verses, regularly arranged, constitute couplets, triplets, and stanzas, &c.

§ 527. The expression of measures, lines, &c., by such symbols as *a x, x a,* &c., is *metrical notation*.

§ 528. *Rhyme.*—We can have English verse without *rhyme*. We cannot have English verse without *accent*. Hence accent is an *essential*; rhyme an *accessory* to metre.

§ 529. *Analysis of a pair of rhyming syllables.*— Let the syllables *told* and *bold* be taken to pieces, and let the separate parts of each be compared. Viewed in reference to metre, they consist of three parts or elements: 1. the vowel (*o*); 2. the part *preceding* the vowel (*t* and *b* respectively); 3. the parts *following* the vowel (*ld*). Now the vowel (*o*) and the parts following the vowel (*ld*) are alike in both words (*old*); but the part preceding the vowel is different in the different words (*told, bold*). This difference between the parts preceding the vowels is essential; since, if it were not for this, the two words would be identical, or rather there would be but one word altogether. This is the case with *I* and *eye*. Sound for sound (although different in spelling) the two words are identical, and, consequently, the rhyme is faulty.

Again—compared with the words *bold* and *told*, the words *teeth* and *breeze* have two of the elements necessary to constitute a rhyme. The vowels are alike (*ee*), whilst the parts preceding the vowels are different (*br* and *t*); and, as far as these two matters are concerned, the rhyme is a good one, *tee* and *bree*. Notwithstanding this, there is anything rather than a rhyme; since the parts following the vowel (*th* and *ze*) instead of agreeing, differ. *Breathe* and *beneath* are in the same predicament, because the *th* is not sounded alike in the two words.

Again—the words *feel* and *mill* constitute only a false and imperfect rhyme. Sound for sound, the letters *f* and *m* (the parts preceding the vowel) are different. This is as it should be. Also, sound for sound, *l* and *ll* (the parts following the vowel) are identical; and this is as it should be also: but *ee* and *i* (the vowels) are different, and this difference spoils the rhyme. *None* and *own* are in the same predicament; since one *o* is sounded as *o* in *note*, and the other as the *u* in *but*.

From what has gone before we get the notion of true and perfect rhymes as opposed to false and imperfect ones. For two (or more) words to rhyme to each other, it is necessary

   a. That the vowel be the same in both.

   b. That the parts following the vowel be the same.

   c. That the parts preceding the vowel be different.

Beyond this it is necessary that the syllables, to form a full and perfect rhyme, should be accented syllables. *Sky* and *lie* form good rhymes, but *sky* and *merrily* bad ones, and *merrily* and *silly* worse. Lines like the second and fourth of the following stanza are slightly exceptionable on this score: indeed, many readers sacrifice the accent in the word *mérrily* to the rhyme, and pronounce it *merrilý*.

      The witch she héld the haír in her hánd,
        The réd flame blázed hígh;
      And roúnd abóut the cáldron stoút,
        They dánced right merrilý.
                           KIRKE WHITE.

§ 530. In matters of rhyme the letter *h* counts as nothing. *High* and *I*, *hair* and *air*, are imperfect rhymes, because *h* (being no articulate sound) counts as nothing, and so the parts before the vowel *i* and *a* are not different (as they ought to be) but identical.

> Whose generous children narrow'd not their hearts
> With commerce, giv'n alone to arms and arts.
> BYRON.

§ 531. Words where the letters coincide, but the sounds differ, are only rhymes to the eye. *Breathe* and *beneath* are both in this predicament; so also are *cease* and *ease* (*eaze*).

> In the fat age of pleasure, wealth, and ease,
> Sprang the rank weed, and thrived with large increase.
> POPE.

§ 532. If the sounds coincide, the difference of the letters is unimportant.

> Bold in the practice of mistaken rules,
> Prescribe, apply, and call their masters fools.
> They talk of principles, but notions prize,
> And all to one loved folly sacrifice.
> POPE.

§ 533. *Single rhymes.*—An accented syllable standing by itself, and coming under the conditions given above, constitutes a single rhyme.

> 'Tis hard to say if greater want of *skill*
> Appear in writing or in judging *ill*;
> But of the two, less dangerous is the *offence*
> To tire the patience than mislead the *sense*.
> Some few in that, but thousands err in *this*;
> Ten censure wrong, for one that writes *amiss*.
> POPE.

§ 534. *Double rhymes.*—An accented syllable followed by an unaccented one, and coming under the conditions given above, constitutes a double rhyme.

> The meeting points the sacred hair dissever
> From her fair head for ever and for ever.
>
> POPE.
>
> Prove and explain a thing till all men *doubt it*,
> And write about it, Goddess, and *about it*.
>
> POPE.

§ 535. An accented syllable followed by two unaccented ones, and coming under the conditions given above, constitutes a treble rhyme.

> Beware that its fatal asc*éndancy*
>   Do not tempt thee to mope and repine;
> With a humble and hopeful dep*éndency*
>   Still await the good pleasure divine.
> Success in a higher be*átitude*,
>   Is the end of what's under the Pole;
> A philosopher takes it with *grátitude*,
>   And believes it the best on the whole.
>
> BYRON.

§ 536. Metres where there is no rhyme are called blank metres.

> Of man's first disobedience and the fruit
> Of that forbidden tree, whose mortal taste
> Brought death into the world and all our woe,
> With loss of Eden, till one greater Man
> Restore us, and regain the blissful seat,
> Sing, Heavenly Muse?
>
> MILTON.

> The quality of mercy is not strained.
> It droppeth as the gentle dew from heaven
> Upon the place beneath; it is twice bless'd,
> It blesseth him that gives, and him that takes
> Tis mightiest of the mighty, it becomes
> The throned monarch better than his crown.
> His sceptre shows the force of temporal power,
> The attribute of awe and majesty,
> Wherein doth sit the dread and fear of kings:

> But mercy is above this sceptred sway;
> It is enthroned in the hearts of kings:
> It is an attribute to God himself;
> And earthly power doth then show likest God's,
> When mercy seasons justice.
>
> SHAKSPEARE.

§ 537. *The last measure in a line or verse is indifferent as to its length.*—By referring to the section upon single rhymes, we shall find that the number of syllables is just double the number of accents; that is, to each accented there is one unaccented syllable, and no more. Hence, with five accents, there are to each line ten syllables. This is not the case with all verses. Some rhymes are double, and the last accented syllable has two unaccented ones to follow it. Hence, with five accents there are to each line eleven syllables. Now it is in the last measure that this supernumerary unaccented syllable appears; and it is a general rule, that, in the last measure of any verse, supernumerary unaccented syllables can be admitted without destroying the original character of the measure.

§ 538. See the verses in the section on double rhymes. Here the original character of the measure is $x\ a$ throughout, until we get to the words *disséver* and *for éver*, and afterwards to *men doũbt it*, and *aboũt it*. At the first view it seems proper to say that in these last-mentioned cases $x\ a$ is converted into $x\ a\ x$. A different view, however, is the more correct one. *Disséver* and *for éver*, are rather $x\ a$ with a syllable over. This extra syllable may be expressed by the sign *plus* ($+$), so that the words in point may be expressed by $x\ a\ +$, rather than by $x\ a\ x$. It is very clear that a measure whereof the last syllable is accented (that is, measures like $x\ a$, *presúme*, or $x\ x\ a$, *cavalíer*), can only vary from their original character on the side of excess; that is, they can only be altered by the addition of fresh syllables. To subtract a syllable from such feet is impossible; since it is only the last syllable that is capable of being subtracted. If that last syllable, however, be the accented syllable of the measure, the whole measure is annihilated. Nothing remains but the unaccented syllable preceding; and this, as no measure can subsist without an accent, must be counted as a supernumerary part of the preceding measure.

§ 539. With the measures *a x*, *a x x*, *x a x*, the case is different. Here there is room for syllable or syllables to be subtracted.

> Queén and húntress, cháste and fair,
> Now the sún is laíd to sleep,
> Seáted in thy silver chair,
> State in wonted splendour keep.
> Hésperús invókes thy light,
> Goddess, exquisitely bright.
>
> BEN JONSON.

In all these lines the last measure is deficient in a syllable, yet the deficiency is allowable, because each measure is the last one of the line. The formula for expressing *fair*, *sleep*, *chair*, &c. is not *a*, but rather *a x* followed by the *minus* sign (—), or *a x*—.

A little consideration will show that amongst the English measures, *x a* and *x x a* naturally form single, *a x* and *x a x* double, and *a x x* treble rhymes.

§ 540. The chief metres in English are of the formula *x a*. It is only a few that are known by fixed names. These are as follows:—

1. *Gay's stanza.*—Lines of three measures, *x a*, with alternate rhymes. The odd (*i. e.* the 1st and 3rd) rhymes double.

> 'Twas when the seas were roaring
>   With hollow blasts of wind,
> A damsel lay deploring,
>   All on a rock reclined.

2. *Common octosyllabics.*—Four measures, *x a*, with rhyme, and (unless the rhymes be double) eight syllables (*octo syllabæ*).—Butler's Hudibras, Scott's poems, The Giaour, and other poems of Lord Byron.

3. *Elegiac octosyllabics.*—Same as the last, except that the rhymes are regularly alternate, and the verses arranged in stanzas.

> And on her lover's arm she leant,
>   And round her waist she felt it fold,
> And far across the hills they went,
>   In that new world which now is old:
> Across the hills and far away,
>   Beyond their utmost purple rim,
> And deep into the dying day
>   The happy princess follow'd him.
>
> TENNYSON.

4. *Octosyllabic triplets.*—Three rhymes in succession. Generally arranged as stanzas.

> I blest them, and they wander'd on;
> I spoke, but answer came there none:
> The dull and bitter voice was gone.
>
> TENNYSON.

5. *Blank verse.*—Five measures, *x a*, without rhyme, Paradise Lost, Young's Night Thoughts, Cowper's Task.

6. *Heroic couplets.*—Five measures, *x a*, with pairs of rhymes. Chaucer, Denham, Dryden, Waller, Pope, Goldsmith, Cowper, Byron, Moore, Shelley, &c. This is the common metre for narrative, didactic, and descriptive poetry.

7. *Heroic triplets.*—Five measures, *x a.* Three rhymes in succession. Arranged in stanzas. This metre is sometimes interposed among heroic couplets.

8. *Elegiacs.*—Five measures, *x a;* with regularly alternate rhymes, and arranged in stanzas.

> The curfew tolls the knell of parting day,
>   The lowing herds wind slowly o'er the lea,
> The ploughman homewards plods his weary way,
>   And leaves the word to darkness and to me.
>
> GRAY.

9. *Rhymes royal.*—Seven lines of heroics, with the last two rhymes in succession, and the first five recurring at intervals.

> This Troilus, in gift of curtesie,
>   With hauk on hond, and with a huge rout
> Of knightes, rode, and did her company,
>   Passing all through the valley far about;
>   And further would have ridden out of doubt.
> Full faine and woe was him to gone so sone;
> But turn he must, and it was eke to doen.
>
> CHAUCER.

This metre was common with the writers of the earlier part of Queen Elizabeth's reign. It admits of varieties according to the distribution of the first five rhymes.

10. *Ottava rima.*—A metre with an Italian name, and borrowed from Italy, where it is used generally for narrative poetry. The Morgante Maggiore of Pulci, the Orlando Innamorato of Bojardo, the Orlando Furioso of Ariosto, the Gierusalemme Liberata of Tasso, are all written in this metre. Besides this, the two chief epics of Spain and Portugal respectively (the Auraucana and the Lusiados) are thus composed. Hence it is a form of poetry which is Continental rather than

English, and naturalized rather than indigenous. The stanza consists of eight lines of heroics, the six first rhyming alternately, the last two in succession.

> Arrived there, a prodigious noise he hears,
>   Which suddenly along the forest spread;
> Whereat from out his quiver he prepares
>   An arrow for his bow, and lifts his head;
> And, lo! a monstrous herd of swine appears,
>   And onward rushes with tempestuous tread,
> And to the fountain's brink precisely pours,
> So that the giant's join'd by all the boars.
>   *Morgante Maggiore* (LD. BYRON's *Translation*.)

11. *Terza rima.*—Like the last, borrowed both in name and nature from the Italian, and scarcely yet naturalized in England.

> The Spirit of the fervent days of old,
>   When words were things that came to pass, and Thought
> Flash'd o'er the future, bidding men behold
> Their children's children's doom already brought
>   Forth from the abyss of Time which is to be,
>   The chaos of events where lie half-wrought
> Shapes that must undergo mortality:
>   What the great seers of Israel wore within,
>   That Spirit was on them and is on me:
> And if, Cassandra-like, amidst the din
>   Of conflicts, none will hear, or hearing heed
>   This voice from out the wilderness, the sin
> Be theirs, and my own feelings be my meed,
>   The only guerdon I have ever known.

12. *Alexandrines.*—Six measures, *x a*, generally (perhaps always) with rhyme. The name is said to be taken from the fact that early romances upon the deeds of Alexander of Macedon, of great popularity, were written in this metre. One of the longest poems in the

English language is in the Alexandrines, *viz.* Drayton's Poly-olbion, quoted above.

13. *Spenserian stanza.*—A stanza consisting of nine lines, the first eight heroics, the last an Alexandrine.

> It hath been through all ages ever seen,
>   That with the prize of arms and chivalrie
>   The prize of beauty still hath joined been,
>   And that for reason's special privitie;
>   For either doth on other much rely.
>   For he meseems most fit the fair to serve
> That can her best defend from villanie;
>   And she most fit his service doth deserve,
> That fairest is, and from her faith will never swerve.
> SPENSER.

Childe Harold and other important poems are composed in the Spenserian stanza.

14. *Service metre.*—Couplets of seven measures, *x a*. This is the common metre of the Psalm versions. It is also called common measure, or long measure. In this metre there is always a pause after the fourth measure, and many grammarians consider that with that pause the line ends. According to this view, the service metre does not consist of two long lines with seven measures each; but of four short ones, with four and three measures each alternately. The Psalm versions are printed so as to exhibit this pause or break.

> The Lord descended from above, | and bow'd the heavens most high,
> And underneath his feet He cast | the darkness of the sky.
> On Cherubs and on Seraphim | full royally He rode,
> And on the wings of mighty winds | came flying all abroad.
> STERNHOLD AND HOPKINS.

In this matter the following distinction is convenient. When the last syllable of the fourth measure (*i. e.* the eighth syllable in the line) in the one verse *rhymes* with the corresponding syllable in the other, the long verse should be looked upon as broken up into two short ones; in other words, the couplets should be dealt with as a stanza. Where there is no rhyme except at the seventh measure, the verse should remain undivided. Thus:

> Turn, gentle hermit of the glen, | and guide thy lonely way
> To where yon taper cheers the vale | with hospitable ray—

constitute a single couplet of two lines, the number of rhymes being two. But,

> Turn, gentle hermit of the dale,
> And guide thy lonely way
> To where yon taper cheers the vale
> With hospitable ray—
>
> (GOLDSMITH)

constitute a stanza of four lines, the number of rhymes being four.

15. *Ballad stanza.*—Service metre broken up in the way just indicated. Goldsmith's Edwin and Angelina, &c.

16. *Poulterer's measure.*—Alexandrines and service metre alternately. Found in the poetry of Henry the Eighth's time.

PART VII.

THE DIALECTS OF THE ENGLISH LANGUAGE.

§ 541. CERTAIN parts of England are named as if their population were preeminently *Saxon* rather than *Angle*; viz., Wes-*sex* (= West *Saxons*), Es-*sex* (= East *Saxons*), Sus-*sex* (= South *Saxons*), and Middle-*sex*, (= Middle *Saxons*).

Others are named as if their population were preeminently *Angle* rather than *Saxon*; thus, the counties of Norfolk and Suffolk once constituted the kingdom of the East Angles, and even at the present moment, are often spoken of as *East Anglia*.

§ 542. It is safe to say that the dialects of the English language do *not* coincide with the distribution of these terms. That parts of the Angle differ from parts of the Saxon districts in respect to the character of their provincialisms is true; but it is by no means evident that they differ on that account.

Thus, that the dialect of Hampshire, which was part of Wes-*sex*, should differ from that of Norfolk, which was part of East *Anglia*, is but natural. There is a great space of country between them—a fact sufficient to account for their respective characteristics, without assuming an original difference of population. Between the *Saxons* of Es-*sex* and the *Anglians* of Suffolk, no one has professed to find any notable difference.

Hence, no division of the English dialects into those of *Saxon* or those of *Angle* origin, has been successful.

Neither have any peculiarities in the dialect of Kent, or the Isle of Wight, verified the notion of the population for those parts having been originally *Jute*.

Nor yet has any portion of England been shown by the evidence of its dialects, to have been *Frisian*.

§ 543. Yet the solution of such problems is one of the great objects of the study of provincial modes of speech.

§ 544. That *Jute* characteristics will be sought in vain is the inference from §§ 7—13.

That differential points between the *Angles* and *Saxons* will be sought in vain is also probable.

On the other hand, differential points between the *Frisians* and *Angles* are likely to be discovered.

§ 545. The traces of the Danes, or Northmen, are distinct; the following forms of local names being *primâ facie* evidence (at least) of Danish or Norse occupancy.

a. The combination *Sk-*, rather than the sound of *Sh-*, in such names as *Skip*-ton, rather than *Ship*-ton.

b. The combination *Ca-*, rather than *Ch-*, in such names as *Carl*-ton rather than *Charl*-ton.

c. The termination *-by* (= *town* ⚹ *habitation, occupancy,*) rather than *-ton*, as Ash-*by*, Demble-*by*, Spills-*by*, Grims-*by*, &c.

d. The form *Kirk* rather than *Church*.

e. The form *Orm* rather than *Worm*, as in *Orms-head*.

In *Orms-kirk* and *Kir-by* we have a combination of Danish characteristics.

§ 546. In respect to their distribution, the Danish forms are—

At their *maximum* on the sea-coast of Lincolnshire; *i. e.*, in the parts about Spills-by.

Common, but less frequent, in Yorkshire, the Northern counties of England, the South-eastern parts of Scotland, Lancashire, (*Ormskirk*, Horn-*by*), and parts of South Wales (*Orms*-head, Ten-*by*).

In Orkney, and the northern parts of Scotland, the Norse had originally the same influence that the Anglo-Saxon had in the south.—See the chapter of the Lowland Scotch.

This explains the peculiar distribution of the Norse forms. Rare, or non-existent, in central and southern England, they appear on the opposite sides of the island, and on its northern extremity; showing that the stream of the Norse population went *round the island rather than across it.*

§ 547. Next to the search after traces of the original differences in the speech of the Continental invaders of Great Britain, the question as to the origin of the *written* language of England is the most important.

Mr. Guest has given good reasons for believing it to have arisen out of a Mercian, rather than a West-Saxon dialect—although of the *Anglo-Saxon* the West-Saxon was the most cultivated form.

This is confirmed by the present state of the Mercian dialects.

The country about Huntingdon and Stamford is, in the mind of the present writer, that part of England where provincial peculiarities are at the *minimum*. This may be explained in various ways, of which none is preferable to the doctrine, that the dialect for those parts represents the dialect out of which the literary language of England became developed.

Such are the chief problems connected with the study

of the provincial dialects of England; the exhibition of the methods applicable to their investigation not being considered necessary in a work like the present.

NOTE.

That *Saxon* was the *British* name of the Germanic invaders of Great Britain is certain.—See § 45.

The reasons which induce me to consider it as *exclusively* British, *i. e.*, as foreign to the Angles, are as follows,—

a. No clear distinction has ever been drawn between, *c. g.*, an *Angle* of Suffolk, and a *Saxon* of Essex.

b. The Romans who knew, for some parts at least, every inch of the land occupied by the Saxons of Germany, as long as there is reason for believing that they took their names from German sources, never use the word. It is strange to Cæsar, Strabo, Pliny, and Tacitus. Ptolemy is the first who uses it.

c. Ecbert, who is said to have attached the name of *Eng*land, or Land of *Angles*, to South Britain, was, himself, no *Angle*, but a West-Saxon.*

* This is worked out more fully in the "Germany of Tacitus, with Ethnological Notes," by the present author.

QUESTIONS ON PARTS IV. V. VI. AND VII.

PART IV.

1. What is Johnson's explanation of the word *Etymology?* Into what varieties does the study fall? What is the difference between *Etymology* and *Syntax?*

2. How far are the following words instances of gender—*boy, he-goat, actress, which?* Analyze the forms *what, her, its, vixen, spinster, gander, drake.*

3. How far is there a dual number in the Gothic tongues? What is the rule for forming such a plural as *stags* from *stag?* What are the peculiarities in *monarchs, cargoes, keys, pence, geese, children, women, houses, paths, leaves?* Of what number are the words *alms, physics news, riches?*

4. To what extent have we in English a dative, an accusative, and instrumental case? Disprove the doctrine that the genitive in -*s* (*the father's son*) is formed out of the combination *father his.*

5. Decline *me, thee,* and *ye.*

6. How far is there a true reflective pronoun in English?

7. What were the original powers and forms of *she, her, it?* What case is *him?* What is the power and origin of *the* in such expressions as *all the more?* Decline *he* in Anglo-Saxon. Investigate the forms *these* and *those, whose, what, whom, which, myself, himself, herself, such, every.*

8. What is the power (real or supposed) of the -*er* in *over,* and in *either?*

9. What words in the present English are explained by the following forms—*sutiza,* in Mœso-Gothic, and *seearpor, neah, yldre,* in Anglo-Saxon? Explain the forms, *better, worse, more, less.*

10. Analyze the words *former, next, upmost, thirty, streamlet, sweetheart, duckling.*

11. Translate *Ida was Eopping.* Analyze the word *Wales.*

12. Exhibit the extent to which the noun partakes of the character

of the verb, and *vice versâ*. What were the Anglo-Saxon forms of, *I can call*, *I begin to call?*

13. Investigate the forms, *drench*, *raise*, *use* (the verb), *clothe*.

14. *Thou speakest*. What is the peculiarity of the form? *We loven, we love*, account for this.

15. *Thou rannest*=(*tu cucurristi*). Is this an unexceptionable form? if not, why?

16. What are the *moods* in English? What the *tenses?* How far is the division of verbs into weak and strong tenses natural? Account for the double forms *swam* and *swum*. Enumerate the other verbs in the same class. Explain the forms *taught*, *wrought*, *ought*, *did*, (from *do—facio*), *did* (from *do—valeo*), *minded*.

17. Define the term *irregular*, so as to raise the number of irregular verbs, in English, to more than a hundred. Define the same term, so as to reduce them to none. Explain the form *could*.

18. What is the construction of *meseems* and *methinks?* Illustrate the *future* power of be. *Werden* in German means *become*—in what form does the word appear in English?

19. *To err is human*,—*the rising* in the North. Explain these constructions. Account for the second -*r* in *forlorn*; and for the *y* in *y-cleped*.

20. Explain the difference between *composite* and *de-composite* words, *true* and *improper compounds*. Analyze the word *nightingale*.

21. How far are adverbs inflected? Distinguish between a *preposition* and a *conjunction*.

22. Explain the forms *there*, *thence*, *yonder*, and *anon*.

23. What part of speech is *mine?*

24. What is the probable origin of the -*d* in such preterites as call-*ed*.

Part V.

1. Explain the terms *Syntax*, *Ellipsis*, *Pleonasm*, *Zeugma*, *Pros to semainomenon*, *Apposition*, and *Convertibility*, giving illustrations of each.

2. What is the government of adjectives?

3. What is the construction in—

a. Rob *me* the Exchequer.—SHAKSPEARE.

b. Mount *ye* on horseback.

c. *His* mother.

  d. If the salt have lost *his* savour.
  e. Myself *is* weak.
  f. This is *mine.*

  4. What are the concords between the relative and antecedent? How far is, *whom* do they say that I am, an exceptionable expression?
  5. *Eteocles and Polynices killed each other.* What is the construction here? *Ils se battaient, l'un l'autre—Ils se battaient, les uns les autres.* Translate those two sentences into English, *My wife and little ones are well.* What is the origin of the word *ones* here? *It* was *those who spoke. These* was *those who spoke.* Why is one of those expressions correct, and the other incorrect?
  6. What is the difference between—

   a. The secretary and treasurer,
    and
   The secretary and *the* treasurer?

  What is that between—
   The first two—
    and
   The two first?

  7. What is the construction of—

    He sleeps the sleep of the righteous?

  8. Whether do you say—It is I your master who command you, or It is I your master who commands you?
  9. Barbican it *hight.* Translate this into Latin.
  10. Explain in full the following constructions—

   a. I have ridden a horse.
   b. I am to blame.
   c. I am beaten.
   d. A part of the body.
   e. All fled but John.

  11. What is meant by the *Succession of Tenses?* Show the logical necessity of it.
  12. Or *hear'st* thou rather pure ethereal stream,
   Whose fountain *who can* tell?—MILTON.

  Give the meaning of this passage, and explain the figure of speech exhibited in the words in Italics.
  13. The *door* being open the steed was stolen.—In what case is *door?*

Part VI.

1. The way was long, the wind was cold.
Express the metre of this symbolically.
2. Define *rhyme*.
3. Give instances of *Service metre, Blank heroics, Alexandrines*.

Part VII.

1. How far do the present dialects of England coincide with the parts, that took their names from the *Angles* and the *Saxons* respectively.
2. What traces of Danish or Norse occupancy do we find in local names ?

NOTES.

[1] The immediate authority for these descents, dates, and localities, is Sharon Turner. They are nearly the same as those which are noticed in Mr. Kemble's *Saxons in England*. In the former writer, however, they are given as historical facts; in the latter they are subjected to criticism, and considered as exceptionable.

[2] It is from Beda that the current opinions as to the details of the Anglo-Saxon invasion are taken; especially the threefold division into Angles, Saxons, and Jutes. These migrations were so large and numerous that the original country of the Angles was left a desert. The distribution of the three divisions over the different parts of England was also Beda's.

The work of this important writer—the great luminary of early England—is the *Historia Ecclesiastica*, a title which prepares us for a great preponderance of the ecclesiastical over the secular history.

Now Beda's date was the middle of the eighth century.

And his locality was the monastery of Wearmouth, in the county of Durham.

Both of these facts must be borne in mind when we consider the value of his authority, *i. e.*, his means of knowing, as determined by the conditions of time and place.

Christianity was introduced among the Anglo-Saxons of Kent A.D. 597. For the times between them and A.D. 740, we have in Mr. Kemble's *Codex Diplomaticus* eighty-five charters, all in Latin, and most of them of uncertain authenticity. They are chiefly grants of different kings of Kent, Wessex, the Hwiccas, Mercia, and Northumberland, a few being of bishops.

[3] Gildas was a *British* ecclesiastic, as Beda was an *English* one.

His locality was North Wales; his time earlier than Beda's by perhaps one hundred years.

He states that he was born the year of the *pugna Badonica*, currently called the *Battle of Bath*.

Now a chronological table called *Annales Cambrenses*, places that event within one hundred years of the supposed landing of Hengist.

But there is no reason for believing this to be a cotemporary entry. Hence, all that can be safely said of Gildas is that he was about as far removed from the seat of the Germanic invasions, in locality, as Beda, whilst in point of time he was nearer.

As a writer he is far inferior, being pre-eminently verbose, vague, and indefinite.

Gildas, as far as he states facts at all, gives the *British* account of the conquest.

No other documents have come down to our time.

Beda's own authorities—as we learn from his introduction—were certain of the most learned bishops and abbots of his cotemporaries, of whom he sought special information as to the antiquities of their own establishments. Of cotemporary writers, in the way of authority, there is no mention.

For the times between the "accredited date of Hengist and Horsa's landing (A.D. 449) and A.D. 597 (a period of about one hundred and fifty years) the only authorities are a few quotations from Solinus, Gildas, and a Legendary Life of St. Germanus."—*Saxons in Engl.* i. 27.

⁴ This account is from Jornandes, who is generally considered as the chief repertory of the traditions respecting the Gothic populations. He lived about A.D. 530. The Gepidæ were said to be the *laggards* of the migration, and the vessel which carried them to have been left behind; and as *gepanta* in their language meant *slow*, their name is taken therefrom.

⁵ Widukind was a monk of Corvey in Flanders, who wrote the Ecclesiastical History of his monastery.

⁶ Geoffry of Monmouth, like Gildas, is a *British* authority. His date was the reign of Henry II. The *Welsh* traditions form the staple of Geoffry's work, for which it is the great repertory.

⁷ The *date* of this was the reign of Marcus Antoninus. Its *place*, the Danubian provinces of Rhætia, and Pannonia. It was carried on by the Germans of the *frontier* or *march*—from whence the name—in alliance with the Jazyges, who were undoubtedly Slavonic, and the Quadi, who were probably so. Its details are obscure—the chief authority being Dio Cassius.

⁸ The reign of Valentinian was from A.D. 365 to A.D. 375.

[9] The date of this has been variously placed in A.D. 408, and between A.D. 395 and A.D. 407. Either is earlier than A.D.

[10] The Saxon Chronicle consists of a series of entries from the earliest times to the reign of King Stephen, each under its year: the year of the Anglo-Saxon invasion being the usual one, i.e., A.D. 449. The value of such a work depends upon the extent to which the chronological entries are cotemporaneous with the events noticed. Where this is the case, the statement is of the highest historical value; where, however, it is merely taken from some earlier authority, or from a tradition, it loses the character of a *register*, and becomes merely a series of dates— correct or incorrect as the case may be. Where the Anglo-Saxon Chronicle really begins to be a cotemporaneous register is uncertain—all that is certain being that it *is* so for the *latest*, and is *not* so for *earliest* entries. The notices in question come under the former class. The Anglo-Saxon Chronicle had been edited by the Master of Trinity College, Oxford (Dr. Ingram), and analyzed by Miss Gurney.

[11] Asserius was a learned Welsh ecclesiastic who was invited by King Alfred into Wessex, and employed by that king as one of his associates and assistants in civilizing and instructing his subjects. Several works are mentioned as having been written by Asserius, but the only one extant is his history of King Alfred, which is a chronicle of various events between the year of Alfred's birth, A.D. 849, to A.D. 889.

Asserius is supposed to have died Bishop of Sherborne, A.D. 910.

[12] The compounds of the Anglo-Saxon word *ware*=occupants, inhabitants, are too numerous to leave any doubt as to this, and several other derivations. Cant-ware=Cant-icolæ=people of *Kent*: Hwic-ware=Hwiccas=*the people* of parts of Worcestershire,* Glostershire, and (to judge from the name) of *War-wickshire* also.

[13] The Annales Saxonici, or Saxon Chronicles, embrace the history of Britain, between the landing of Cæsar and the accession of Henry II. They are evidently the work of various and successive writers, who were Saxon ecclesiastics. But nothing certain can be affirmed of the authors of their respective portions.—See Note 10.

[14] See Note 2.

[15] Adam of Bremen was a Minor Canon of the Cathedral of Bremen, about the years 1067—1077. He travelled in Denmark, and was in great favour with King Sweyn of that country. He wrote an Ecclesiastical History of the spread of Christianity in the North, to which he appended a description of the geography, population, and archæology of Denmark and the neighbouring countries.

* Preserved in the name of the town Wick-*war*.

[16] Ethelward was an Anglo-Saxon nobleman, who wrote a chronicle of events from the creation of the world to the death of King Edgar, A.D. 875.

[17] The following is a specimen of the Frisian of Gysbert Japicx, in metre. It is part of a rustic song, supposed to be sung by a peasant on his return from a wedding feast. Date about A.D. 1650.

> "Swiet, ja swiet, is't oer 'e miete,
> 'T boáskiere fóar ó jonge lie,
> Kreftich swiet is't, sizz ik jiette,
> As it giet mei alders rie.
> Mai óars tiget 'et to 'n pléach,
> As ik óan myn geafeunt seach."

Translation of the same from Bosworth's *Anglo-Saxon Dictionary*, p. lxxiii.

> "Sweet, yes, sweet is over (*beyond*) measure,
> The marrying for the young lede (*people*);
> Most sweet is it, I say yet (*once more*),
> When (*as*) it goes with the rede (*counsel*) of the elders.
> But otherwise it tends to a plague,
> As I saw on (*by the example of*) my village fellow."

[18] Of the early constitution of states of East Friesland, we have a remarkable illustration in the old Frisian Laws. These are in the native Frisian tongue, and, except that they represent republican rather than monarchical institutions, are similar in form, in spirit, to the Saxon.

[19] The great blow against the sovereignty of Rome, and the one which probably prevented Germany from becoming a Roman province, was struck by the Cheruscan Arminius against Quintilius Varus, in the reign of Augustus. The date of the organized insurrection of Arminius was A.D. 9; the place, the neighbourhood of Herford, or Engern, in Westphalia. Drawn into an inpracticable part of the country, the troops of Varus were suddenly attacked and cut to pieces—consisting of more than three legions. "Never was victory more decisive, never was the liberation of an oppressed people more instantaneous and complete. Throughout Germany the Roman garrisons were assailed and cut off and, within a few weeks after Varus had fallen, the German soil was freed from the foot of an invader.

"Had Arminius been supine or unsuccessful, our Germanic ancestors would have been enslaved or exterminated in their original seats along the Eyder and the Elbe. This island would never have borne the name of

England, and we, this great English nation, whose race and language are now overrunning the earth, from one end of it to the other, would have been utterly cut off from existence."*

[20] *Heliand* is the gerund from *helian*=*heal,* and means *the Healer* or *Saviour.* It is the name of an old Saxon poem, in alliterative metre, of the tenth or eleventh century, in the dialect supposed to have belonged to the parts about Essen, Cleves, and Munster in Westphalia. It is a sort of Gospel Harmony, or Life of Christ, taken from the Gospels. It has been edited by Schmeller.

[21] Hildubrand and Hathubrant, father and son, are two legendary heroes belonging to that cycle of German fiction of which Theodoric of Verona is the centre. A fragment containing an account of their hostile meeting, being mutually unknown, in alliterative metre, represents the *fictional* poetry of the old Saxons in the same way (though not to the same extent) that the Heliand represents their sacred poetry. The "Hildubrand and Hathubrant" have been edited by Grimm.

[22] In a language which for a long time was considered to be the Dutch of Holland in its oldest known form, there is an imperfect translation of the Psalms; referred by the best writers on the subject to the reign of Charlemagne, and thence called the Carolinian Psalms. The best text of this is to be found in a Dutch periodical, the *Taalkundig Magazijn.*

[23] *Beowulf* is by far the most considerable poem, not only in Anglo-Saxon, but in any old Gothic tongue. It has been admirably edited and translated by Mr. Kemble. The subject is the account of Beowulf, an Angle hero— Angle but not English, as the scene of the poem is on the Continent. In its present form it shows traces of the revision of some Christian writer: the basis, however, of its subject, and the manners it describes, are essentially Pagan. The most remarkable feature in the poem is the fact that no allusion is made to England—so that, *Anglo-Saxon* as the work is—it belongs to the Anglo-Saxons of Germany before they became English.

[24] A Gospel Harmony translated from the one of Tatian, exists in a dialect too little purely High German, to pass absolutely as such, yet less *Low* German than the Dutch of Holland. This belongs to the *Middle* Rhine, and is called *Frank.*

[25] The Alemannic is the German of the *Upper* Rhine; the dialect out of which the Bavarian and Swiss grew. Its chief specimens occur in—

---

* "The Fifteen Decisive Battles of the World," by Professor Creasy.

a. The Glosses of *Kero*—
b. The Psalms by a monk named *Notker.*
c. A life of *Anno* of Cologne.
d. The Song of Solomon, by Willeram.
e. *Musrpilli*, an alliterative poem.
f. *Krist*, a Life of Christ, by Otford, and others less important.

Most of these (along with Tatian), are to be found in **Schilter's** *Thesaurus.*

www.ingramcontent.com/pod-product-compliance
Lightning Source LLC
Chambersburg PA
CBHW030546300426
44111CB00009B/876